COMIX

The Underground Revolution

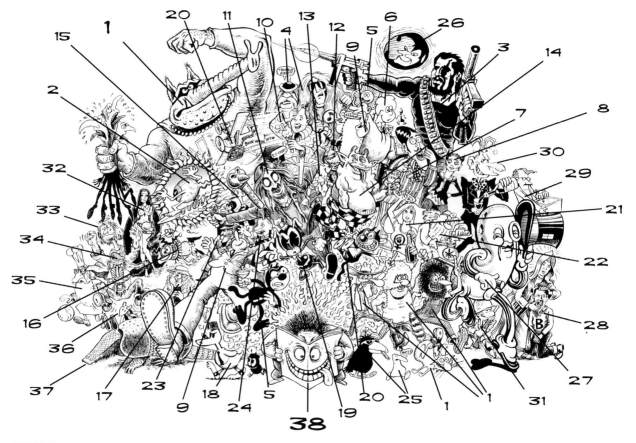

KEY TO COVER CHARACTERS

1 Wonder Warthog [left] and
   The Fabulous Furry Freak Brothers and
   Fat Freddy's Cat *(Gilbert Shelton)*
2 Surfing Eyeball *(Rick Griffin)*
3 Trashman *(Spain Rodriguez)*
4 Ogoth and Ugly Boot *(Chris Welch)*
5 Sunshine Girl [top] and
   Waldo the Cat *(Kim Deitch)*
6 Barefootz *(Howard Cruse)*
7 Snappy Sammy Smoot *(Skip Williamson)*
8 Heroine *(Suzy Varty)*
9 Mr. Natural [top] and
   Keep On Truckin' *(Robert Crumb)*

10 Zippy the Pinhead *(Bill Griffith)*
11 Chester P. Hackenbush *(Bryan Talbot)*
12 Mickey Rat *(Robert Armstong)*
13 Cheech Wizard *(Vaughn Bode)*
14 The Checkered Demon *(S. Clay Wilson)*
15 Nard 'n' Pat *(Jay Lynch)*
16 Jester *(Knockabout)*
17 Pudge, The Girl Blimp *(Lee Marrs)*
18 Dirty Duck *(Bobby London)*
19 Coochy Cooty *(Robert Williams)*
20 Thunderdogs [top] and
   Firkin the Cat *(Hunt Emerson)*
21 Suzie Slumgodess *(Trina Robbins)*
22 Dr. Atomic *(Larry Todd)*
23 Dan Maniac *(Mike Matthews)*

24 The Firm *(Mike Weller)*
25 Crow [left] and Largactylite *(Edward Barker)*
26 Moon *(Dan O'Neill)*
27 Mr. Peanut *(Victor Moscoso)*
28 Binky Brown & the Virgin Mary *(Justin Green)*
29 Denis and his Kitchen Sink *(Denis Kitchen)*
30 Arnold Peck the Human Wreck *(Willy Murphy)*
31 Dopin' Dan *(Ted Richards)*
32 The Leather Nun *(Dave Sheridan)*
33 The Adventures of Jesus *(Foolbert Sturgeon)*
34 Gregor the Purple-Assed Baboon *(Greg Irons)*
35 God Nose *(Jack Jackson)*
36 Maus *(Art Spiegelman)*
37 Armadillo *(Jim Franklin)*
38 **YOU!**

COMIX

The Underground Revolution

Dez Skinn

THUNDER'S
MOUTH
PRESS

Published in the United States by
Thunder's Mouth Press
An imprint of Avalon Publishing Group
245 West 17th Street, 11th floor
New York, NY 10011-5300

1 3 5 7 9 8 6 4 2

Library of Congress Control Number 2003113700

ISBN: 1 56025 572 2

Commissioning editors: Will Steeds, Chris Stone
Researched and designed by Quality Communications Ltd.
Cover illustration by Hunt Emerson
Repro by Anorax Imaging
Printed in Portugal by Printer Portuguesa Lda
Distributed by Publishers Group West

About the Author

Dez Skinn's career in the comics industry spans more than 30 years. Currently editor of leading trade magazine *Comics International* (www.comicsinternational.com) he was previously Editorial Director of Marvel UK where his Stan Lee-coined 'Sez Dez' column had a monthly audience of 500,000. Titles he has created include *Dr Who Weekly*, *House of Hammer*, *Hulk Comic*, *Starburst* and *Warrior*, while he has also edited the likes of *MAD Magazine*, *Buster*, *Conan*, *Star Wars Weekly*, *2000 AD Presents*, *Judge Dredd*, and *Spider-Man*. He has won more than 20 Eagle awards, the awards for excellence in the comics industry. His co-created *V for Vendetta* is currently optioned to Warner Brothers.

Acknowledgements

Elated but frustrated… It's been a fantastic experience putting together an introductory book on underground comix for a 21st century audience, most of whom were probably not even conceived by the Summer of Love. But it's been equally frustrating, realizing how much amazing material couldn't be shoehorned in.

While I've grabbed cover credit for this taster of the swinging sixties, it's been very much a team effort, from initial synopsis through to squared-up sized-up pages. For their invaluable research input, I'd like to thank Raoul Collins, Frank Plowright, Jonathan Weeks and Julie Collier. For their knowledge, memories and way with words, Trina Robbins, Mike Conroy, Tim Pilcher and Will Rogers. For their visual dexterity, Gary Lawford and Steve Turner. For kicking things off in style—both then and now—Denis Kitchen. And for a truly superb cover visual, Hunt Emerson.

Heroes of the Revolution all!

Contents

Foreword

Sometimes cultural phenomena appear with relative spontaneity. A youth movement, political tumult, rapidly changing sexual politics and mores, open drug use and an incipient art form all converged in America in the late '60s.

Underground comix was the bastard child of a wayward generation.

As someone who was there near the very beginning I can say with certainty that there was no grand conspiracy, no secret cell activity and no intellectual summit. Even the beginning, if one must define the beginning, is murky. Robert Crumb's first **Zap**, appearing during San Francisco's fabled summer of love in 1967, is widely regarded, and rightly so, as the catalyst for the stream of work that followed.

But the medium's relatively short evolution includes earlier independent efforts by artists like Frank Stack, Joel Beck and Jack Jackson.

College humor magazines also played a key role. Several underground artists, such as Gilbert Shelton in Austin, Texas, cut their teeth on such titles. My own early efforts appeared in a college satire magazine called **Snide** [1967].

Regional underground newspapers bloomed seemingly overnight, both in major cities and college towns, providing vehicles and audiences for other young cartoonists. But the comicbook, the cheap newsprint pamphlet so reviled by our parents' generation, quickly evolved as the format of choice.

Harvey Kurtzman's role as the "father-in-law" of underground comix cannot be overemphasized. **MAD**—his brilliant early 1950s invention—mesmerized a generation with topics never before addressed in comics, and his dissection of famous cartoon characters was both howlingly funny and an eye-opening course in strip anatomy, galvanizing a new generation of cartoonists. **MAD**, as one commentator put it, was a sub-machine gun attack on American culture when unquestioning conformity was the rule of the land.

> "...a sub-machine gun attack on American culture."

In the late '50s two other Kurtzman satire publications, **Trump** (all too briefly) and the low-rent **Humbug** followed **MAD**, with the same essential crew of geniuses who could not help but inspire the Young Turks in the wings. Crumb has said that **Humbug**, quite simply, changed his life. As it did my own.

Kurtzman's final foray into satire magazines was **Help!** [1960-65] which gave Crumb, Shelton, Beck, Jay Lynch and Skip Williamson their first national exposure. It was there that I first saw their cartoons, not long before their appearances in underground comix.

Some of these young contributors to **Help!**, along with Art Spiegelman and Jay Kinney corresponded and networked through miniscule circulation fanzines. Others worked in isolation.

My own first effort, **Mom's Homemade Comics** ("Straight from the Kitchen to You") was written and drawn in 1968 in a virtual vacuum

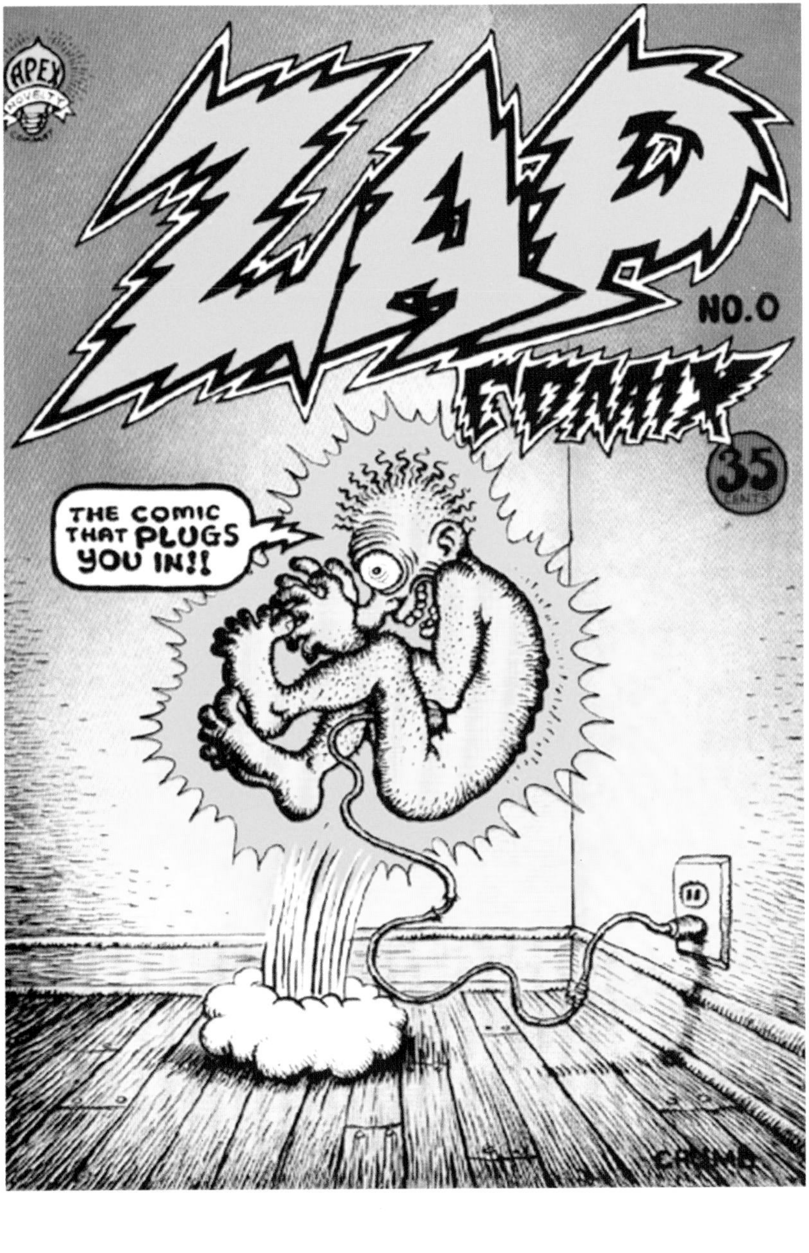

ABOVE AND LEFT: The artwork was lost before it could be printed, so R. Crumb's intended launch edition of Zap Comix (left) was not the first issue actually to hit the streets.

Replacement work was produced for the February 1968 published Zap #1 (above) and when the missing originals were discovered, they were published as the 35c Zap #0 (left). Currently in its 11th edition, it now carries a $2.75 cover price.

in Milwaukee, Wisconsin. When I self-published it in 1969 I was aware of only one other similar effort, **Bijou Funnies** #1, which I discovered in a Milwaukee bookstore that supported small presses. I soon came into contact with Lynch, Williamson and Dan Clyne in nearby Chicago. We were all delighted to meet kindred spirits and the network continued to grow.

Lynch (who kept track of such things) informed me that **Mom's Homemade Comics** was the eighth underground comic. There was a sense something was happening in the comics realm but we were also swept up in a larger anti-war movement and cultural upheaval and the comix component was not, at least early on, a self-conscious movement.

In 1969 and 1970 my focus was on creating a sequel to **Mom's** and to establishing a new alternative newspaper in Milwaukee (**The Bugle**). I was also a socialist candidate for public office. But the West Coast publisher I trusted to reprint **Mom's** #1 and to solely publish **Mom's** #2 did not treat me in the egalitarian manner I expected of a counter culture entity, so I withdrew my work from them. Reluctantly, I determined to self-publish again.

My initial efforts to distribute **Mom's** had been surprisingly successful, but it was my goal to be a cartoonist, not a businessman. As fate would have it, Lynch and Williamson had problems with the same California publisher. Learning of my new effort, they asked if I would take over publishing **Bijou**. With extreme naivete and without full comprehension of what I agreed to do, I overnight became a publisher, though a two-headed man I remained. Soon afterward, in 1970, R. Crumb visited, and gave me his latest comic to publish (**Home Grown Funnies**). I never looked back.

It is for others like Dez to bring objectivity to any overview of underground comix. Complete artistic freedom remains the hallmark of underground comix. Part and parcel with such freedom was widely varying content, too often narrowly stereotyped as graphic violence, drug-induced imagery, obscenity and/or misogyny. Any history of underground comic books will have an understandable emphasis on an examination of the aesthetics and content of the oeuvre. In this brief foreword I would like to address a much less sexy and less volatile but fundamentally important aspect of underground comics: the economics. Oscar Wilde astutely observed that when bankers dine together they discuss art and when artists dine together they discuss money. Cartoonists are no different.

> Oscar Wilde astutely observed that when bankers dine together they discuss art and when artists dine together they discuss money.

The comic strip, and its younger cousin the comic book, were such new art forms when I began my career that the first modern strip cartoonist, Jimmy Swinnerton, a centenarian, was still alive. Underground cartoonists were part of the first generation of cartoonists to have a sense of their profession's history. Before the proliferation of books *about* comics, we certainly recognized and appreciated the often-magnificent talents that came before us. But we were also acutely aware of the dark side of the profession. Young and idealistic, we brought an outsider's objectivity to a niche publishing world we both loved and rejected. We knew that copyrights to comics were historically—almost without exception—owned not by creators but by publishers or syndicates.

We knew, for example, that *Superman* creators Jerry Siegel and Joe Shuster signed away their rights as very young men, and over the years received only a pittance in comparison with their publisher, DC Comics. We knew that our creative inspiration, Harvey Kurtzman, left **MAD** because of an equity dispute with EC publisher Bill Gaines, and we saw that Kurtzman remained financially precarious while Gaines, whose business was saved by Kurtzman's **MAD**, made millions. And we observed that even the most successful newspaper strip artists, with very few exceptions (Al Capp, Will Eisner and Milton Caniff), were unable to wrest ownership of their own famous creations.

From the start, every cartoonist in the counterculture understood that the old economic system was unacceptable. As an artist first, and a publisher second, I understood that creators on principle should own their own copyrights and trademarks.

Kitchen Sink Press and other underground publishers paid artists a royalty, generally 10% of cover price, a system modeled on the literary book world. Artists who were tempted to create work-for-hire assembly line pages in a "house style" for Marvel or DC knew the bottom line trade-off: more money up front from the giant house but nothing down the road.

The best-selling underground artists under the royalty system, over time, ended up with page rates far superior to the mainstream counterparts' flat rates *and* the artists owned their property. Further, while the mainstream publishers kept all original art, underground publishers returned it. And when there were opportunities to sell foreign, merchandise or ancillary rights, the underground cartoonist maintained ultimate control.

Ultimately the pressure from the upstarts grew too great for even the largest superhero publishers to bear and the system reformed. Today almost all large publishers pay freelance writers and artists some sort of royalty, compromise to a large degree on ownership issues, return all original art and have broadened their editorial bases. Alongside these giants, independent publishers in the pure underground tradition continue to proliferate.

The "revolution" in comic books is most easily seen in terms of the increasingly literary subject matter, the wonderfully idiosyncratic writing and art styles and the physical formats. But behind the scenes another revolution took place, one that addressed creator equity issues, arguably an issue as important as intellectual freedom itself.

Denis Kitchen

Denis Kitchen

ABOVE: Foreword author Denis Kitchen's first foray into counter culture publishing, Mom's Homemade Comics #1 [1968].

INTRODUCTION

Putting the 'x' into Comix

*Forebears and influences, roots and derivations... How the comix phenomenon came to be, owing as much to **Surfer** and **Custom Rodder** as it did to **The East Village Other** and **The LA Free Press.***

UNDERGROUND comix. To an earlier generation, those two words represented an escape, an answer, an alternative. But most people today are more likely to lump them in with porn magazines, just a pile of sexist titilation and rude drawings with a few words to hold it all together. Give somebody an underground comic to read and the chances are they'll skip through the visuals, looking for the naughty bits. The "nudge, wink, know what I mean, squire" *Monty Python*-style curiosity inherent in everybody.

Sure, the graphic depiction of sex was one of the barriers that those rascally cartoonists smashed asunder, at a time when the glossies offered very softcore material by today's standards. But almost every new medium finds easy money from sex. Videos were considered backstreet dodgy goods when that industry started up. Before the high street video megastores legitimized the business, if you spotted anybody with a video case under their arm, it was a definite "nudge wink" contender. Telephone companies latched on to sexy chatlines as a major money spinner within months of privatization similar to the current domination of the internet by porn merchants.

> "Comix—the X suggesting x-rated or an adult readership... special books."
>
> *...Jack (Jaxon) Jackson*

But the underground, in its lifestyle and its components was much more. The teenage college crowd was still a relatively new mass market in the 1960s, with independent spending power and eager to test itself by rebelling against tradition. It had been freed up by a new kind of music, by the creation of improved contraception through The Pill, and its heroes were no longer middle-aged actors and singers. Even the country's leader was much younger and a renowned rebel against traditional values. When the beatnik and mod eras mutated into the hippie movement, and the new establishment became vilified through its politics and policing of such, equally new role models were needed. Rebels, with a cause.

Through their instant accessibility by telling stories in pictures, comix became a perfect vehicle for a new way of thinking, a powerful tool not only to break the sex taboos, but also to present entire lifestyle manuals to the nascent peace and love generation. Not through the stagnating empire of Superman and Batman, but through street comix, introducing leaderless youth across the world to an almost-mythical alternative culture. In the same way punk rock shocked and revitalized the music industry ten years later, underground comix presented a heady alternative to the moribund mainstream, which was content to repeat a sanitized version of a formula which had peaked 20 years earlier.

Love blooms on a street called Haight

While New York was traditionally the nexus of four-colour comicbooks, San Francisco is always considered to be the birthplace of the underground comix revolution, focused in an area known as Haight-Ashbury.

That term, "Haight-Ashbury," probably bears some explanation for out of towners. Described by today's commentators as "the world's first psychedelic city-state," the Haight-Ashbury was little more than a few square blocks that stretched from the edge of Golden Gate Park for around a half mile down Haight Street.

On Haight Street there were sidewalk cafés, head shops such as the Psychedelic Shop selling drug-related paraphernalia, poster shops like the Pacific Ocean Trading Company and hip boutiques such as The Blushing Peony. Running parallel to Haight Street is the Panhandle, a very narrow slice of Golden Gate Park which was the site of many free concerts and protest rallies. Its counter cultural ethos proved irresistible to the restless youth of the '60s. From across the world, they flocked to Haight-Ashbury with the district's population exploding from 15,000 in 1965 to almost 100,000 by the summer of 1967.

Naturally, this made the 'Haight' not only a nexus for the underground comix scene, with artists drawn together to create an

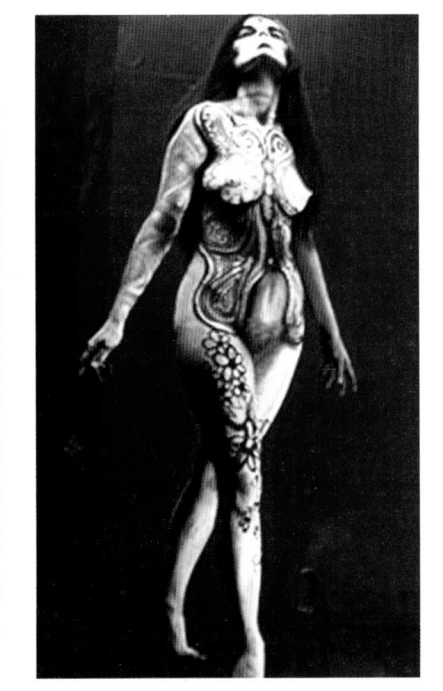

informal collaborative network, but it was also home to such diverse icons of the period as LSD guru Timothy Leary, beat-generation author Allen Ginsberg, infamous serial killer Charles Manson, **Interview with a Vampire** author Anne Rice and rock legends The Grateful Dead, Frank Zappa and Janis Joplin.

Notably, R. Crumb moved in, becoming the midwife to underground comix, bringing it kicking and screaming into the world in 1967 after an incredibly lengthy gestation period. It had been conceived in Texas in the early '60s with the parents of this illegitimate child being artists Frank Stack and Jack "Jaxon" Jackson, while its grandparents were the outrageous **Tijuana Bibles** of the 1930s.

Death Rattle artist Jaxon sums up the difference between comix and comics: "Comix—the "x" suggesting x-rated or an adult readership—was our spelling for alternative books so readers would know at a glance that these were special books, different than regular comicbooks. The subjects were dope, sex and altered consciousness of some sort as opposed to mainstream subjects."

The overground comics industry had started by collecting and reformatting newspaper strips in the 1930s. When these 64-page resized compilations had voraciously eaten up all the available strips featuring Tarzan, Flash Gordon, Popeye and their like, new material was sought. This led to their publishers flourishing in the 1940s with anthology titles ranging from crime, adventure and westerns to horror, romance and,

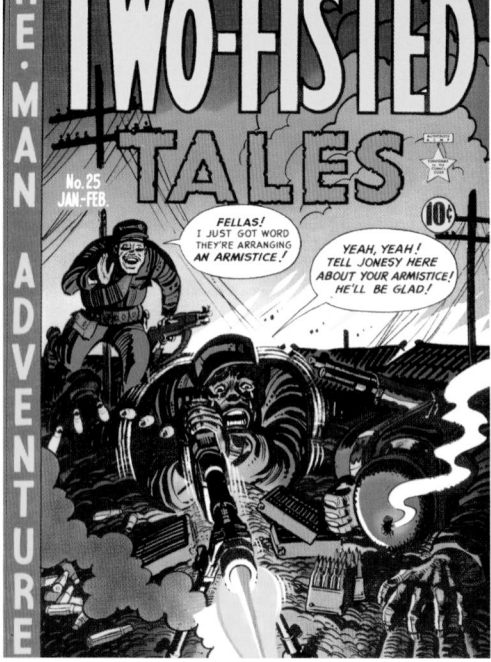

thanks to cornerstones like Superman and Batman, the format's very own invention of masked men in tights—superheroes.

Within a year, the popularity of this new breed of more-than-human hero brought with it a dramatic sea change as the generic anthology format, with its variety of content, gave way to single character comics.

But 1930s rebel cartoonists were even faster than the mainstream in recognizing the potential of a stand-alone format, albeit a totally illegal one.

The spoof series of **Tijuana Bibles**—also known as **Eight-Pagers** because of their flimsy page count—were under-the-counter pamphlets featuring outrageously pornographic strips.

With over 1000 titles produced to fulfil a prurient need, the targets went beyond ficticious comics characters, humiliating movie stars, politicians and crime tzars alike through their sexually explicit stories. Not surprisingly, they were produced by anonymous writers and artists wanting to protect themselves from inevitable lawsuits. No one even knew where they came from, although the anything-goes border town of Tijuana was the rumoured source, earning them their name.

Sold only by backstreet porn vendors, the **Bibles** are an obvious precursor to the comix of the 1960s. However, because of their dodgy content, they were almost impossible for '50s kids to find and many comix creators growing up then refute their effect on the development of the undergrounds.

Unlikely as it may sound, many of them credit Chuck Jones' *Bugs Bunny, Daffy Duck* and *Road Runner* cartoons as influences, the 1940s shorts still being screened in cinemas during the '50s. But they did feature a theme that comix would adopt, rooting for the underdog and promoting the rebel's cause—one man (or animal) against society.

Artists including *Pogo* creator Walt Kelly, political cartoonist Jules Feiffer and the young Al (*L'il Abner*) Capp are also cited as major influences while inspirational characters include George Herriman's *Krazy Kat*, Winsor McCay's *Little Nemo in Slumberland* and the Donald Duck comics produced by Carl Barks. But even more influential were the early 1950s EC comics.

Labelling them Educational Comics, format pioneer M. C. Gaines believed comicbooks could be a useful teaching tool and published such titles as **Picture Stories from the Bible** [1942]. When he died in a boating accident in 1947 his son, William M. Gaines, took over. "I hated the business so much I visited the office only once a week to sign the payroll checks," he quipped.

> **Mad** switched from colour comicbook size to black and white magazine to avoid the comic code censors.

Gaines Jr quickly changed the EC name to stand for Entertaining Comics and within five years transformed his father's lacklustre line into lurid but groundbreaking successes. Through such comics as **Tales from the Crypt**, **Crime Suspenstories**, **Two-Fisted Tales** and **Weird Fantasy**, a host of talented writers and artists strove to shock with graphic horror and at the same time, through the quality of their work, raise the level of visual storytelling.

"The EC comics had an air of disreputability," remarks **Trashman**'s Spain Rodriguez. "And, y'know, I was a little reluctant to look at them. But once I started, I got everything I could get my hands on. The science fiction ones were, well... my parents didn't mind them so much, but they didn't like all this crime comic stuff."

Illustrating the rampant paranoia of the States during the 1950s Cold War era, Spain adds, "At some point my mom thought that EC comics were a communist influence!"

Cartoonist turned fine artist Robert Williams also acknowledged the importance of EC when he recently listed his major influences, "Comic books, movies, and things like that... Automobile racing, airplane and aircraft warfare, things that affect a kid. War comics, and EC comics."

Smut comics pioneer S Clay Wilson was a big EC fan: "There was a teenage babysitter who looked after me and my younger siblings who had a great cache of ECs that she would let me have free access to."

Giving an indication of how graphic and how memorable the strips could be, Skip (**Smoot**) Williamson said, "The EC horror story that implanted itself most vividly in my unfledged psyche was one drawn by Jack Davis featuring a baseball game where intestines were the baselines, a human heart was home plate and a head was the ball." This 1953 comic was the ultra-scarce **Haunt of Fear** #19, reprinted in 1993 as **Haunt of Fear** #3.

Slipped in among the O Henry-style twist ending gore stories there were also politically controversial strips taking a stand on war, the Holocaust and racial prejudice. Their storymakers included many US comics legends but the one who had the most impact on the nascent comix creators was Harvey Kurtzman. He is often cited as the father of underground comix—begging the question of just how many parents did it have. Kurtzman suggested "brother-in-law" as more appropriate.

As editor, chief writer and occasional artist of EC's war titles **Two-Fisted Tales** and **Frontline Combat**, Kurtzman brought a new level of realism to the genre, raising it above the "heroic G.I. single-handedly wipes out Nazi horde" cliche strips.

TOP: Publisher William Gaines (left) and editor Al Feldstein at the 1951 EC Christmas party. Harvey Kurtzman (top right) looks pretty MAD about missing out.

ABOVE: Dr Fredric Wertham almost destroyed the comics industry with his book, Seduction of the Innocent [1953].

FACING PAGE: Terry Beatty's 1981 Kitchen Sink homage to Kurtzman's original MAD #1 cover [1952].

But while Kurtzman and EC were busy raising standards, a rash of cash-in publishers had climbed on the gravy train of horror and crime comics producing gross visuals from hack scripts. This led to a public outcry against the entire industry.

Psychiatrist Dr Fredric Wertham was a leading comics critic. His 1954 book **Seduction of the Innocent** claimed that reading comics inevitably led to juvenile delinquency. It became a catalyst for Senate hearings to investigate the alleged link. These resulted in comics publishers banding together to form the Comics Code Authority as a self-imposed censorship body. The CCA cover seal of approval was created to restore distributors faith in comics and reassure young readers' concerned parents.

Immediately, distributors refused comics without the cover seal, bringing about the closure of all but the most vapid titles.

As *Trashman* creator Spain Rodriguez remarked, "As far as EC Comics go, what they were trying to do was make comics for adults. Guys in the armed forces were reading ECs. But the comics got swept into a kid's ghetto." Emphasizing the dumbing down of the medium and the ceiling being enforced on its audience, he added, "The Comics Code Authority was a brutal effort to shove all that stuff to the kids."

One of the major casualties of the new direction was EC Comics. Gaines had been a vocal advocate of the industry's right to publish what material it saw fit—even speaking out at the Senate hearings. Recklessly, he continued publishing without Code approval but within a year was down to one title, and that radically reshaped. Converted to a black and white magazine it escaped comics censorship.

Launched in 1952 with Harvey Kurtzman as editor, EC's **MAD** was originally a humour comicbook with satirical art by Wally Wood, Jack Davis, Will Elder and others whose work had been more associated with horror, science fiction and crime comics. Irreverent, anarchic and anti-establishment, the kids loved it.

"It totally flipped me out," said **Bijou Funnies** co-founder Jay Lynch.

"I remember thinking **MAD** was one of the few comics that didn't talk down to its audience, I dug it. When I was a kid, seeing something like that made me want to be a cartoonist."

To avoid scrutiny by the Comics Code Authority and escape the fate of the rest of the EC line, following its 24th issue **MAD** switched size and format from standard colour comicbook to black and white magazine. As a full-sized periodical, it enjoyed the benefits of better newsstand display and a higher cover price with only monochrome production costs.

However, within four issues of the format change, Kurtzman suddenly resigned from **MAD** over disagreements with publisher Gaines about editorial content. But his influential role in the industry continued to grow. Staying with satire, he joined forces with **Playboy**'s Hugh Hefner in 1957 for the short-lived **Trump**. When that failed after only two issues Kurtzman co-published **Humbug** with cartoonist Arnold Roth, who was to be heavily involved in his next project.

"An older brother of a friend of mine quit reading comics and gave me his collection, which included a run of **Humbug**," said Kitchen Sink's Denis Kitchen. "These left a most definite impression. I had seen a couple of them when they first came out but I was too young to really appreciate them. But by 1963 or so the exquisite Elder/Davis/Roth stories and parodies made sense to me. They spoke a truth to me. I was certain what I wanted to be… a cartoonist."

Humbug survived only 11 issues [1957-58] but, undaunted, Kurtzman launched **Help!** five years later for **Famous Monsters of Filmland** publisher James Warren. While being more reliant on photostrips than comic strips, it is notable for featuring some of the first professional art by Robert Crumb, Skip Williamson, Jay Lynch and Gilbert Shelton. Under art editor Terry Gilliam, who spent three years there (writing, designing and drawing—but being paid very little) **Help!** featured a young John Cleese in a photo strip as a guilt-ridden man having an affair with a small doll.

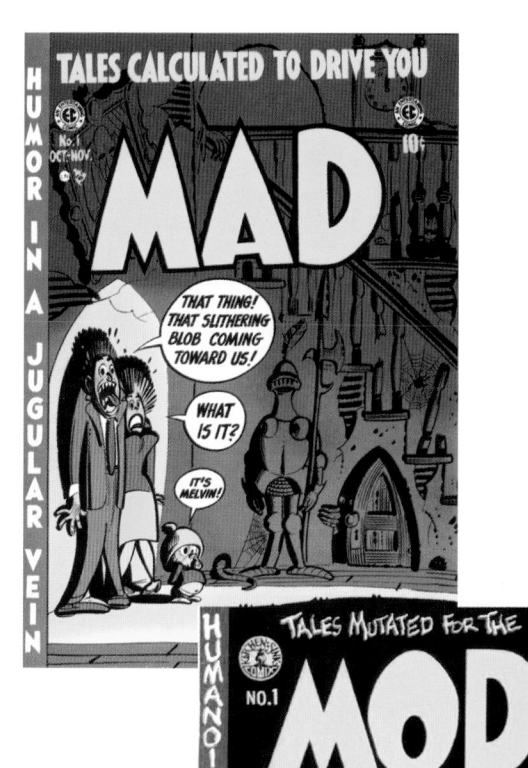

The magazine closed in 1965 after 26 issues, leaving Kurtzman free to continue with his paying work, the **Playboy** strip *Little Annie Fanny* which he and Will Elder produced from 1962 until 1988.

Minneapolis-born Gilliam, out of work and out of town, decided to travel further afield and, via California, landed in London in 1967.

Failing to find work in magazines and not knowing anybody else, he called John Cleese, who was by then a primetime BBC1 satirist, part of the team on David Frost's *That Was The Week That Was*. Cleese recommended him to a friend's in-development TV series, *Do Not Adjust Your Set*. The friend, Humphrey Barclay, was an amateur cartoonist and seeing Gilliam's work, offered him a job as writer/animator for the series. The writing pool also included Eric Idle, Terry Jones and Michael Palin. Without realizing it, Kurtzman had been a catalyst in bringing together a key part of the UK's foremost underground comedy team, *Monty Python's Flying Circus*.

Coincidentally, Cleese was not the only photo model from a Kurtzman magazine to star in *Monty Python*. Carol Cleveland, the series' female stooge, had appeared as a 15-year-old Miss Teen Queen in **MAD** Magazine in 1958.

About **Help!**, Kurtzman went on record to say, "We had a great collection of people. We worked with a whole galaxy of actors and actresses who went on to great things. And cartoonists! We worked with Robert Crumb and Gilbert Shelton. We were the first to publish *Fritz the Cat*... it was just amazing the caliber of people we had. We practically used the whole of what developed into the comics underground: Skip Williamson, Denis Kitchen, Jay Lynch, Bob Grossman and on and on and on."

Jay Lynch believes **Help!** was a milestone in the development of comix. "Skip and I had been brought up on a steady diet of Harvey Kurtzman. At that time, 1960-61, we decided that along with Shelton and Joel Beck we should send material to him. For a lot of the original underground artists, the first national magazine they got stuff in was

Help!, so in a sense it was probably the first underground comic."

While Kurtzman's experimental humour magazines were coming out of New York, over on the West Coast, the kids were beginning to take things into their own hands. By the early '60s the surfing scene was riding the crest of a wave and magazines appealing to surfers—who saw themselves outside the established community—were everywhere.

The pithily and aptly-titled **Surfer** magazine integrated comic strips and cartoons with photos and features and gave a 16-year-old Rick Griffin his first professional writing and drawing exposure.

Another bunch of west coast rebels with their own niche titles were the hot rod and dragster freaks, spearheaded by Ed 'Big Daddy' Roth.

Coochy Cooty Men's Comics creator Robert Williams: "I used to be art director for Ed 'Big Daddy' Roth, and that was very much an underground think tank down in Maywood. Roth was this very important seminal character in the underground. During 1959 to 1961 Roth was doing monster T-shirts. He would go to car shows, set up an airbrush, and just paint shirts for people. They caught on really big. So he started doing decals, and then selling these shirts through the mail. It became an institution in the early Sixties. He used very low-brow subject matter. There's a lot of beer cans, open wounds, warts, monsters with drool coming out, and popping eyeballs, like in the work of Basil Wolverton who was an influence on Roth and me too.

"Stanley Mouse, Rick Giffin, Victor Moscoso, Alton Kelly, and Wes Wilson did the very first psychedelic posters. Mouse is one of the better ones, on par nearly with Rick. He started out doing hot rod T-shirts, as a competitor with Roth. My work back then was kind of like a Wally Wood style, the EC science fiction comics artist who was a big influence on me too. But when psychedelics came along, it opened up the world of color and shape—an emphasis was put on things that were really not paid attention to before."

Explaining psychedelia, he added, "The predominant thing about psychedelics is harsh contrast, working one color against another.

ABOVE: Coochy Cooty by Robert Williams [1970], yet another swipe at the monolithic Disney corporation. You did recognize those gloves and booties, didn't you?

FACING PAGE: Through his HELP! magazine [1960], Harvey Kurtzman brought together two of the Monty Python team, John Cleese and Terry Gilliam.

ABOVE: A 1961 magazine advertisement for Ed "Big Daddy" Roth's hot rod and dragster T-shirt designs, with artwork by Robert Williams.

FACING PAGE: An early '60s Shelton designed poster for Shiva's Headband (top). While the title would have a different meaning now, Drag Cartoons (below) featured work by Peter Millar who not only drew them, but raced the cars as well.

That had been done by the German Expressionists, but it wasn't done like this. The German Expressionists like to get one color against another color to make it ugly—real dark green against harsh pink, for example—and it would be this real obtrusive thing. But our psychedelic art wasn't like that, it was colors at their maximum. It's like 100% yellow against 100% red."

Roth is now an Utah elder in the Church of Mormon, "Depressing, isn't it?" says Williams. He calls his old art director a pornographer, while Williams calls him a religious zealot. But in the early 1960s Roth built up a prominent brand name, and among his many enterprises was **Big Daddy Roth's Magazine**, which not only included strips by comics legends Alex Toth, Reed Crandall and Russ Manning, but also the work of a young Rick Griffin. Its editor was Pete Millar who went on to publish **Rod & Custom** featuring early work by Rand Holmes and **Drag Cartoons**, which in 1966 began running Tony Bell and Gilbert Shelton's *Wonder Wart-Hog*, a seminal underground strip that had previously appeared in **Help!** and The Texas Ranger.

The pre-**Freak Brothers** Shelton—who became editor of **Speed and Custom** and **Custom Rodder**—was also a member of what has become known as the Texas Mafia, a group of cartoonists including comix pioneers Frank Stack, Jack Jackson and Fred Todd. Between 1962 and 1963 Shelton had also been editor of **The Texas Ranger**, a humour magazine produced by students at the University of Texas.

Very much the forerunners of underground comix in terms of their irreverent attitude if not content, campus magazines were a key focus for social and political agitation. **The Texas Ranger**'s contemporaries included the University of California at Berkeley's **The Pelican**, which published early work by Joel Beck and John Thompson, Los Angeles' **Occidental College Fang**—edited by Terry Gilliam—and **The Harvard Lampoon**, which begat **National Lampoon**. Other key rag mags included **Voo Doo** at M.I.T., Ohio State's **Sundial**, **Chaparral** at Stanford and **Satyr** at U.C.L.A.

In 1962 Shelton's Wonder Wart-Hog strips appeared in **Bacchanal**, a short-lived off-campus mag. When that failed after two issues, the strip carried on in **The Texas Ranger** and **Charlatan**, a University of Oklahoma student title that went independent when its editor Bill Killeen took to the road. Among others supplying material to both titles were Lynch and Beck as well as Skip Williamson and Art Spiegelman.

After **The Texas Ranger**, Shelton became involved in starting up **The Austin Iconoclastic** and, when that folded after 12 issues, he opted to publish a collection of *The Adventures of Jesus*, a strip Stack had been drawing since 1961.

Cited as the first underground comic despite a print run of only 50 copies, **The Adventures of J** appeared in 1964. It was credited to F. S. (Foolbert Sturgeon) a pseudonym the cartoonist hid behind to protect his university tenure. In parallel to this, Jack Jackson was working for the government during the early 1960s and under his alias, Jaxon, self-published his strips in **God Nose (Snot Reel)** later in 1964. Many feel this to be the first of the undergrounds by virtue of its strips being originated for the title rather than reprinted from other sources.

Jaxon says he produced it because, "Underground comix developed out of the Sixties counterculture movement as an alternative to the type of comicbooks being offered by the big companies like Marvel and DC. We tried to appeal to the hippie audience that could find nothing about its lifestyle in other media of the time."

As the various members of the Texas Mafia began to head out on individual treks that would ultimately reunite them in San Francisco, major changes were starting to happen. The advent of offset printing reduced the cost of small print runs and this was the catalyst that generated the underground press and its weekly newspapers.

In 1965, politically aware tabloids began appearing everywhere. The **Los Angeles Free Press, Berkeley Barb** and New York's **East Village Other** were the forerunners with the **San Francisco Oracle, Chicago Seed**, Detroit's **Fifth Estate** and many more following within months.

Mr. Natural, disguised as a vacuum cleaner salesman, talks to the Housewives of America.

"The comics I did during this period were sociopolitical type comics with a few 'mystical' pages," said John Thompson, a prolific producer of psychedelic posters who would go on to provide strips for the **East Village Other**. "I feel my humorous comics work for the **Barb** weekly was significant in what I did. Both Joel Beck and myself were the first to publish counterculture comics in the hippie tradition there."

While the plethora of underground newspapers all featured comics and cartoons, it was the tabloid-sized **East Village Other** that led the way. It devoted full pages to strips and in 1966 even commissioned an all-comics issue. Manuel "Spain" Rodriguez was a regular contributor as were Trina Robbins, Kim Deitch, Nancy Kalish and Vaughn Bode.

Bode would later become editor of the first issue of **Gothic Blimp Works**, the comic tabloid launched less than a year after **Zap** had sparked off the demand. California-based Robbins, creator of the comic **It Ain't Me Babe**, recalls Manhattan's **EVO** as not being as politically aware as the **LA Free Press**. "It was more about hippie politics. Off the Pigs was their editorial policy."

Describing his introductory meeting with **EVO** editor Walter Bowart, **Maus** creator Art Spiegelman said, "When I first went there, Bowart said he liked my comics, but to do some with sex and dope in them, of which I had no experience. I didn't know where to approach the comics from. I wandered away and came back about two years later after a lot of experience with both, and started drawing for them."

EVO also featured early work by Robert Crumb, who said Bill Beckman's *Captain High* strips, which also appeared in the newspaper, were "the first underground of hippie-type comic strips I ever saw."

Crumb to the fore

The far-from-hip cartoonist had been introduced to a national audience via men's magazine Cavalier, which had made him something of a celebrity when it published his *Stoned* strip in October 1967.

He was also becoming well known among the emergent hippies

through his work for the **East Village Other** and, more significantly, for the Philadelphia underground newspaper **Yarrowstalks**. In the autumn of '67 **Yarrowstalks** devoted its entire third issue to Crumb comix for which the cartoonist was paid with 500 copies of the paper. These he hawked around San Francisco's head shops with great success.

Inspired by this demand and encouraged by Don Donahue and Charles Plymell, who were to become his publisher and printer, the cartoonist began creating material for his own comic.

Donahue and Plymell were both looking for new material for their own underground newspapers when Plymell showed Donahue some of Crumb's work in **Yarrowstalks** #1.

"It was the *Head Comix* page," explained Donahue. "It was the first thing I ever saw by Crumb. I had never seen anything like it before. Charlie and I both went out of our heads. It was one of the heaviest things we'd seen around in a long time.

"We assumed R. Crumb had to be a pseudonym, because it fitted in with the work," he continued. "It didn't seem like a real name. Later on we saw another thing by the same guy in **East Village Other**. I thought he must be an old man, because that's the way it looked. Maybe he'd been drawing for comic books back in the '20s and '30s and he went berserk or something."

Determined to get some of Crumb's work for their own titles, the pair set about tracking down the cartoonist. When they found him it was not in Philly or New York as they expected, but just a few blocks away in San Francisco's Haight-Ashbury district.

As Crumb recalls, "I did this comic for this guy named Brian Zahn in Philadelphia. First I did some stuff for his underground newspaper. He came back and said, 'Hey, people really like that stuff a lot! Why don't you send a whole comic?'"

So Crumb was ready when Donahue and Plymell tracked him down. He had been working on the comic book for Zahn but had had a false start when the artwork for the original first issue went missing along

ABOVE: R. Crumb's cover to Yarrowstalks #3. The artist was paid in copies which he then sold on.

FACING PAGE: A huge range of alternative newspapers, including The East Village Other, Georgia Straight and San Francisco Oracle provided an outlet for the early work of many leading underground cartoonists.

with its intended publisher. "I did two comics **Zap** #0 and **Zap** #1. I sent him **Zap** #0 and told him another was ready as soon as that one sold. **Zap** #0 was stolen by this guy Zahn."

By pure luck, the only art Crumb had made photostats of was for this very issue. "I never heard from Zahn again, so when I met Don Donahue and Charlie Plymell, they printed **Zap** #1."

With Apex Novelties, Donahue became a pioneer comix publisher. "Plymell split and Donahue took over. Plymell just left town. I don't know where he went, he was one of those old beatnik guys," Crumb recalls. Donahue's take was, "I hired Charlie Plymell to run off the cover and pages. I couldn't pay him, having zero capital, so I gave him an expensive tape recorder." He added that the birth of the undergrounds was "a joke that got out of hand." He maintains that Crumb had been sitting around drunk one night and came up with the idea of doing a comic book and, as he had a multilith, Donanhue printed it.

Crumb disagrees, saying his first comic was "a thrill, an exciting thing. We just started small. It wasn't a joke. We wanted to get a comic book out."

Whatever the reason for starting it, **Zap** #1 was an instant hit as the cartoonist and his heavily pregnant wife discovered as they sold copies out of a pram they pushed through the crowds attending a street party on San Francisco's Haight.

As Plymell recalled, "Crumb and Dana did spend a few hours on February 25th with the baby carriage down there on Haight Street, that's true. But we sold the bulk of them to Bob Rita over at Third

World Distribution on Haight Street for cash. From there they went all over the country. The hippie vendors from all over the Bay Area went there to pick up their stuff."

The bulk bought by Bob Rita is said to be 4,000 of the 5,000 print run, meaning that Crumb and friends still managed to sell an impressive 1,000 copies themselves. However Plymell believes that because of paper wasted in learning how to print it, the final count was 1,500 or less. Either way, demand was such that it was reprinted two months later.

"The thing about **Zap**," explained Donahue, "about underground comix in general, is here is this whole medium of expression that had been neglected for so long or relegated to this very inferior position and nobody had done much with it. And all of a sudden someone did start something with it, and then there was this explosion."

The impact of Zap

Spain—whose tabloid **Zodiac Mindwarp** was conceived as a comic although the printer couldn't handle it—said of the early days, "The '60s seemed to have this underground resonance; this psychedelic thing that's hard to put your finger on. It seemed to have escaped all this boring post-Comic Code format. Before **Zap**, comics were hardly ever worth reading."

Zippy creator Bill Griffith says, "Crumb spoke for everybody. Plus he had the guts to do these comicbooks. He reinvented the comicbook. Took it over just as other people of his generation took over music. He just said, 'No, you can't have it that way. We're gonna make it the way we want it!' That's an incredible thing to have done.

There are very few people that you can say literally became the starting point for a whole movement. I mean there are people who will tell you that the very first underground comic book was **God Nose** by Jaxon, or was **Lenny of Laredo** by Joel Beck, but Crumb had the real big vision, the burning vision. Like I said, he reinvented the form."

The reaction to **Zap #1** by prolific poster artist Victor Moscoso was, "Far out! I was familiar with Crumb's artwork because I had seen it in **Yarrowstalks**. And when I was in New York in '67, I saw Crumb's work, like *Life Among the Constipated*. I couldn't tell if it was an old man drawing young, or a young man drawing old. Just like the old-time comics on acid. Crumb was very enamored of the archaic comics, the early comics and newspaper strips, just like he was with early music. But what really got me was the format. Color cover, black and white newsprint inside for only 50 cents. Cheapness equals availability. Availability equals distribution. You can get rid of millions of them for 50 cents. If we had to charge $5, we wouldn't have sold as many. Not only that, it smelled like comics did when I was a kid. Newsprint has a certain smell, a certain feel. I love the cheapness."

Talking about how he became involved in the comic, Moscoso continued, "Then Crumb found us and invited us in. He knew who we were. After all, we were famous. Griffin and I were famous in **Zap #2**. **Zap #1** was a sellout on the Haight-Ashbury. It was because of me and Griffin being in **Zap #2** that made it so easy to get the backing. And where were they distributed? The Print Mint was to be the distributor. They were distributed in poster shops, where Moscoso and Griffin posters were selling like hotcakes. Anything with Moscoso and Griffin on it, at that time, would sell. So, we come out with a comic. Who are these guys? Crumb, Wilson — holy shit! 'Head First.' God! That's disgusting, and then **Zap #3**, *Captain Pissgums And His Pervert Pirates?* Oh, my God! This is going to ruin our children. Crumb and Wilson were taking on the taboos straight on. And at that point I thought the taboos were all illusions, until Crumb did *Joe Blow*. Then

ABOVE: EVO's first issue of Gothic Blimp Works [1969], the only one Vaughn Bode managed to edit.

FACING PAGE: Joel Beck's cover to his Lenny of Laredo, one of the early ones [1965]. Beck was working on a sequel when he died in 2000, aged 56.

I realized, OK, you can chop off a guy's penis and eat it. That's all right. But you can't fuck your children. There are limits in this civilized society. It's interesting, that's the way it works. They sold even more because of it of course, but you couldn't buy it over the counter."

But Crumb disagreed about The Print Mint as a distributor for **Zap**. "When we first started **Zap**, the first thing Don Schenker wanted us to do was make a contract so that all the comix from then on would be done by The Print Mint. If we'd gone along with that, that company would have turned into the biggest rip-off tyrants you ever saw! They paid the best, that's the truth. They tried pulling some shit all along the line though. I don't think they're any more just than anyone else. They're more efficient though."

First among equals, ergo ego

Moscoso on working together on **Zap**: "I don't remember any ego problems, because we were all equals. We were not impressed by Crumb, the way some people might be impressed by Crumb, because he was just another artist. I don't give a shit if he created the format for **Zap**. Rick and I were famous before he was. You're not going to impress me, Buster. I was not intimidated. In fact, I did him a big favor, by helping make him a star faster than he would have been otherwise by tying into the poster distribution, which bypassed the Marvel and DC Mafia."

Meanwhile, back in Texas, Gilbert Shelton had already tried newsstand comix in 1967 with two 64-page magazines, **Fearless Fighting Foul-Mouthed Wonder Wart-Hog, the Hog of Steel** and **Wonder Wart-Hog Quarterly** #2 (Millar Publishing), which had helped plunge the publisher into bankruptcy. But, with Crumb's success, Shelton saw undergrounds as a way forward.

Over in Illinois, Jay Lynch and Skip Williamson had been contributors to the **Chicago Mirror** in 1974. Also inspired by Crumb's **Zap** #1, they transformed the satire magazine into **Bijou Funnies** and launched it with an issue that featured their work plus Jay Kinney, Crumb and material from Shelton's then unpublished **Feds 'n' Heads**. Predating **Zap** #2, it is heralded as the first example of the cooperative nature inherent within a new style of publishing.

Shelton then self-published **Feds 'n' Heads**, which resurrected Wonder Wart-Hog and introduced the Fabulous Furry Freak Brothers to the world. Then he headed for San Francisco.

Once there he made a deal with The Print Mint to publish future issues of his title. He also arrived in time to contribute a *Wonder Wart-Hog* strip to the third issue of **Zap** [1968].

As Crumb remarked about the whole **Zap** group in 1974, "After a while, it got to be a tight thing and other people wanted to get in. It got messy. So there was a push to come out more often—so we could all make more money. But nobody wanted to let the other artists in on it so we could have eased the burden of getting the stuff out. **Zap** sold because of the title. Wilson said, 'You can't degrade the magazine because the title sells!' I said we wouldn't necessarily be degrading it because we were letting other artists in. If they were good, it was okay. But who was going to decide on who was a good artist? It got to be a fucking hassle. I didn't want anything to do with that, so I just washed my hands of the whole business."

RIGHT: "We didn't very often ask each other for advice," says Moscoso about the time Crumb asked for his thoughts about the original Zap #1 cover [top]. "I looked at it and said, 'It don't look right, Robert. The guy is in a fetal position with electricity surrounding him, so to have the chord go into his ass doesn't make as much sense as if it went into his umbilical cord.' And he actually took my advice."

FACING PAGE: Rip Off Press opens for business (above). Rip Off co-founder Gilbert Shelton's early colour experimental work on Feds 'n' Heads (below).

Tijuana Bibles

America's forbidden funnies from the '30s to the '50s

THE Tijuana Bibles have acquired a legendary status as arguably the earliest form of US underground comix and certainly the most outrageous. Anonymously produced from the 1930s through to the 1950s, they were cigarette-packet sized eight-page booklets, running one comic strip picture a page, dedicated to poking fun at every icon imagineable. Breaking both sexual taboos and legal copyrights—with it taking almost 50 years of litigation to prove them protected by the First Amendment—they parodied almost 1000 subjects, from Adolf Hitler and Al Capone to The Marx Brothers and Mickey Mouse.

Pop artist Roy Lichtenstein summed them up by saying, "Sex can be seen as absurd and comical... The Tijuana Bibles have a charming, harmless naughtiness that portrays a hidden side of their era."

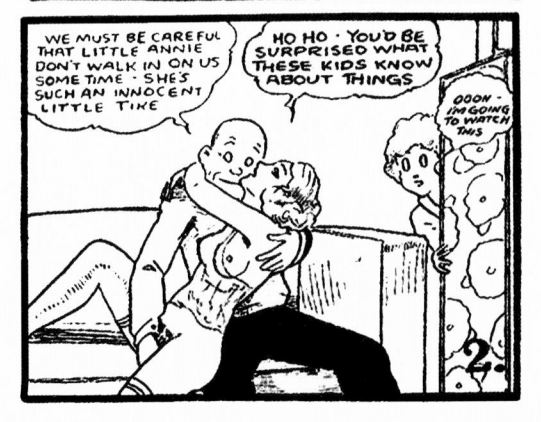

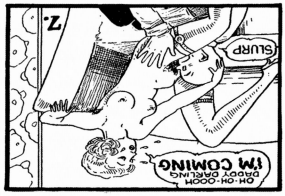

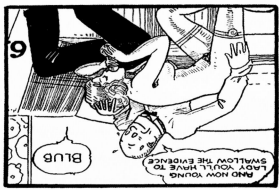

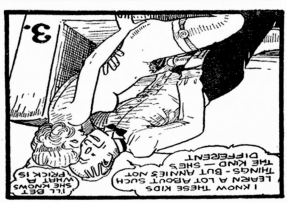

Chapter 1:

Heroes of the Revolution

The major players

"A painfully shy out-of-it nerd ...a lonely maladjusted weirdo with heavy Catholic guilt." ...CRUMB ON CRUMB, PRE-ZAP, DRUGS AND ROCK N ROLL

They didn't really know what they were doing. They got ripped off, busted, screwed and shafted by just about everyone. But out of the counter culture revolution emerged a handful of heroes.

NO more publishers... no more editors... no more deadlines or late cheques. And, most importantly of all, no censorship. School's out, for the summer of love.

Attracted to the freedom of doing their own thing, a new generation of cartoonists from across America rose to the heady challenge of producing a unique range of comix, branded X for their generation.

Some said their piece then faded into obscurity, others basked in their 15 minutes of fame. But a handful made a lasting impact, both on comics and the international art world in general.

R. Crumb

Gawky, introverted and frustrated. Myopic, short-haired and nerdy—a 1940s leftover with funny moustache and beaten-up hat. Not a description you'd associate with the age of peace, love and beautiful people. Yet the greatest success of the San Francisco '60s comix scene, the one man most identified with the times fits that unlikely description, Robert Crumb.

Living the American dream, Crumb not only fulfilled his wildest desires, he surpassed them. Shoehorned into a dull job in a quiet town, he escaped to became the darling of the hippie revolution, achieving ultimate acclaim as probably the 20th century's greatest cartoonist.

Born in Philadelphia on August 30th, 1943, he was the third of five children to career marine Charles Crumb Sr and his wife Beatrice. By the age of three, he was a keen artist, already drawing his own comics. But it wasn't until 1962 that he began to earn a wage from his hobby. Moving to Cleveland, Ohio in 1962, he worked for The American Greetings Corporation under the sort of factory line conditions that existed in many industries from clothing to animation.

Artists worked in lines of cubicles, each merely adding an identical detail to every card, all under the watchful eye of the studio manager who maintained quality control over the end product. This was the kind of soul-destroying arrangement which could totally shatter the ambition of any would-be creative artist. But as bad as this would be to any contemporary cartoonist, this was the Swinging Sixties, the era of free love, teenage liberation and drug experimentation. But not for Crumb and Cleveland, Ohio. As he recalls, in the early 1960s he was "a painfully shy out-of-it nerd... a lonely maladjusted weirdo with heavy Catholic guilt."

In 1963 Crumb spent six lonely months in his sleazy batchelor pad on Cleveland's East Side. It was there he fell in love with Dana Morgan "also a horny young virgin, looking for love in a sad, jaded world."

They married in 1964, and divorced in 1977 when Crumb fled to France to postpone payment on a $30,000 tax bill on his *Keep on Truckin'* poster. A federal judge had ruled that, as Crumb had never registered copyright, the image was in public domain so a substantial portion of Crumb's royalty payments suddenly dried up.

Dana Crumb on their early days said, "One thing led to another and

Living the American Dream, Crumb not only fulfilled his wildest desires, he surpassed them.

ABOVE: As Bob Dylan once sang, "Sometimes even the President of the United States has to go naked." A self-portrait from R. Crumb Sketchbook volume 6 (Fantagraphics).

LEFT: One of R. Crumb's most iconic images, the Keep On Truckin' poster appeared on countless walls during the '60s but the artist ended up not getting a penny. A US judge declared the image to be in the public domain.

we were married on September 11, 1964. The wedding was sad and silly. We moved to New York and lived in my Aunt Leah's Lincoln Center apartment for about four weeks while we made plans to go to Europe and live there for as long as we could on our savings, the money gleaned from returning all of our wedding presents. We booked a passage on a Norwegian freighter with eight other passengers and off we went. Big dreams and scared shitless. We spent nine months walking all over Europe. Harvey Kurtzman sent us to Bulgaria for ten days."

Kurtzman, as editor/creator of **MAD**, had been Crumb's boyhood idol. By now the 21-year-old was drawing the first commissioned *Fritz the Cat*, a character he had been developing in notebooks since 1959. This was for mens' magazine **Cavalier**. Also in 1964 he had submitted strips to Kurtzman, at the time producing **Help!** magazine. "We really like the cat cartoon," wrote Kurtzman. "But we're not sure how we can print it and stay out of jail."

When **Help!** folded just after Crumb returned from his nine-month European honeymoon, he stayed in New York to find other work, including a period drawing trading card art for Topps Bubble Gum. But he found little else and soon returned to Cleveland.

There, he went back to American Greetings for eight months. It was, he said, the last time he ever held down a nine-to-five job.

Restless, he started frequenting bars and one afternoon in January 1967 two friends told him they were splitting for San Francisco that night. With less than $8 in his pocket, he went with them, without so much as a phone call to his wife. A year later, he was a famous cartoonist.

By February 1968, Dana had gone to San Francisco to join her husband at the time of **Zap** launching. "We folded and stapled all 5000 copies ourselves," Crumb remarks. Following its success, his output was prodigious. Across the years his creations included **Motor City Comics**, **Uneeda Comix**, **Homegrown Funnies**, **Big Ass Comics** and **Weirdo**.

Fulfilling a prurient demand for such, he also focused on the easy money aspect of publishing: sex. When aspiring artist Mary Fleener wrote to Crumb for advice on her *Li'l Mofo* strip, he replied, "Draw it the way you want it to look." Most importantly he told her, "Sex sells, Fleener; sex sells." Taking his own advice, Crumb went to the extreme, launching **Snatch Comics, Jiz** and **Cunt Comics**, which kicked off a whole wave of underground sex titles.

As comics shockjock S Clay Wilson recollects, "When I met Crumb we talked, smoked some pot and drew some cartoons. Later, I talked Crumb—a repressed Catholic choirboy—into drawing dirty… That is, drawing anything that occurred to him, without censorship or concern for an imagined audience. He took my advice and did so with relish."

In an interview in **East Village Other**, a Trina Robbins quote is thrown at Crumb, accusing him of hostility towards women in his work. Instead of defending himself, he openly replies, "No, I'm just me—26 years old—and I am hostile towards women."

LEFT: A Crumb classic: Mr Natural's 719th Meditation from Zap #6 [1973].

FACING PAGE: An R. Crumb self-portrait, taken from Last Gasp's Tales from the Leather Nun [1973].

Crumb created a swathe of bizarre characters who, being way out racist and sexist, would have great difficulty being accepted were they created today. These included Angelfood McSpade, Honeybunch Kaminski, Mr Natural, Shuman the Human, Whiteman and the Snoid. Most were conceived while Crumb was having a bad acid trip in 1965. This was his first experience of LSD and he reflected afterwards on how it brought home his feeling of displacement, "The whole world I was living in just seemed like a puppet show, a tragic farce."

Crumb even became a youth culture hero outside of comix, through posters of his skewed vision being as crucial on every dorm wall as Che or Dali. Top pinups included the classic *Keep on Truckin'*, plus *Tommy Toilet, Stoned Again* and *A Short History of America*.

Perhaps it was not his vision which was skewed, but his life. John Thompson, cartoonist, a year after the launch of **Zap**: "Bob [Crumb] had been experimenting with what were then called 'conciousness-expanding drugs,' which worried Dana. She told me that on his trips, Bob sometimes felt he was the incarnation of a 1930s cartoonist and, on some occasions, that he was a 1930s cartoon reborn as a human."

Thompson also commented on Crumb's wife, "I met his extremely glum and quite overweight wife. Dana had dark stringy hair and looked miserable—very out of place in the exotic Haight. Bob told me a few months after they were married, he rode home as usual on the bus. But instead of getting off at his stop, he got off at the end of the line and walked west, and kept walking and hitchhiking with no destination in mind, ending up at Haight Ashbury. He phoned Dana a couple of weeks later and she was frantic. He said he'd left his life in Cleveland behind him. But Dana, who was pregnant, came out to the West Coast to join him. This, Bob explained, was why Dana looked so miserable."

By 1974 Dana—now described as a Barbara Stanwyck-type character—had been with Crumb on a secluded Californian farm. "The way things are going, I want to get this place workable... so it'll support itself and me," he said, having little faith in his future in comix.

Keith Green of the Cartoonists Co-Op Press arrived to interview him there and discovered Dana had bought a cow that had gone mad.

Colourfully, she told Green she planned to "Chase it down, blow its brains out, slit its throat and get the good-for-nuthin' horse to haul it back to the ranch for burgers."

Gilbert Shelton

As Frank Stack summed it up, "In my opinion, Crumb is the best comicbook artist who ever lived—and Shelton is his best competition."

Born in 1940 in Houston, Texas, Gilbert Shelton hated superhero comics ("too silly") and introduced his Superman parody, Wonder Wart-Hog, in a 1961 issue of **The Texas Ranger**, the University of Texas's student magazine which he was to edit after Frank Stack from 1962 to 1963. The Hog of Steel went on to appear in **Bacchanal**, an off-campus magazine, and **Charlatan**, another student title, as well as **Drag Cartoons** and **Help!** while the cartoonist himself followed another passion and became editor of **Speed and Custom** and **Custom Rodder**.

One of the lucky ones, Shelton was drafted in 1964—a time when the Vietnam crisis was hotting up—but the army only kept him for a few days. "They said I was medically unfit. Maybe they didn't like the fact that I admitted taking drugs like peyote and LSD," he confessed.

A member of the "Texas Mafia" along with Jack Jackson, Dave Moriarty, Frank Stack and Fred Todd, Shelton is another person credited with publishing the first underground. 1964's **The Adventures of J** was a small 50 copy print run collection of *The Adventures of Jesus*, a strip Stack had been drawing since 1961.

In 1967, Shelton convinced Millar Publishing to get his seminal

LEFT: Gilbert Shelton's Wonder Wart-Hog "the world's awfullest smelling superhero" from the cover to The Print Mint's Best of Wonder Warthog II [1973]; art by Tony Bell.

FACING PAGE: An early 1960s shot of Gilbert Shelton which defies description.

underground creation onto the newsstands. **Fearless Fighting Foul-Mouthed Wonder Wart-Hog, the Hog of Steel** was followed by **Wonder Wart-Hog Quarterly** #2 but distribution problems for the 64-pagers meant little more than 25% of each issue's 140,000 copies were sold.

The following year, after a brief attempt to run his own head shop in Austin, Shelton was inspired to write and draw his own comic by the first issue of **Zap** and by **R. Crumb's Head Comics**, a mainstream collection of the cartoonist's early work published by Viking Press.

His self-published **Feds 'n' Heads** starred Wonder Wart-Hog but also introduced Phineas, Freewheelin' Franklin and Fat Freddy—the "Loveable" Furry Freak Brothers as they were then known, but under any name probably the most recognizable characters to come out of the entire underground scene. With a title of his own under his belt, Shelton then headed for San Francisco where he contributed a *Wonder Wart-Hog* strip to **Zap** #3. In 1969 he joined forces with Jackson, Todd and Dave Moriarty to set up Rip Off Press, a major publisher of underground comics which has survived relatively intact to this day.

Nowhere near as prolific as Crumb, he still contributed to a variety of titles, among them **Anarchy Comics**, **Arcade**, **Bijou Funnies**, **Cascade Comix Monthly**, **Facts O' Life Sex Education Funnies** and **Tales from the Ozone**. But it was the launch of his archetypal hairy hippie trio's own comic which set things rolling.

The first issue of **The Fabulous Furry Freak Brothers** appeared in 1971 reprinting strips from **The LA Free Press** and **High Times** newspapers and from comix including **Yellow Dog**, **Radical America Komiks**, **Zap** and **Rip Off Comix**. With #4 [1975], the title began running new material so Shelton needed help, first from Dave Sheridan and later Paul Mavrides.

It took 27 years for **Freak Brothers** to reach #13 but it did spawn two spin-offs along the way. **The Adventures of Fat Freddy's Cat** ran six issues from 1977 to 1986 while two issues of **Fat Freddy's Comics & Stories** appeared in 1983 and 1986.

The Freak Brothers comic has now been superceded by **Not Quite Dead**, launched in 1993 and as sporadic as its predecessor with only four issues having appeared to date. Probably inspired by Shelton's own not-inconsiderable musical talents, it features the exploits of "The World's Most Experienced Rock Band" who, collectively, have more than 800 years experience —most at the end of the business where a really good gig is a biker funeral with plenty of free beer.

Rick Griffin

While S. Clay Wilson can take credit for expanding comix boundaries, Rick Griffin's influence is one of style rather than content.

Born outside Palo Verdes, California in 1941, Richard Alden Griffin became a surfer in his early teens. An avid **MAD Magazine**-inspired cartoonist with an interest in hot rod cars and motorbikes, he was soon decorating vehicles as well as providing visuals for members of the surfing community, including freelance work for **Surfer** magazine during his last few High School years. Following graduation, he became staff artist on **Surfer**, where he created a mascot—his personally trademarked Murphy gremlin. It became an integral part of the Californian surf scene and he continued to produce new strips and visuals of it through to the late '80s.

Griffin not only provided artwork for Ed "Big Daddy" Roth, the main man in customized cars, he also contributed to such titles as **Car Toon Magazine** and **Hot Rod Cartoons**.

His embryonic psychedelic style became fully developed following his 1966 move to San Francisco. In 1967 he created a poster for *Pow-Wow: A Gathering of the Tribes for a Human Be-In*, the event which kicked off the Summer of Love.

Drawing on diverse influences including Native American culture, the Californian surf scene, 19th century graphics and the burgeoning flower power movement, he incorporated beetles, skulls, vivid colours and wild lettering into his posters promoting concerts by such rock legends as Jimi Hendrix and the Grateful Dead. He created the cover logo for **Rolling Stone** magazine as well as many album sleeves, the best-known being for the Grateful Dead's *Aoxomoxoa*.

In a 1967 partnership with Alton Kelly, Stanley Mouse, Victor Moscoso and Wes Wilson, Griffin founded the Berkeley-Bonaparte distribution agency. These artists were recognized as the "Big Five" of psychedelia, and used the company to print and sell their far out designs. Its most famous poster is Griffin's *Flying Eyeball*—also known as *Bill Graham #105*, being the 105th poster created for the legendary Philmore Auditorium promoter. It was created for a 1968 concert by Hendrix, John Mayall and Albert King and is much sought after by fans and modern art museums alike.

Griffin produced only a small amount of comix work. Epitomized by his own **Tales from the Tube**, his work also appeared in **Zap**—where he often collaborated with Moscoso—and **Snatch**.

Moving to southern California in 1969, Griffin started down a path that would lead him to become a Born Again Christian, a conversion he documented in 1972's **The Man from Utopia**. His newfound faith was

Continued on p40

Happy hippie, surf king and psychedelia star, Rick Griffin (facing page) plus two of his comix covers (right) and his mind-blowing centrespread from Tales from the Tube (over).

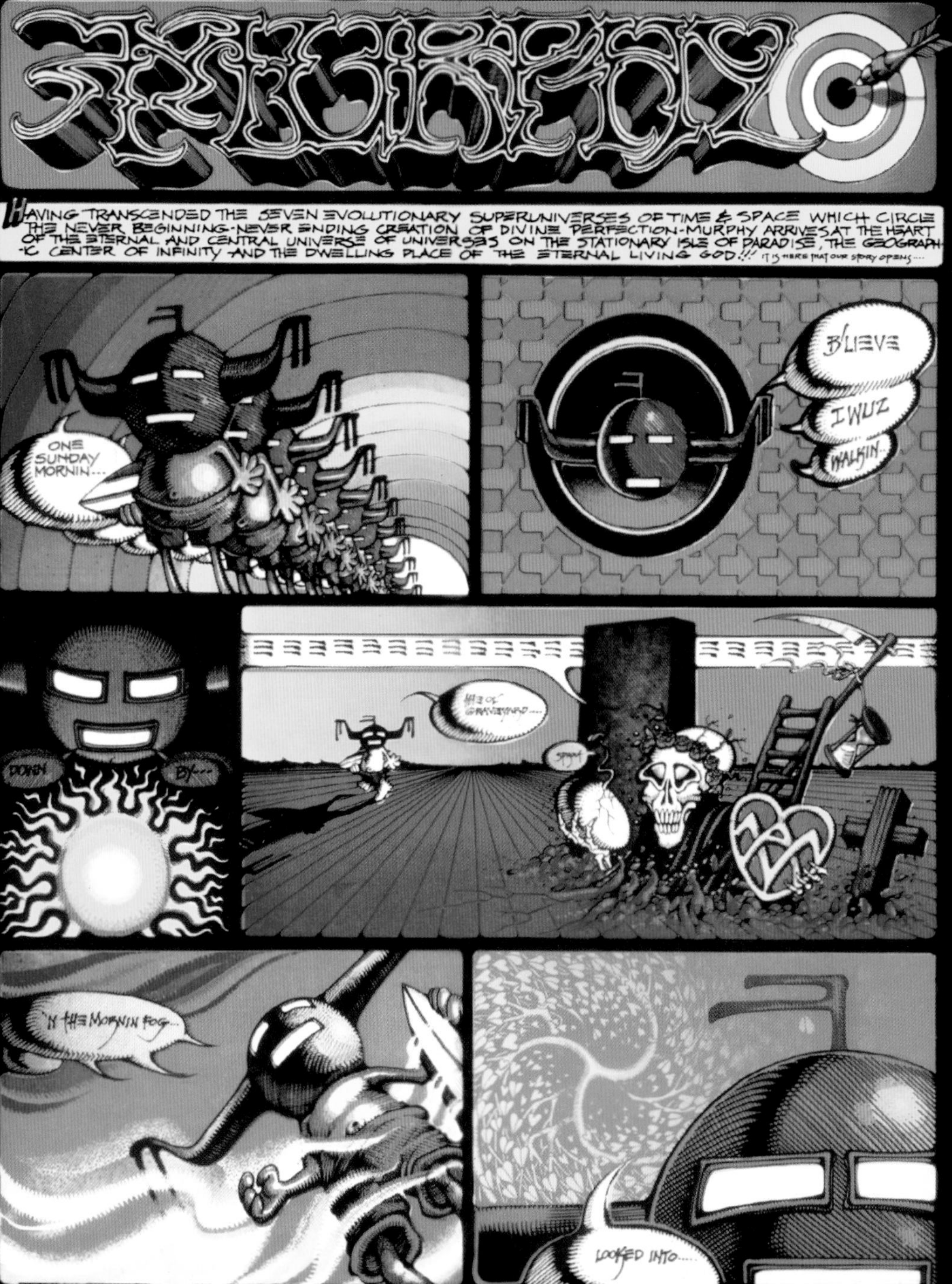

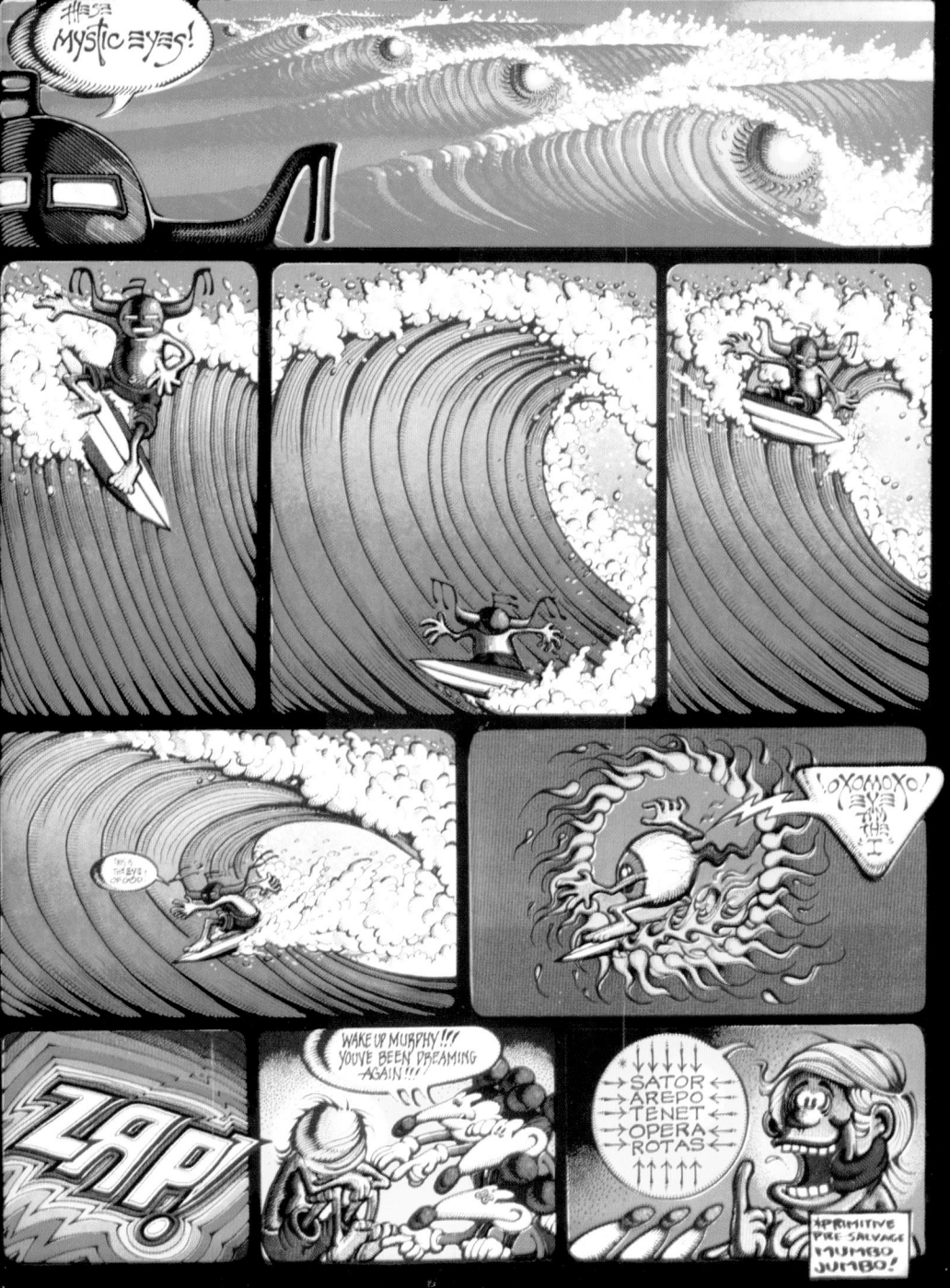

also reflected in *Omo Bob Heads South*, his last **Zap** story for #6 [1973], and in his continuing contributions to **Surfer Magazine**.

As art director by Maranatha Music from the late '70s through to the mid-80s, Griffin produced album covers, posters and flyers for Christian singers while in 1980 he illustrated **The Gospel of John**, a book published by The Word for Today. For the following ten years he worked mainly for secular projects and companies.

His final work before his death in a motorbike accident in 1991 was, ironically, a self-portrait he entitled "Heaven's Gate."

Denis Kitchen

Unlike Shelton, who rationed his output to increase his quality of life, Denis Kitchen put aside his drawing board in favour of a publisher's desk. It was a decision that would lead him out of the underground and into the mainstream limelight as an advocate of the comics medium.

Born in Milwaukee in 1946, Kitchen's first foray into publishing was a magazine he produced while still at school. "My main creative outlet was **Klepto**, which I typed and illustrated on multi-colour carbon-like sheets," he explained. "I printed and collated them in the office of a sympathetic secretary. And then I carefully hawked up to 200 eager classmates. The school did not approve."

Kitchen's career path became clear when he was given a run of Harvey Kurtzman's **Humbug**. "These left a definite impression. I had seen a couple of **Humbug**s when they first came out in 1957-58 but I was too young to appreciate them. But by 1963 or so the exquisite Elder/Davis/Roth stories and parodies made sense to me. They spoke a truth to me. I was certain what I wanted to be: a cartoonist."

A journalism graduate, Kitchen never immersed himself totally in the counter culture movement. Singlehandedly he wrote, drew, published and distributed his first title, **Mom's Homemade Comix** [1969], but even as his "hippie empire" grew, he produced commercial work for straight magazines and other establishment outlets.

The San Francisco-based Print Mint produced its own edition of Kitchen's first issue as well as publishing **Mom's Homemade #2** and this increased profile brought him to the attention of such cartoonists as Jay Lynch and Skip Williamson. Crumb told Kitchen his sense of humour was "something unique in all of comicdom. Don't even ask me how, but keep it up! And don't listen to anybody! Do it your way!"

It was advice he probably took to heart in 1970 when, like Crumb, he became disenchanted with Print Mint's accounting methods. His unhappiness led him to consider self-publishing **Mom's Homemade** #3—which eventually appeared in 1971—but his raised profile began to attract others to what he had dubbed Kumquat Productions. "For some reason we thought Kumquat had a vaguely erotic tone."

Kumquat produced single issues of **Quagmire** and **Smile**. Although neither was a success, Kitchen had more titles lined up and realized the expansion would need funding. As a result, in 1970

Let's Be Honest

YOU MAY THINK THAT BEING THE HEAD OF AN UNDERGROUND PUBLISHING COMPANY IS A LOT OF FUN. WELL, LEMME TELL YA... IT'S NOT!

IT'S A SUPREME HASSLE IS WHAT IT IS... EXCUSE ME. RING

HELLO. HEF? HOWYA DOIN' BABY? TONIGHT? ... LISTEN, WHY DONCHA COME HERE? SURE! ... AND BRING A LOTTA GIRLS. YEAH... LATER!

LIKE I WAS SAYING... IT AIN'T A BARREL OF MONKEYS. FOR INSTANCE— I HAVE TO SLIP OUTTA MY COMFORTABLE SUIT INTO THESE BELL-BOTTOM JEANS CAUSE SOME CARTOONIST IS COMING IN WITH A NEW UNDER-GROUND COMIC BOOK.

HE'S HERE, MR. KITCHEN.

HEY! WHAT'S HAPPENIN'?!

GOT A NEW BOOK HERE.

GROOVY!

CAN I GET AN ADVANCE?

WELL, TIMES ARE TOUGH... BUT I'LL TELL YA WHAT— HERE'S A TWENTY OUTA MY OWN POCKET.

DENIS, YER A SAINT.

MISS CHEEVER— HAVE HIGGINS BRING THE LIMO AROUND. GET THIS BOOK TO THE PRESSES... HAVE 'EM RUN HALF A MILLION. AND WIRE THIS TO MY SWISS ACCOUNT. I GOTTA RUN NOW.

YES SIR.

I TELL YA, HEF... PUBLISHING IS A REAL FUCKIN' HASSLE.

I KNOW WUCHA MEAN.

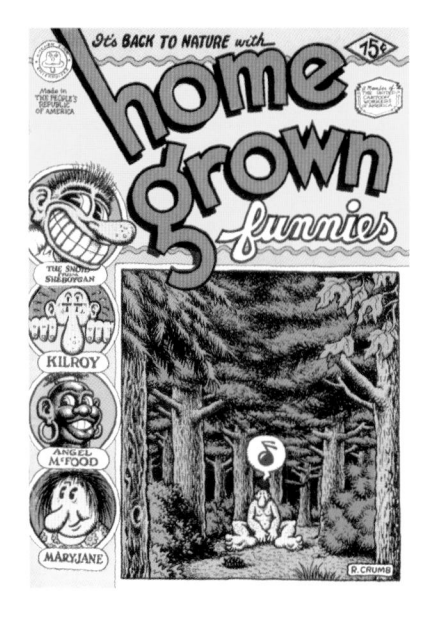

ABOVE: The cover to R. Crumb's Home Grown Funnies. The 1971 comic went on to sell over 160,000 copies, making it Kitchen Sink's biggest seller.

LEFT: Kitchen levels with his readers on the "problems" of being a comix publisher in a strip from Snarf #2 [1972].

FACING PAGE: Denis Kitchen (left) meets Stan Lee to discuss the 1974 launch of Marvel's Comix Book.

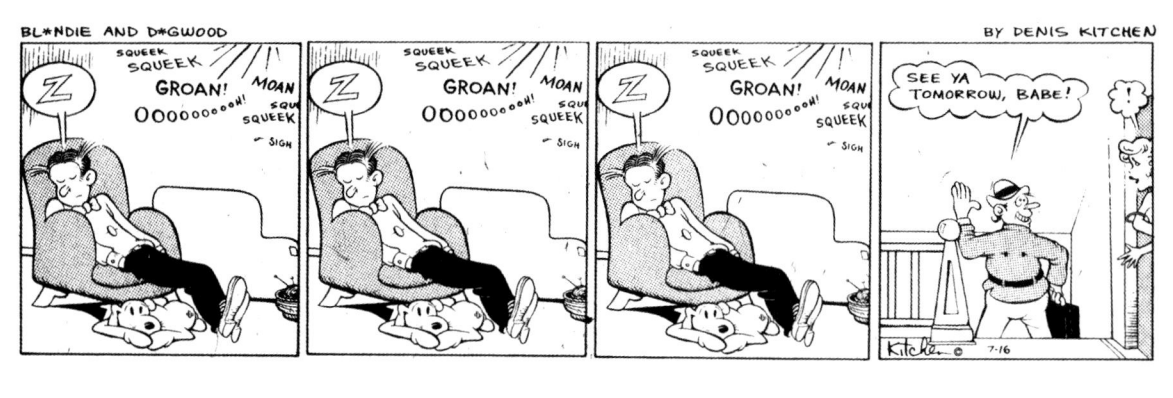

Krupp Comic Works Inc was formed, merging the existing Kitchen Sink Press (the comix publisher); Strickly Uppa Crust (a head shop); The Cartoon Factory (a commercial art studio); plus Ordinary Records, Krupp Mail Order and Krupp Distribution.

Also in 1970 Kitchen co-founded **The Bugle-American**, a Wisconsin-based alternative weekly newspaper that lasted seven years and before it folded, he co-founded another local weekly, **The Fox River Patriot** [1976]. But over three decades Kitchen's main focus has always been on publishing comics and books.

Despite being outside of the key San Francisco and New York scenes, Kitchen Sink attract top name creators. Crumb, Shelton, Lynch, Williamson, Art Spiegelman, Justin Green, S Clay Wilson, Kim Deitch, Rich Corben, Trina Robbins and Joel Beck were among the impressive lineup of cartoonists contributing to a wave of titles that soon established the newcomer as one of the top four comix publishers alongside Rip Off Press, Last Gasp and The Print Mint.

Spiegelman considered the mid-West location to be an important component in Kitchen Sink's identity. He observed, "It [**Mom's Homemade** #1] seemed so sweet, so good-natured, so benign

> "I remember feeling rather pissed off at the relative lack of madness and urgency in those books."...*Art Spiegelman*

compared to the more extreme, obscure, sardonic and twisted thrashings that made up much of the first waves of underground comix coming out of the East and West Coasts.

"The books that followed also radiated a general good-naturedness, a *liberal* rather than a radical vision of what comix might be," he continued. "Here were comix not from the outhouse but the… kitchen.

In fact, I remember feeling rather pissed off at the relative lack of madness and urgency in those books.

"At the same time," Spiegelman added, "I was grateful that kindred souls had formed a Comix Commando Unit out in the heartland; a safe haven in my crosscountry Volkswagen runs between **The East Village Other** and **The Berkeley Barb**. Those comix coming out of the beer capital were an integral part of the very real revolution happening in comix."

One of Kitchen Sink Press's first productions was **Bijou Funnies** #5 [1972] edited by Jay Lynch and featuring Crumb, Williamson and Green. It was soon followed by a title that was to be Kitchen Sink's all-time top title, **Home Grown Funnies**, racking up an impressive 160,000. sales. It did so well because in addition to a Crumb three-page short

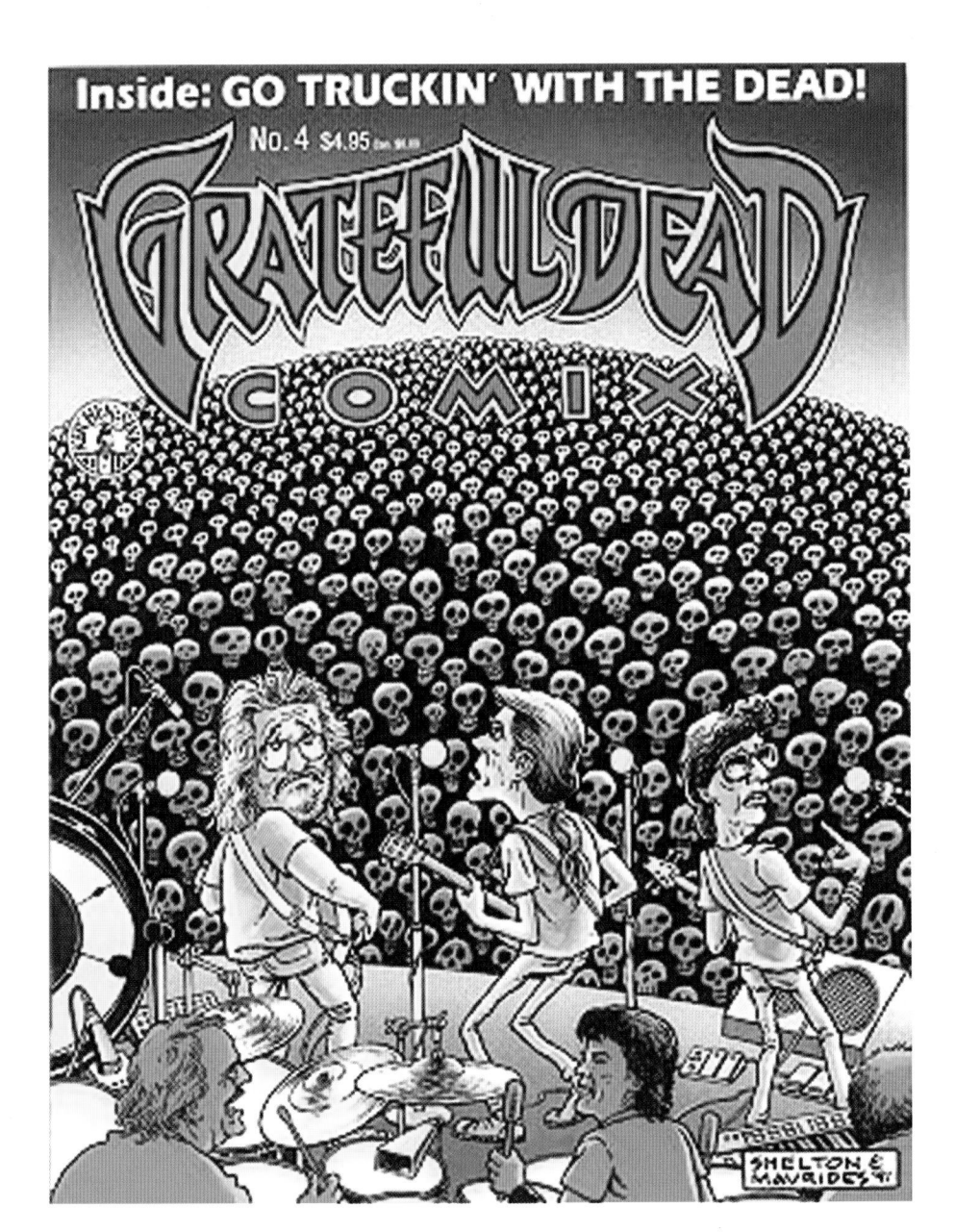

LEFT: Kitchen Sink kept on trucking into the '90s with such titles as Grateful Dead Comix. Cover art for #4 by Gilbert Shelton and Paul Mavrides.

FACING PAGE: Denis Kitchen parodies an icon, the Blondie & Dagwood newspaper strip, in an example of what Art Spiegelman refers as his good-natured humour. From Snarf #2 [1972].

featuring *Mr Snoid* and *Angelfood McSpade*, the rest of the comic was given over to the legendary *Whiteman Meets Bigfoot* story. It tells how everyman caucasian Whiteman is kidnapped by the dark, large, furry and female Yeti. Eventually Whiteman falls in love with her and lives happily ever after. Not your regular cynical Crumb short strip.

Kitchen followed up with Crumb's **Projunior**, the nine-artist anthology **Hungry Chuck Biscuits**, local discovery Jim Mitchell's **Smile** and **Teenage Horizons of Shangrila**. On a roll, in 1972 he put out **Bizarre Sex** and **Death Rattle** featuring early Corben horror and the three issue **Snarf** anthology. He also released the unique and now very scarce one-shot **The Great Marijuana Debate**. True to its title it featured alternating drawn-up opinions from Kim Deitch and Denis Kitchen (pro-grass) and Jay Lynch and Peter Poplaski (anti-grass).

But boom turned to bust in late 1973. The comix industry was devastated as a result of a US Supreme Court ruling that allowed local communities to determine what was obscene. Artists wanted to draw, readers wanted to read but retailers, not knowing what was safe any more, were afraid to stock any adult titles whatsoever.

Unable to find a market for his comics, Kitchen faced a bleak future until help came from an unexpected quarter when Marvel Comics editor-in-chief Stan Lee called. The end product was a Marvel underground title, **Comix Book** [1974]. It only lasted three issues before, as Trina Robbins put it, Stan Lee woke up, exclaimed "Good grief, what have I done?" and cancelled it. *[Comix Book feature, page 150.]*

Kitchen published two more issues of **Comix Book** [1975] before **Kurtzman Komix**, a 1976 collection of early *Hey Look!* and *Pot Shot Pete* comic strips. In 1978 he took over publishing Will Eisner's **The Spirit** magazine—compiling old Sunday sections—from Warren Publications, then boosted his collected newspaper strip line with Milton Caniff's **Steve Canyon**. Finding a

NANCY   by KITCHEN

AUGUST 9   —DENIS KITCHEN

viable mainstream/nostalgia market for household names, he added compilations of *Flash Gordon, L'il Abner, Alley Oop, Secret Agent X-9, Nancy, Batman* and *Krazy Kat*.

Not neglecting his roots, throughout the '80s and '90s Kitchen also supported the new wave of alternative cartoonists, publishing early work by Charles Burns, Mark Schultz, Peter Bagge, Drew Friedman and Dan Clowes. He also kept the fading embers of the underground still smouldering by launching a shedload of decidedly adult comix; among them **Dope Comix, Gay Comix, Blab!, Omaha the Cat Dancer, Melody, French Ticklers, Buzz** and **Grateful Dead Comix**.

Unfortunately Kitchen Sink collapsed in 1999. Part victim to a major industry recession, its downfall was also a result of boardroom manoeuvres by outside investors, brought in to fund an ambitious but untimely expansion. Before its decline, Kitchen founded the Comic Book Legal Defense Fund of which he remains president. Set up in 1986, it serves to defend the industry's First Amendment rights.

Vaughn Bode

A key influence on today's graffiti artists, with derivations of his style seen across the world, Bode's work has influenced street sprayers as varied as Dondi, Kel, Noc, Seen, Tracy and Can Two.

Born in Utica, New York in 1941, Bode described himself as "an extremely introverted kid, completely unable to relate to the world around me." Having been drawing since the age of five, his solution

ABOVE RIGHT: Vaughn Bode, by his occasional collaborator, the acclaimed Jeff Jones.

RIGHT: Bode's 1963 take on Love Is... using a Hate Is... theme, Das Kampf.

FACING PAGE: Nancy becomes the target of another of Kitchen's "good natured" parodies.

was to create his own fantasy world populated with strange little creatures. In 1957 he designed a funny little wizard wearing only a huge yellow star-spangled hat. Evolving to the stage where he was no more than a hat, two orange legs and an orange weiner, he became one of Bode's most enduring characters, Cheech Wizard—the name being inspired by a can of Cheechy Nuts. A Mr Natural on acid with often incomprehensible storylines, he had his own monthly strip in **National Lampoon** from 1971-75, gathered by Company & Sons in a 1975 oneshot and Rip Off Press in four issues, 1986-1987.

His 52-page self-published **Das Kampf** [1963] was one of the first underground comics. A parody of the *Love Is...* strips, it put a twist on Londoner Kim Casali's insanely popular little series by renaming the theme *Hate Is...* In keeping with the oneshot's title, Bode cover credited himself with a phonetic spelling of his first name, Von.

In 1969 his *Deadbone* strip began in the science fiction digest **Galaxy Magazine**, running until 1971, while his *Deadbone Erotica* strip gave him a far greater audience, replacing Crumb's *Fritz the Cat* in **Cavalier**. A busy year for Bode, he was also the founding editor of **Gothic Blimp Works**, the short-lived comix supplement to the **East Village Other**, while another men's mag, **Swank**, launched his and Bernie Wrightson's *Purple Pictography* strip. Eros Comics collected the 1971-72 series in 1991. His **Junkwaffel** #1-4 were published by **Last Gasp**, while his **Lizard Zen, Erotica** and **Schizophrenia** collections have been among 11 Bode titles produced by Fantagraphics.

In 1972, he created a unique form of entertainment, Bode's Cartoon Concert. Bawdy and erotic in nature, it was a mixture of reading and performance in which he brought his characters to life via slide projection while narrating and playing their roles, speaking the language of his creations. His shows were performed at colleges and comics conventions throughout the United States and Europe until shortly before his untimely death in 1975.

As well as seen on walls across the world, Bode's art lives on

ABOVE AND LEFT: Respect. Can kings West and Wane acknowledge their debt to Vaughn Bode.

FACING PAGE: A fantastic vista from Bode's Deadbone.

through his son, Mark, who has developed his father's Cobalt 60 concept into a line of comics and has revived Cheech Wizard for his forthcoming Fantagraphics book, **The Lizard of Oz**.

S. Clay Wilson

Underground artists thought they were breaking barriers when they launched their response to Code-approved neutered mainstream titles. Then Wilson arrived and showed them pretty quickly that they'd hardly scratched the surface. On meeting Crumb, Wilson recalls, "He thought my stuff was great. We probably smoked a joint and started drawing, babbling away. Then Crumb said, 'Why don't you draw some strips, we'll expand **Zap!**'"

It was the end product—*Head First*—Wilson's outrageous knob-chopping and chewing one-pager in **Zap** #2 that inspired Crumb to go for it and exorcise his own sex hangups through print. "I was just completely blitzkrieged by the guy," Crumb remarked.

Born in Lincoln, Nebraska in 1941, Steven Clay Wilson studied fine arts at the University of Nebraska until he protested against the university's requirement for all male students to undergo training with the ROTC [Reserve Officer Training Corp]. He dropped out only to be called up by the army anyway. There he learned to be a medic and viewed explicit movies about combat wounds and other gory aspects of medical life, material that would serve him well when dreaming up his shocking and violent comix.

RIGHT: Wilson looks on (top) in a 1973 photo by Rebel Visions author Patrick Rosenkranz while The Chequered Demon (below) struts his stuff on the landscape-format #1 [Last Gasp, 1977].

FACING PAGE: One of S. Clay Wilson's outrageous creations, the scantily-clad sci-fi heroine Star-Eyed Stella.

Returning to university, he graduated in 1964 with a Bachelor's degree in Fine Arts. A variety of jobs followed, so in 1968 Wilson moved to San Francisco to take up a new career as a comix artist.

Praised by his contemporaries for breaking taboo sex barriers in art, his most famous underground character is the raunchy Checkered Demon character, which starred in its own outrageous three-issue title between 1977 and 1979. Wilson was also responsible for the creation of Starry-Eyed Stella, Ruby the Dyke, the Hog Ridin' Fools and the attractively named Captain Pissgums. Wilson's work has appeared in such titles as **Yellow Dog, Tales of Sex and Death** and **Comix Book**, Marvel Comics' short-lived attempt to market comix to a mainstream audience.

Spain Rodriguez

Born in 1940 in Buffalo, New York, Manuel "Spain" Rodriguez grew up on a diet of CC Beck's **Captain Marvel** comics, but only if his father didn't find them and tear them up. An avid biker with an art school background, he hung out with the Road Vultures Motorcycle Club and his violent experiences with the gang have been reflected in much of his comix work.

His first published strip was *SUNY Daze*, for student newspaper **The Spectrum** but when he moved to New York City in 1965, he began contributing cartoons to subversive newspaper **The Militant**. In the wake of Crumb, he then approached **The East Village Other.** Asked by its publisher to produce material for a comic tabloid supplement, Spain created **Zodiac Mindwarp** across a six month period. Published in 1967 it was a forerunner to **EVO**'s second attempt at a tabloid comic,

the short-lived **Gothic Blimp Works** [1969] which folded at issue 8.

Following the spin-off, Spain's art began appearing in **The East Village Other** itself and in 1968 his *Brink of Doom* strip was responsible for the underground paper's first bust. A frame in which the main character, Big Rod Pernil, was depicted going down on a woman included explicit sound effects and offended the Brooklyn District Attorney. The subsequent trial resulted in a Not Guilty verdict.

In 1969 Spain moved to San Francisco, where, like so many artists he had strips published in a variety of comix, among them **Anarchy, Subvert** and **Tales of the Leather Nun**. Another key contributor to **Zap**, his work included *Mara, Mistress of the Void* and *My Secret Date with Linda Blair*, a sex fantasy about meeting the *Exorcist* actress.

Spain's choice of subject matter has certainly been diverse, ranging from the inevitable bikers to strips featuring futuristic science fiction whores. But undoubtedly his best known character is Trashman, the artist's blue collar international terrorist. Introduced in **The East Village Other**, this "Agent of the 6th International" is best summed up as a communist counter culture James Bond revolutionary. And very much a figurehead for a political standpoint. As Spain explains, "In any kind of army the bands are important, because they kind of lift the morale of the troops. It's important to have that sort of thing, so the role I saw that Trashman had was an encouragement to our side."

In 1994, Spain produced the auto-biographical **My True Story** which included a retelling of his exploits with the Road Vultures as well as his coverage of the violence during the 1968 Democratic Convention in Chicago as a reporter for **The East Village Other**.

ABOVE: All tooled up and ready for action: Trashman, Agent of the 6th International.

LEFT: Spain's Trashman gets down to business on the cover to Subvert Comics #1 [Rip Off Press, 1970].

FACING PAGE: Spain Rodriguez, photographed by Patrick Rosenkranz [1973].

Admitting that Trashman is used to express his political views, Spain commented in a 1999 interview, "In the most recent **Zap**, Crumb is asking Trashman, 'Are you still a socialist?' Of course Trashman is still a socialist, as am I." Spain's most recent Trashman story appeared in the Fantagraphics comic **Zero Zero** #2.

Art Spiegelman

Spiegelman's body of underground comix work is comparitively small but he has gone on to become a major force in raising public awareness of comics and acceptance of the medium as an art form. Born in Stockholm, Sweden in 1948, Arthur Spiegelman and his parents emigrated to America in 1951.

An art and philosophy major, despite his family wanting him to become a dentist, he began contributing to undergrounds in 1968, fresh out of college. Using a variety of pseudonyms, including Joe Cutrate, Skeeter Grant and Al Flooglebuckle, he worked on such titles as **Bizarre Sex**, **Real Pulp Comix** and **Young Lust**. For Kitchen Sink's anthology **Sleazy Scandals of the Silver Screen** he not only worked alongside Griffith, Deitch and Spain, but edited the title which exposed the dark side of Hollywood and included the Fatty Arbuckle rape scandal, the excesses of Liberace and Clara Bow taking on an entire football team.

His long-term creative consultancy role for Topps Gum [1965-87] peaked with his and Mike Newgarden's co-creation of the vile and disgusting Garbage Pail Kids as a reaction to the sickly sweet Cabbage Patch Dolls.

In 1975, Spiegelman and Bill Griffith co-founded **Arcade, The Comix Revue**, an influential stab at finding a mass market for the then-dying underground comix movement. Inspired to "show how it should be done" by Marvel's attempt to go underground with **Comix Book**, **Arcade** pulled in all the key creators who had refused to work for the established overground press. It didn't fare much better than the New York hybrid and was cancelled in 1976 after only seven issues. Having provided a quality package, its regular contributors included Crumb, Kim Deitch, Spain, Robert Williams, Gilbert Shelton and S. Clay Wilson.

Spiegelman then went on to launch **RAW** in 1980. A tabloid avant-garde comix magazine which he produced with his wife, Françoise Mouly, it introduced the work of scores of second-generation comix creators to a newsstand readership. Among those featured across its 11 issues were Chris Ware, Dan Clowes, Charles Burns and David Mazzuchelli as well as overseas contributors including France's Jacques Tardi and Holland's Joost Swarte. *[See Chapter 9 for further details.]*

Spiegelman's public profile was boosted considerably in 1986 by the publication of **Maus: A Survivor's Tale**. A graphic novel based on the experiences of his parents as concentration camp survivors, it began life before **RAW** as a short story in the 1972 Apex deliberately misspelled **Funny Aminals** oneshot and had been reprinted for a wider audience in Marvel's **Comix Book** #2. A comics breakthrough, the writer/artist's opus won a 1992 Pulitzer Prize. *[See feature, page 214.]*

His work has since appeared in many periodicals including *The New*

Yorker, where he was a staff artist/writer from 1993-2003. In his lecture *Comix 101*, Spiegelman explores the evolution of comics, while explaining the value of the medium and why it should not be ignored. He believes that in our post-literate culture the importance of the comic is on the rise, stating, "Comics echo the way the brain works. People think in icono-graphic images, not in holograms, and people think in bursts of language, not in paragraphs."

Hunt Emerson

Far smaller than the San Francisco explosion, the UK underground comix market had difficulty finding its own identity. But if any UK cartoonist had an impact on the scene it was Hunt Emerson.

Born in Newcastle-upon-Tyne in 1952, he moved to the Midlands where he became involved with the Birmingham Arts Lab in the early '70s. Quick on the draw, his first published work was 1974's **Large Cow Comix**, rapidly followed by **Outer Space Comix, The Adventures of Mr Spoonbiscuit, Pholk Comix** and, in 1975, **Zomik Comix** and **Dogman**.

A fervent fan of undergrounds, Emerson co-organized 1976 and 1977's Konvention of Alternative Komix with Chris Welch, best known for **Ogoth and Ugly Boot** [Cozmic Comics, 1973].

In 1981, Rip Off published **Thunderdogs**, Emerson's first full-length comic, reprinted by Knockabout in the UK in 1993. Knockabout's lengthy association with Emerson began with publishing his **Big Book of Everything** [1983] and they have been his main publisher ever since.

His 1986 **Jazz Funnies** starring cool cat Max Zillion is his favourite creation: "Max Zillion is like jazz—wild, full of soul, and always broke. Alto Ego is his horn, his friend, and the brains of the outfit." Since then his steady output has included **You Are Maggie Thatcher** [a role-playing magazine with author Pat Mills, Titan, 1987] and Knockabout's **The Rime of the Ancient Mariner**, **Casanova's Last Stand**, **Citymouth** and an adaptation of D H Lawrence's **Lady Chatterley's Lover**.

As well as Max Zillion his other major creations betray his feline

ABOVE: Emerson's cover to Knockabout Comics #1.

LEFT: Large Cow Comics [1974], Emerson's first published comic work.

FACING PAGE: Art Spiegelman, [1969], photo by Bhob Stewart.

love though **Calculus Cat** [1987], **PussPuss** [1994] and his wider-circulated *Firkin the Cat*, which has appeared monthly in the men's mag **Fiesta** since 1981 as well as in a recent collection and seven issues of its own Knockabout comic.

Bryan Talbot

Considered the "godfather" of modern British comix, Talbot's work bridges the early '70s underground movement and the birth of the **2000 AD** generation in the late '70s.

His first published art appeared in the **British Tolkien Society Magazine** in 1969. In 1972, with fellow student Bonk he produced a weekly strip for the college newspaper. This was collected as the self-published **Bog Standard Comix** in 1977. After college, he created, wrote and drew the Chester P. Hackenbush trilogy about a "psychedelic alchemist" and his talking hash-pipe for **Brainstorm Comix** #1-3 [Alchemy, 1976-77]. This strip was also reprinted in one volume, **Brainstorm**, in 1982 and Hackenbush later appeared in an homage as Chester Williams for the comic **Swamp Thing**, written by Alan Moore.

In 1978, Talbot's *Flash Gordon* spoof **Frank Fazakerley** appeared in the science fact and fiction mag **Ad Astra**. Again this was reprinted in one book, by the Preston Speculative Fiction Group in 1991.

1978 was a pivotal year for Talbot as, through a seven-page Moorcock a la Corben-style strip for **Near Myths** *[The Papist Affair]*, he lay the groundwork on what would become his epic *Adventures of Luther Arkwright* saga. The 41-page serial ran across the five published issues, and was reprinted and expanded in 1981 in the experimental comics magazine **Pssst!**.

The following year the first collected volume of **Luther Arkwright** was published making this and Raymond Briggs' **When The Wind**

Blows possibly the first UK graphic novels.

Talbot then wrote and drew *Scumworld* for a year for the tabloid rock newspaper **Sounds** until the editor left for heavy metal mag **Kerrang** and took Bryan and his strip with him. Unfortunately, despite a brief of making the strip "as near to the knuckle as possible without us getting busted," management dropped the strip a few weeks later, saying it was "too heavy" for them.

In 1983, through author Pat Mills he began working for the weekly sci-fi comic **2000 AD** drawing *Nemesis the Warlock* and *Judge Dredd*.

Returning to his indie roots and Luther Arkwright, he completed the story in nine issues for indie publisher Valkyrie Press. This was followed by a three volume collection in Britain and a US monthly reprint of the series from Dark Horse. The story's blend of SF, historical, espionage and mystical themes, combined with experimental narrative techniques, was a seminal work with many of today's leading comics creators including Alan Moore, Garth Ennis, Grant Morrison and Neil Gaiman admitting to being influenced by it.

Over the past 25 years Talbot has created strips for US and UK titles as diverse as **Imagine**, **Street Comics**, **Slow Death**, **Vogarth**, Paradox Press's **Big Books**, **The Radio Times**, **Wired**, **Knockabout**, **IT** and **The Manchester Flash**.

Recent work includes the multi-award winning **Tale Of One Bad Rat**, a moving story about child abuse, Beatrix Potter and redemption. It was produced for Dark Horse Comics, the head of which—Mike Richardson—thought he was buying a new Arkwright series. When he asked when Luther would appear, Talbot said, "In my next story." True to his word, he did return to Arkwright next, with the 284-page opus **Heart of Empire** which Dark Horse was only too happy to publish.

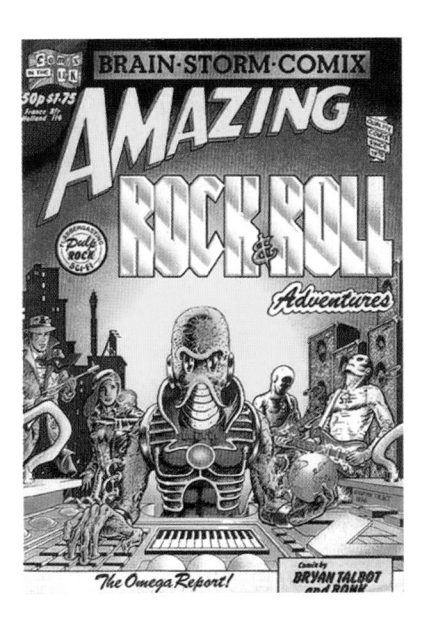

ABOVE: The cover to Amazing Rock & Roll Adventures [1977]; art by Talbot. The Alchemy published comic—actually Brainstorm Comix #6—features another of the artist's creations: Ace Wilmslow, the alien-fighting rock journalist.

LEFT: What a long strange trip it's been. Talbot's psychedical alchemist Chester P Hackenbush comes back to reality with a crash in a page from Brainstorm Comix#1 [Alchemy, 1975].

FACING PAGE: Looking more rock star cool than struggling underground comix artist, Bryan Talbot in the late 1980s.

Taking the Mickey

One comic incurred the wrath of corporate America in 1973. Disney won more than $1 million in damages over the defiling of Mickey Mouse's "innocent delightfulness" as a horny doper.

THE general public didn't pay too much attention to the attacks underground comix made on its cultural totems. Nobody outside of the underground took much of it seriously. After all, these cartoonists were rebels, they were wanting to shock everybody by being outrageous so it was expected of them. Then one madcap bunch overstepped the mark.

As insensitive as much of the industry's sex, drugs and violence-laden work was by today's standards, few got into hot water. Then, in 1971, a San Francisco collective of talented artists decided to mess with a multi-national known for its litigious nature.

When Mickey Mouse was portrayed having oral sex with Minnie, Disney was not amused. The two issue story also had the pair involved in the illegal drugs trade and Donald Duck and Goofy featured as peeping toms known as the Nameless Perverts. The Air Pirates group was responsible for the deed.

Led by Odd Bodkins creator Dan O'Neill (perp behind the

Mickey and Minnie two-parter), they included Gary (Nameless Perverts) Hallgren, Bobby London and Ted Richards—whose Dopin' Dan was introduced in their first issue of **Air Pirates Funnies**.

Disney struck back. Its lawyers hunted down the Pirates and hit them with an injunction, stopping distribution of the first two issues and production of any more. Disney also began a massive lawsuit.

When the Pirates declined a 1975 offer of an out of court settlement, a Californian judge ruled in Disney's favour, determining it a clear case of copyright infringement. In 1979 a US Supreme Court refused to hear the collective's appeal and upheld the lower court's decision.

But O'Neill wouldn't quit. He joined the Mouse Liberation Front and in defiance of the court ruling spoofed more Disney characters for a 1979 issue of **CoEvolution Quarterly**.

For this, he was threatened with a jail sentence in 1980. So he finally cut his losses, agreeing to cease and desist.

Artt: R. Crumb, Bizarre Sex #8, [1980].

Chapter 2:

Can't Get Enuff

Sex in comix

"We did not self-censor ourselves. It was just that after a while we got it out of our systems." ...VICTOR MOSCOSO ON THE ZAP ARTISTS

Throbbin' cocks chopped… giant alien pussies lasciviously attacking skyscrapers… What better way to shock your parents than with graphic depictions of fuckin', suckin' and a bizarre array of sexual deviations that Mom and Dad had probably never even heard of, let alone tried.

HIPPIES rebelled totally against the beliefs of previous generations. Anti-war, anti-corporation, anti-system, anti-The Man. So when it came to sex, at a time when their parents had been uptight and repressed conservative prudes, the attitude was "anything goes." Through comix they viciously attacked everything and anything that was held dear, so it was no accident they were outrageously blatant in their contempt for, and disregard of, the sexual taboos of the past.

Sure, there were stories about drugs and politics and corruption in the undergrounds. But if you had a message to preach, you needed to get more than the converted in your audience. Whereas sex would sell itself. No great depth, no hidden meaning, no angry voices screaming defiance. All it took was a salacious cover and an outrageous title for an instant sell-out. Not a lot of imagination is required to guess the sort of visuals accompanying R. Crumb's strip, *The Grand Opening of the Great Intercontinental Fuck-In and Orgy-Riot* [**Snatch Comics** #1, 1969] or his *The Family that Lays together Stays together* [**Snatch** #2, 1969].

As Crumb realized early on that sex sells and makes cash, his sordid subject matter also served as a form of catharsis to purge his sexual neurosis. The 1930s **Tijuana Bibles** might have done it first, but they were about to be updated and upstaged with what the **Zap Comics** creator and those who followed him were willing to show.

> ## "The Only Comic You Can Eat!"
> ### …cover line,
> ### *Cunt Comics* #1

Heavily influenced by Robert Williams and S Clay Wilson—who he credits for starting off the "smut revolution" in comix—Crumb began producing material that, until then, had been the preserve of hard-core porn merchants.

In 1968, he launched the first of three titles which proudly carried the Smut Peddlers of America logo: **Snatch Comics**. The next two were **Jiz Comics** (don't ask!) and the even more blatantly-named **Cunt Comics**, which—if the title wasn't enough to outrage mainstream America—carried the cover banner line *The Only Comic You Can Eat!*

Initially published through Don Donahue's Apex Novelties with later editions coming from Print Mint, it is hardly surprising that all three created a furore in the media and with just about every city's local law enforcement.

Despite these pressures, **Snatch** outlived its sister titles by lasting to issue #3. As well as Crumb, the first issue also featured work by the unrelenting Wilson who revealed, "R. Crumb said he likes to masturbate to his comics; are they fantasies for you? Yeah, you draw the babe that you want to show up. But you better be careful what you draw because a lot of the time she does show up."

Rory Hayes' *Prick Sick* featured later in the series although most of his material would never see print as he was a heavy contributor for the unreleased **Cunt Comics** #2. For **Jiz Comics** Crumb created

ABOVE: Unused Snatch Comics #2 cover art by Crumb, featuring the ever-popular Honeybunch Kaminski.

LEFT: Cover to Snatch Comics #3 [Apex, 1969] with cover art by R. Crumb.

ABOVE: S. Clay Wilson's pirates cover for the Special 69 Zap #3.

RIGHT: Three decades later and the shock value of Head First is still not diminished [Zap #2, 1968]. Writer/artist S. Clay Wilson: "The Japanese used to do that all the time with the exaggerated cocks. But now they've become so westernised they even airbrush out the pubic hair."

FACING PAGE: Spain Rodriguez' first title, EVO's Zodiac Mindwarp. When it was sent to the printers as a comicbook, they objected about it being in bad taste. So it was printed tabloid size.

The Adventures of Dicknose, which featured a black guy endowed with an overly large proboscis which served his horny pursuits just as well as his lower manhood.

Zap #3's *Special 69* issue (even though it was released in 1968, the cover tag-line played on the linking of the sexual position and the imminent year change) kept the fornication flag flying after the benchmark had been set in the previous issue with S. Clay Wilson's *Headfirst*. The tastless tale of a pirate flaunting his mammoth male member and his shipmate slicing its tip off, eating it, and then announcing "The head tastes best," was the catalyst for a wave of prurient material from Crumb. It also upped the ante for the rest of the **Zap** bunch.

During a rare comment on his comix work, Moscoso recollects, "First Wilson comes out with the Checkered Demon, then Captain Piss Gums in which he is drawing my worst fantasies! Frankly, we didn't really understand what we were doing until Wilson started publishing in **Zap**. I mean, he's not a homosexual, yet he's drawing all these homosexual things. He's not a murderer, yet he was murdering all these people. All the things that he wasn't, he was putting down in his strips. So that showed us that we were, without being aware of it, censoring ourselves."

Spurred on by what he was "getting away with," Wilson wrote and drew *Captain Pissgums and his Pervert Pirates* for **Zap** #3. This was a chapter-length strip in which the good captain and his crew take on Captain Fatima's Dyke Pirates in a rug-munching, tit-twirling, cock-biting slugfest. Another single page shocker for the issue was *Come Fix* in which one woman gives another a full service to check out that her cock transplant is fully functional.

Pushing the velvet envelope

But stretching society's limits was not the provenance of **Zap** alone. Communication Co's **The Life and Loves of Cleopatra** was self-published in 1967 by Harry Driggs, art director of **Good Times**, another of San Francisco's underground newspapers. The "historical" oneshot contained images of a blatantly pedophilic nature; but it was still reprinted in a joint venture by Apex Novelties and the San Francisco Comic Book Company in 1969. Spain Rodriquez wasn't going to be left behind either. With his explicit **Jiz Comics** strip, *Modern Love*, he warned of what was to follow with the first page banner line, "He promised me love but gave me nine inches."

1969 was notable for two things in comics; the Apollo moon landings creating a market for sci-fi comics, and the release of the

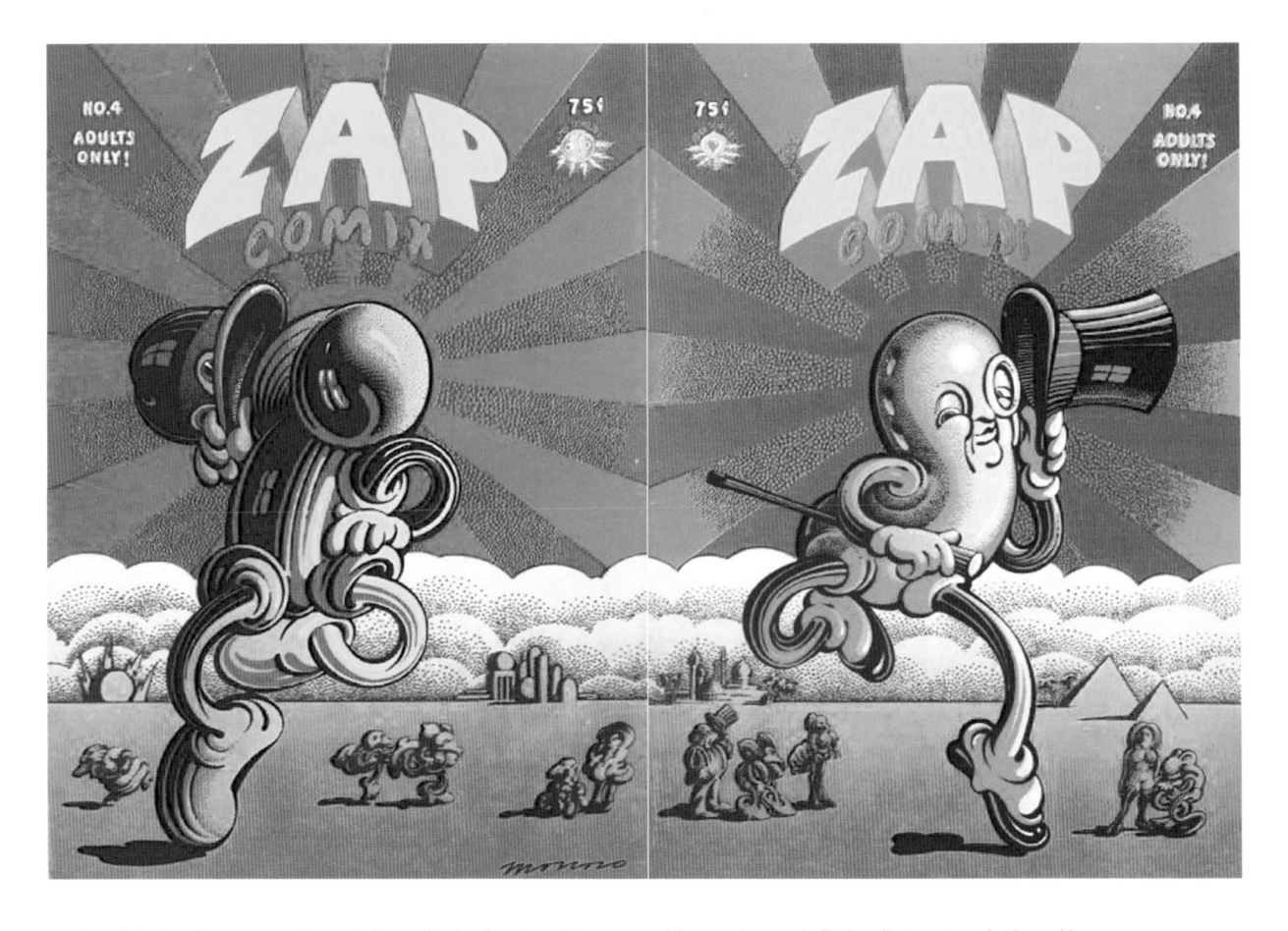

much anticipated **Zap** #4 sending notaries in the legal system into orbit along with Armstrong and Aldrin. Having already publicized his preference for big black women with huge asses through the introduction of Angel Food McSpade in **Zap** #2, Crumb proved he attacked every creed equally with the first appearance of Horny Harriet— a similarly-endowed white girl—who indulges in an act of bestiality. But it wasn't that which upset everybody. It wasn't even Spain's *Mara, Mistress of the Void*, which took the previous year's comic-based blockbuster movie **Barbarella** ten steps further with an even more gratuitous sex story in outer space. Even smut king S. Clay Wilson's *A Ball in the Bung Hole* raised only a few eyebrows, despite a prince being shot in the winking eyeball at the tip of his one-eyed trouser snake via the quim of a servant girl who is performing fellatio on him.

As ever, it was left to Crumb to inadvertently leave his **Zap** mentors behind in the filth league by producing a lengthier sequel to *The Family that Lays Together* Stays Together centrespread from **Zap** #2. *Joe Blow* blew away any remaining vestiges of decency and shattered the last taboo when he showed a wholesome-looking family indulging in a variety of incestuous activities. In the eyes of the law (despite justice being supposedly blind) it was enough to lure the cops away from the donut stands and into head shops and book stores from California to New York, with the intent to bust anybody stocking the issue.

Even with all the heat that **Zap** was bringing down on undergrounds, there were still other avenues for comix creators to explore. Vaughn Bode's *Deadbone Erotica* was picked up by newsstand soft porn mag **Cavalier** as a replacement for Crumb's *Fritz the Cat*, which it had begun running in 1968. Despite where it appeared, it was much gentler and less salacious than almost anything appearing in comix, resembling his *Purple Pictography*, which the self-styled cartoon guru later produced with mainstream comics artist Bernie Wrightson for **Swank** from 1971.

Back on the West Coast, despite or probably because of the **Zap** #4 busts, the range of underground comics kicked into overdrive, but this was happening at the cost of originality. Crumb was more than happy to turn out torrid sex tales, particularly for his own titles. He felt that his female fans had enjoyed his cuter earlier work. "I got too much love. I had to make them back off by showing them this

RIGHT: S. Clay Wilson's A Bolt in the Bung Hole strip appeared in 1968's Zap #3. Nothing has been the same since. In his defence, he once said, "Yes, I did take acid, dope, speed, every drug known to man. And yes, I did get more pieces of ass than you've had hot dinners."

LEFT: You may never want to eat peanuts again. Victor Moscoso's unmistakable style on the wraparound art for Zap #4: Front cover [right] Planter's Mr Peanut, an icon since 1916, is revealed on the back cover [left] to be a prancing prick.

ABOVE: The Checkered Demon #2. The pint-sized bad ass takes on bikers, slavers and aliens. Then in #3 he heads for the future to find more victims to fuck and fight.

RIGHT: Crumb's All Meat Comics from Big Ass Comics #1 [1969].

FACING PAGE: Big Ass Comix #2 [Rip Off Press, 1971]. The second all-Crumb issue from his 'smut period.'

other side of myself—a real weirdness. And they did indeed back off. My popularity went down quite a bit when **Big Ass Comics** came out."

Across the two issues of the Rip Off title [1969-71] Crumb continued to drool over big women while adding his passion for young—but still big—girls in the semi-autobiographical *Honeybunch Kaminski, the Drug-Crazed Runaway* for **Uneeda Comix** [Print Mint, 1970]. Promoted in posters as "jail bait of the month," she became a minor icon herself and one of the artist's recurring characters. Crumb continued to keep up the smut quotent for three issues of **Mr Natural** [San Francisco Comic Book Co, 1970-77] and both issues of **Motor City Comics** [Rip Off, 1969-70].

Suprisingly, it took almost another decade for S Clay Wilson's own raving, racist, sexist creation to acquire his own title. Between 1977 and 1979 Last Gasp published three issues of **The Chequered Demon**. Not for the faint hearted, Wilson continued to offend everybody with this title, abounding with racist caracatures, degrading sex bouts and ultra-violence as the diminutive demon fights and fucks bikers, slavers and aliens. Giving the scarey impression he's still holding back, he once said, "It's too bad there's so much censorship over here because in Europe anything goes." Europe should be thankful that he's American!

In an anarchic alternative industry born out of a need to counterbalance the repetitive mundanity of mainstream comics, this process was itself occurring in the new subject matter. Drugs were still being touted in titles to reflect the creators and readers main predilictions, but the sex titles sold better and the theme was dominating anthologies. So much so that new release jam issues were dropping all non-sex stories just to focus on often specific lurid carnal desires. Quite a few had a clever title, but featured little beyond poorly rendered art and stories that bore no relevence to the comics' specific theme. But the better produced ones successfully bore the brunt of the industry's pending implosion, and this can be attributed to their delivering the cover-promised goods and can be seen by the number of them passed from one dying publisher to the next.

Among them was **Young Lust** which got through four publishers and eight issues before folding in 1993. Launched in 1970, it was the brainchild of Jay Kinney and Bill Griffiths, who produced the first issue between them with such classic lines as "Two weeks ago he was dry-humping me in the elevator—now I'm lucky if he can remember my goddam name!"

Roger Brand, Paul Mavrides, Justin Green and Griffiths' wife, Nancy, were among those who joined in for later issues along with Crumb, Spain and Larry Todd.

It contained such strips as *Love-Nest for Three!, Too Fucked Up to Love!* and *Little Sister loses her Hymen* alongside such features as *Kinky Klothes for Kute Kittens* and ads that offered an artificial penis in 30 seconds or jobs in sexual telepathy.

A former assistant to Wally ("Woody") Wood and Gil Kane—two mainstream comics legends—Roger Brand contributed to **Witzend, Tales from the Leather Nun, Insect Fear** and **Real Pulp Comics**.

Maintaining the theme he went from working on **Young Lust** to editing his own title **Tales of Sex and Death** for Print Mint [1971], who in turn also became the publisher of **Young Lust**.

Tales of Sex and Death kicked off in 1971 although its second (and final) issue didn't appear until 1975, living up to its raunchy "coming late" ethos. Brand's sauce achieved a Wood-like style, alongside Kim Deitch, Spain, Wilson and Green, whose *Soupygoy* was a Superboy parody subtitled *Alias Kent Lark—Boy Voyeur* with the high school-goer's alter ego using his x-ray vision to do what any boy would.

A worthy entry among the underground sex comix was 1972's **Facts O' Life Sex Education Funnies**. Published by Rip Off Press, it featured a motley lineup of comix characters in public service strips including *Fat Freddy Gets The Clap, Fertile Fanny,* Strawberry Fields in *Preggers, Bitsy The Teenage Bunny, The Abortion Game* and Clarence Crablice in *Sins of the Flesh*. Contributors included Shelton, Crumb,

pig-tailed Pirate Shary Flenniken and her henchmen Gary Hallgren and Bobby London plus The 40-Year Old Hippie's Ted Richards.

One which kept it up longer than most was **Bizarre Sex** which had a 10 issue run from 1972 to 1982. Unusual in that it didn't come from California, it was published by Milwaukee, Wisconsin-based Kitchen Sink Enterprises. As a result, its early issues especially didn't feature material from many of the usual gang of suspects, but instead had a formidable lineup all of its own, including contributors destined for their own major and minor stardom. In fact, issue #1 had a lineup of relatively unknown artists, with only Richard "Grass" Green, of 1973's **Good Jive Comics** being the exception.

In the early day absence of Crumb, Shelton, Spain or Moscoso, it presented Howard Cruse's popular *Barefootz* from issue two onwards as well as Joe (Art Spiegelman) Cutrate's *My Heart Skipped A Beat for a Meat-Beating Fiend!*, Richard "Grass" Green's *Incest*, Mike Vosberg's *Mail Order Brides*, Trina Robbins' *Feminist Hookers From Outer Space* and *The Adventures Of Kinky* plus early instalments of Harvey Pekar's life in *How'd Ya Get Inta This Bizness Ennyway?*

Later issues featured a swathe of classic-titled strips as the number of contributing artists grew. Crumb came on board for *Josephine The Cross-Eyed Quadroon in "Shakin' The Afri-Can"* [#5], **The Cartoon History of the Universe's** Larry Gonnick drew *Effluvium* [#6],

ABOVE: A pin-up of Honeybunch Kaminski, "Jail Bait of the Month."

LEFT: R. Crumb's "Honeybunch Kaminski The Drug-Crazed Runaway" from Uneeda Comix [1970].

FACING PAGE: Red Guard Romance by Jay Kinney and Bill Griffith. Splash panel taken from Young Lust #5, [Last Gasp 1975].

Fred Hembeck added his *Sextraterrestrial* [#7] and Art Spiegelman provided *Pluto's Retreat* [#8].

Bizarre Sex #9 alone justified the title's existence, being totally given over to introducing Kate Worley and Reed Waller's outrageous *Omaha the Cat Dancer*. A furry animal turned exotic dancer, she is one of the few underground comix characters to outlive her roots. While the covers to her comics were always of the plain-brown-wrapper school, the beautifully drawn content was totally explicit. Following **Bizarre Sex** #10, where Omaha appeared alongside William F. Loeb's *Rex Mason, Boy Transvestite* and Guy Colwell's *Hornies*, she sashayed into her own title in 1984 and appeared in 19 issues before it was cancelled in 1993. Fantagraphics relaunched it the following year but managed only four issues. Created by Worley and Waller and inspired by Fritz the Cat, **Omaha** is best summed up as an erotic soap opera full of nubile animals of all sexual persuasions.

Omaha was the first of a number of comix that integrated sex into a storyline rather than just for shock value. Among the others were **Melody**, **Cherry** and **Doll**. **Melody** was very much a sister underground comic to **Omaha the Cat Dancer**. It also told the x-certificate story of a stripper, and was also written by a woman and drawn by a man. But there the similarity ends. While Omaha was pure—or not so pure—fantasy, **Melody** provided the autobiographical story of an actual nude dancer from Quebec named Sylvie Rancourt, stage name Melody. Her sex-filled true story was drawn by veteran Montreal cartoonist Jacques Boivin across 10 Kitchen Sink issues from 1988 to 1994.

Coming from Last Gasp in 1987, **Cherry** was launched as **Cherry Poptart** but with a truncated title from #3 following an injunction from Kellogg's. Presumably the breakfast cereal giant was afraid of confusion between an underground comic and a breakfast snack. Created by Larry Welz—who had a brief 1960s underground fling with **Captain Guts** [1969]—it is drawn in a style reminiscent of the innocuous, kiddie friendly Archie Comics titles. The far from

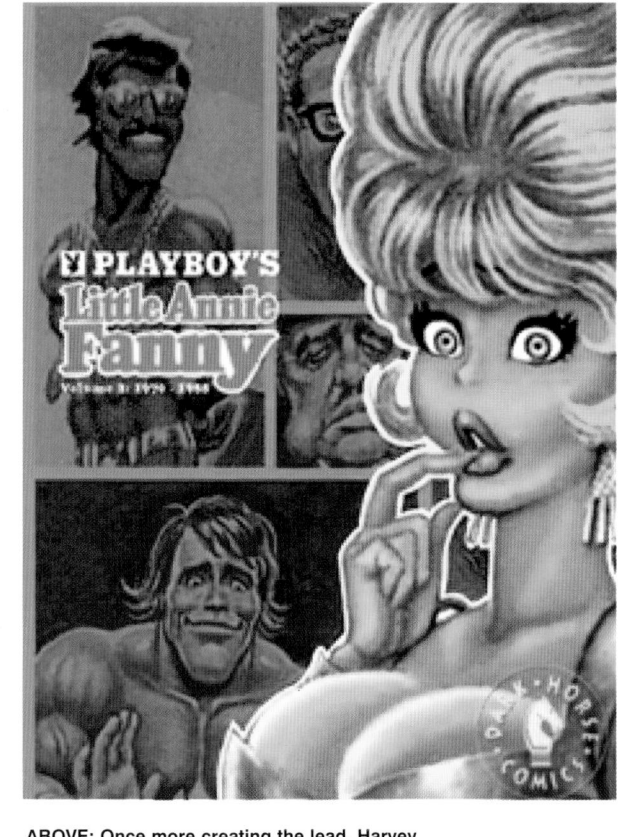

ABOVE: Once more creating the lead, Harvey Kurtzman's Little Annie Fanny for Playboy magazine. The strip ran from October 1962 to September 1988—a full five years before the underground artists began to produce their own sex comics. Shown here is the recently released second Dark Horse collection.

FACING PAGE: A typical scene from erotic furry comic Omaha by Reed Waller and Kate Worley. The series closed in May 1995 when the creators fell out. Worley continues to write comics for artist husband James Vance, but Waller vowed never to draw a comic again.

ABOVE: Crumb reminds us all of our childhood [1971].

RIGHT: The unstated simplistic art style belies the message. Cherry #12 by Larry Welz [Last Gasp, 1991].

FACING PAGE: Field Use, a wonderful piece of 1972 Vaughn Bode nonsense.

innocuous, kiddie friendly series follows the eternal 18-year-old as she, along with her divorcee mother and various nubile friends, has it off in all manner of salacious ways. Stylistically and thematically, it follows the sort of strips Welz and Larry Sutherland produced for such titles as Last Gasp's earlier **Bakersfield Kountry Komics** oneshot [1973].

Cherry, still batting and currently up to issue #22, spawned a spin-off title in 1992. Intended to feature stories by writers and artists other than Welz, **Cherry's Jubilee** was launched by Tundra Publishing before being picked up—along with its parent title—by Kitchen Sink, which published **Cherry** #14-15. Obviously feeling the character well-enough established, writer/artist Welz began self-publishing his series with his wife from #16, cancelling the spin-off with #4.

Guy Colwell's **Doll** is not so much a sex comic as an exploration of men's sexual attitudes towards women. Apart from the occasional knob shot, being a sensitively erotic story it hardly warrants its 'Adults Only' label. Published by Rip Off Press, it tells the story of a hyper-realistic sex doll, the tragically deformed man she was created for and the porn magazine publisher who bankrolled her creation and then wanted her for himself. It ran eight issues from 1988 to 1991.

Comix that didn't have staying power and fell by the wayside in the '70s included **Sex and Affection** (C P Family Publications, 1974) and the off-beat **Amputee Love** which was also cut off in its prime. Published by Last Gasp in 1975, it was the work of Rich and Rene Jensen, both of whom were amputees and proudly told of their uninhibited sexual exploits in graphic detail.

Ful-Horne Productions' three-issue **White Whore Funnies** [1975-79] really pushed the boat out with totally offensive covers, but again just traded on the name and had a poor interior standard.

Another latecomer but foremost in terms of outrageous content was Keith Green's **Felch Cumics**. Published in 1975, it featured work by head boys Williams, Wilson, Crumb, Osborne, Lynch, Stout and Spain among others on such strips as *The Felching*

Vampires meet the Holy Virgin, *The Felching Family Robinson, Phelch Phunnies, Stop Jacking Off* and *Clean Me Out*. It was blatantly dedicated to felching.

Even 1950s EC comics legend Wally Wood joined in with **Gang Bang**, just about as exploitative as a sex comic could be. Published by Nuance, its three issues were entirely the work of the veteran EC Comics artist and **MAD** contributor who parodied popular cultural icons through such stories as *So White and the Six Dorks, The Farmer's Daughter, Prince Violate, Stuporman Meets Blunder Woman, Flasher Gordon, The Sexual Revolution* and *Flesh Fucker Meets Women's Lib*. Even though Wood got in on the act late with this rampant 1979-1981 sexfest, the quality of Wood's style stood out from the rest thanks to his workmanship, but it was equally unnerving as the strips looked more like an explicit version of *Bewitched* due to his traditional '50s style.

The wimmin's point of view

Women comix creators responded with less graphic but still risqué material in such titles as **Tits 'n' Clits**, which ran seven issues from 1972-1987, and the two-issue **Wet Satin** [1976-78].

Tending to be less prurient than its masculine-driven equivalents, **Tits & Clits** still ran such strips as *Fonda Peters Vaginal Drip, Maxine*

and Dennis Visit Touch Much Spa, Vibrator Cozys and *The Miss Universal Udder Contest*.

Trina Robbins joined the fray with **Wet Satin: Women's Erotic Fantasies** [1976]. This featured strips with such titles as *Nose Fuck, The Cock-Pit, Feline Frolic* and *Nifty Ways to Cleave your Lover*, produced by a host of female creators showing they had as much gusto as men, including Marrs, Farmer, Gebbie and Mary Wilshire.

Despite having no qualms about Kitchen Sink's undergrounds—even **Bizarre Sex**—the publisher's printer refused to have anything to do with it, resulting in the comic being printed in California. *[See Chapter 6, Wimmen's Comix, for the full story on page 167.]*

Gay comes into play

While most underground titles stuck to heterosexual antics, gay sex wasn't overlooked although only a couple of comix were devoted to it. The first of these was **Gay Heart Throbs**, launched by Ful-Horne Productions in 1976. Edited by Larry Fuller, it ran three issues until 1981.

Among the contributors to the title were Danny Bulanadi—who went on to draw for Marvel Comics—and Bill Plimpton as well as the undoubtedly pseudo-nonymous Wiley L Spade, Larry Ben Gaye and Ray Horne. Going for the same over the top humour vein as the women and straight male cartoonists, their slapstick

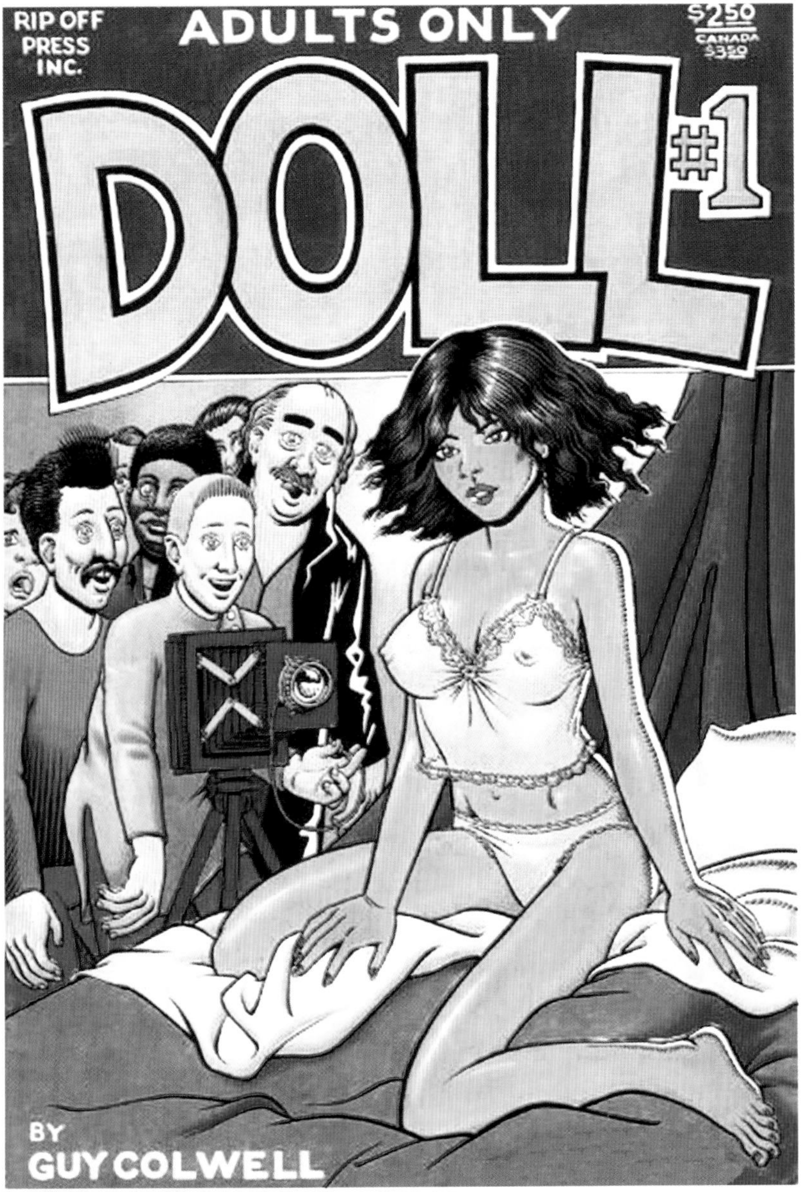

ABOVE: Gay Hearthrobs from Ful-Horne Productions, 1976. A 44-page jam issue from the underground's gay artists.

LEFT: Doll #1, written and drawn by Guy Colwell for Rip Off Press [1989].

FACING PAGE: Crumb's Ruff Tuff Creampuff was the odious embodiment of all of the politicians of the time who the artist despised. The strip was reprinted in The Complete Crumb Volume 6 [1991].

strip titles included *The Brothers Rim in Late One Night, Oedipus Ritz, The Closet, Kid Cunt, The Real Mother Trucker* and *The Fun Adventures of Ozzle and Harrial Bumsterp*.

However, a far more successful title was **Gay Comix**, which was launched in 1980 by Kitchen Sink. Taken over with 1985's #6 by Bob Ross, the publisher of San Francisco's **Bay Area Reporter**, it didn't run out of steam until in 1998 after an impressive 25 issues and one 1992 special. The series focused more on the experience of being gay than sex, although such strips as *Stains on the Sofa, Gerbil Love, Wee Wee's Gayhouse, Household Sadists* and *Blubber in a Rubber* did add a touch of raucous variety to the mix.

Its artists, who weren't obliged to be gay to contribute, included Donna Barr—whose own **Desert Peach** tells the story of the fictional gay brother of German World War II hero, Erwin Rommel, aka the Desert Fox—plus Cruse, Roberta Gregory, Randy Holmes, Andy Mangels, Lee Marrs, Trina Robbins, Howard Stangroom (editor of **Buddies**, the **Gay Comix** UK counterpart) and Reed Waller and his then-wife, **Omaha the Cat Dancer** writer Kate Worley.

Others with more mainstream comics credits also worked on the title. Among them were Tony Harris—better known for his art on DC's **Starman**, DC/Vertigo editor Joan Hilty, **The Maxx** creator Sam Kieth, veteran Marvel and DC superhero artist George Pérez,

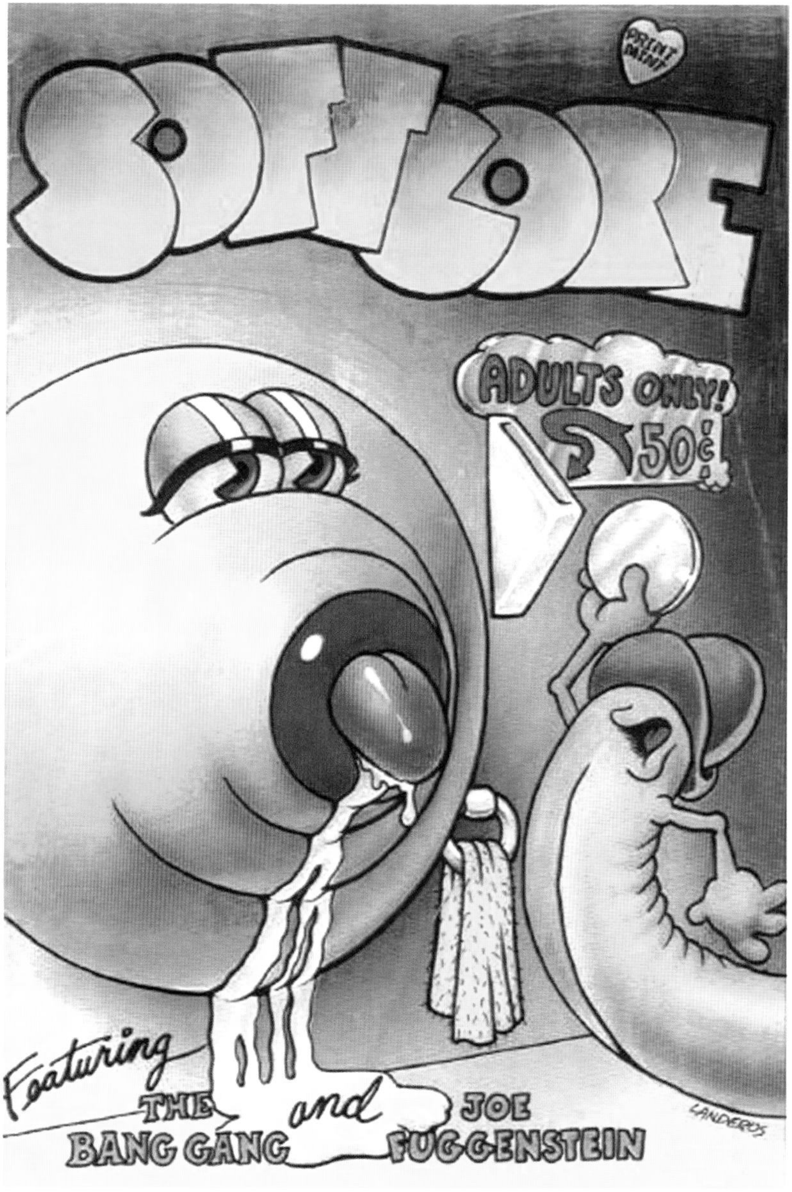

TOP: Amputee Love #1 written and drawn by amputee victims [Last Gasp 1975].

ABOVE: Young Lust #4 [Print Mint 1974].

LEFT: Softcore was a Print Mint title [1973]. Artist Rob Landeros went on to become a wildly successful computer games creator.

FACING PAGE: Justin Green's Soupygoy shows what all boys would probably do with superpowers. [Tales of Sex & Death, 1971].

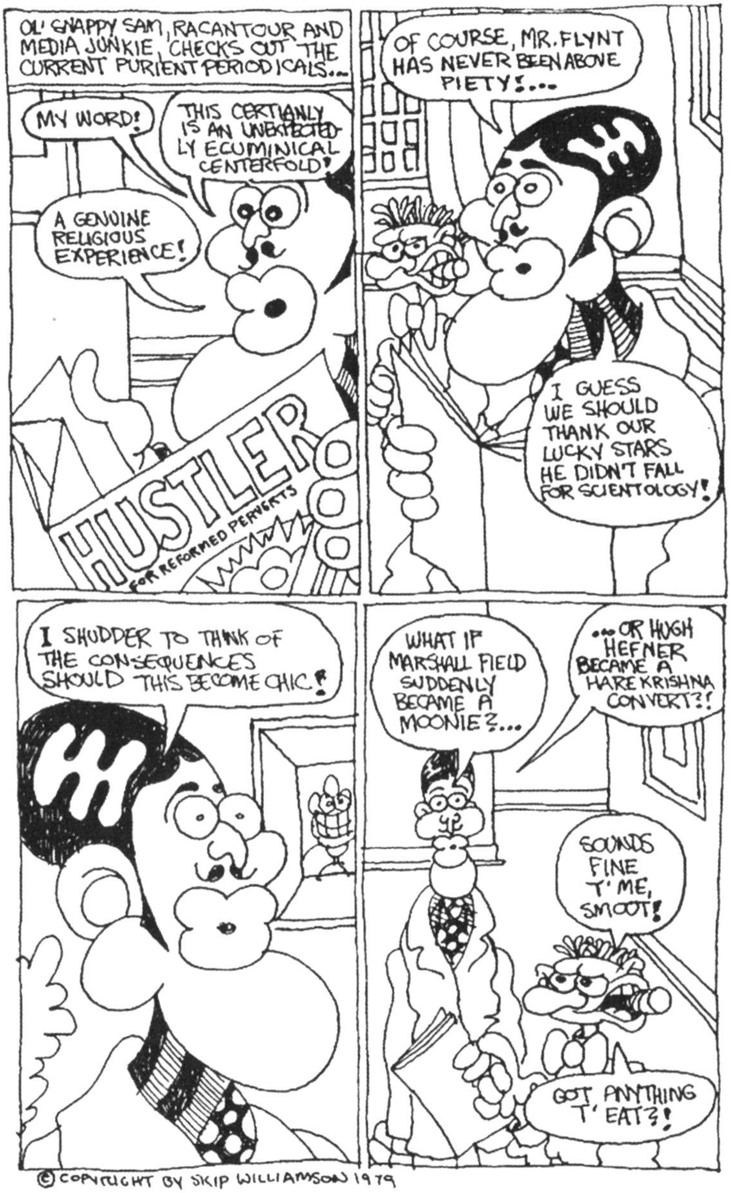

P Craig Russell—revered for his comics adaptations of opera and of Michael Moorcock's **Elric** stories—and Eric Shanower, who adapted L Frank Baum's **Oz** books into comics.

Gay Comix #1 and #25 featured strips by Mary Wings, whose **Come Out Comix** [1973] was the first lesbian-oriented underground comic, which she created as a reaction to a lesbian story by Trina Robbins in **Wimmen's Comix** #1.

Anything you can do, we can't

Following the collapse of the domestic underground comix market Crumb continued to produced his more personal work for a wider audience. Although sales had shown that sex comix sold, it was often hard to get them into other countries, with the UK targeted by overzealous customs officers enforcing outdated censorship laws.

There were transatlantic ripples when Crumb's work was also the primary catalyst for the 1973 prosecution under the UK's Obscene Publications Act of **Nasty Tales**—a British underground that mainly reprinted US material. London's Meep Comix Group title had included the *Grand Opening of the Great Intercontinental Fuck-In and Orgy-Riot* in its first issue and that led to a lengthy and highly publicised trial, which amazingly resulted in a Not Guilty verdict.

UK creators tended to steer clear of overt sexual material although Antonio Ghura and Mike Matthews pushed the boundaries in their **Truly Amazing Love Stories**, **Napalm Kiss** and **Horrific Romance Comics**.

LEFT: Skip Williamson's Snappy Sammy Smoot (who was brought to life by Carl Reiner on TV's Laugh-In in the '60s) plus "Williamson paints a nude" [1968].

RIGHT: The "Wimps" cover to Bizarre Sex #4. Beneath the plain wrapper lurks a '50s SF trash movie spoof cover with a gigantic pussy spaceship enveloping the top of the Empire State Building. The cover line reads "It Came From Alpha Centauri Looking For Love."

INKWELL

2.00

ADULTS ONLY!

#1

STEPHEN GUY ENTERPRISES $

BIZARRE SEX No. 4

Retailer: Remove this outer cover at your own risk!

75c

outer 'wimp' cover

One of the leading lights on the UK comix scene found a mainstream outlet for his sexually themed work. With writer Tym Manley, Hunt Emerson created the *Firkin the Cat* strip for **Fiesta**, a soft-core men's magazine. Introduced in 1981, the strip—a tongue-in-cheek look at human sexual behaviour—is still running today. The cartoonist has also adapted a classic 1928 novel, made notorious by its uninhibited descriptions of sex. Emerson's comix version of D H Lawrence's **Lady Chatterley's Lover**—itself subject of a trial under the Obscene Publications Act—was published by Knockabout in 1986. A large format graphic novel, it was followed in 1993 by a sequel of sorts, **Casanova's Last Stand**, which Emerson based in part on the notorious lover's memoirs. *[For more on UK comix trials and tribulations, see Chapter 7 on page 178.]*

Sex comix legacy

Recently sex comix have been through a renaissance, outside of the UK which continues to struggle against a repressive and puritanical establishment which still views comics as being only for kids.

In the US, there are now whole lines of porn titles, king among them being Eros Comics. An imprint which subsidizes the publication of Fantagraphics Books highly regarded alternative comics, it publishes such titles as **Alice in Sexland**, **Were-Slut**, **Footlicker**, **Pleasure Bound** and **Bizarre Bondage** as well as **Head**, **Rear Entry**, **Boffy the Vampire Layer**, **Housewives at Play** and **I Wanna Be Your Dog**.

Carnal Comics' output on the other hand is devoted to the porn movie industry. As well as comics dedicated to such stars as Anna Malle, Annie Sprinkle and Kimberley Kupps, it also publishes a number of series including **Legends of Porn: A Cartoon History**, **Porn Star Fantasies** and **Superstars of Erotica** among others.

Even the mainstream porn industry got in on the act with both *Penthouse* and *Hustler* releasing their own short-lived spin-off adult comics. With ultra-slick production values and the massive backing of their parent titles, these contained strips by major international talent. But while smaller companies continue, both giants folded due to poor editorial decisions rather than due to a lack of sales.

With the continuing relaxation of censorship laws, what was once taboo is becoming increasingly acceptable and, where they were once groundbreaking and controversial, sex comics are likely to gain acceptance as society in the English-speaking world mellows to the level it reached long ago in most of mainland Europe.

HIS FIRST DAY IN THE CITY

GOSH, A 'COUNTRY-TYPE' HOOD SURE GET LOST 'ROUND HERE!

BIG CITY WOMAN

HERE'S HOPE'N!

SALVADOR BETTY

ABOVE: Denis Kitchen's cover to Bizarre Sex #1, which hit the shelves of selected stores in a blaze of glory in 1972.

LEFT: Good Jive #1, with cover art by Richard "Grass" Green [Pooo Bear Productions, 1973].

FACING PAGE: A classic piece of Robert Williams artwork highlighting the perils of big city living. From Snatch Comics #3 [Apex, 1969].

STAYS together!

GOO

~~~ R. Crumbski

SNATCH COMICS

NO. 2   75¢

JANUARY 1969

HELLO '69!

©1968 by R. SCRUM

LEFT AND ABOVE: When Crumb set out to offend everybody... with January 1969's Snatch Comics #2, a comic that was reprinted at least six times, despite being banned almost everywhere! Behind the outrageous cover, as well as letting his smut-guru S Clay Wilson join in, Crumb produced the infamous two pager [left] possibly dooming any hope of widescale distribution of comix forever.

"I never did an incest story," says Moscoso. "And Crumb never did an incest story again, as far as I know. However, we did not self-censor ourselves. It was just after a while we got it out of our systems."

The Two Lives of Fritz the Cat

The career of one of its highest profile characters had already burnt out by the time the comix revolution kicked in.

CRUMB created a host of characters that fuelled criticism of him being sexist, racist and homophobic. The likes of Angelfood McSpade, Bigfoot, Whiteman, Honeybunch Kaminski and the Ruff Tuff Creampuff had their fair share of critics. But the biggest critic of a Crumb creation turned out to be the artist himself.

Fritz the Cat made his first public appearance in Harvey Kurtzman's **Help!** #24 [1965] in the two-page *Fred the Teenage Girl Pigeon* strip, Crumb's first sale to the Warren humour magazine. Unnamed at the time, the amoral anthropomorphic hipster was the latest incarnation of a comix version of a family pet, introduced by Robert and his brother Charles Crumb in their home made **Crumb Brothers Almanac** [1959].

Although many of the stories Crumb produced between then and 1965 have not survived, a 1964 strip in which the wisecracking feline takes a trip around the world and comes home to seduce his sister resurfaced in 1969's **R Crumb's Comics and Stories**. But it was those reprinted in the 64-page **Head Comix** [Viking Press, 1968], and by Ballantine Books in **R Crumb's Fritz the Cat** [1969] that brought both

Crumb and his screwin' smokin' creation to the attention of the mass media and ultimately drove the writer/artist to a nervous breakdown. Those, plus the ones the cartoonist wrote and drew in 1967 for "gentlemen's magazine," **Cavalier**.

"It happened real fast," Crumb said, "Within six months it went from me, my wife, [**Zap** publisher Don] Donahue, and a couple of other people hand-stapling comics and selling them on the street... to having all these fast-talking lawyers fighting over the rights and sleazy guys offering big money contracts."

Among those who approached Crumb was Ralph *(Heavy Traffic)* Bakshi, who went on to be "heavily influenced" by Vaughn Bode's work on his *Wizards* [1977] and *Lord of the Rings* [1978] animated flops. Crumb described him as "a schlock-meister, a no-talent bum."

Bakshi wanted the pot 'n' pussy-obsessed cat as the star of the first full-length X-rated animated feature. Crumb wasn't interested but his wife Dana had her husband's power of attorney and signed the rights over to the producer/director.

The result was the 78-minute 1972 *Fritz the Cat* movie, detailing the cool cat's encounters with dope, the police, life in Harlem and biker Angels. "Flawed but engaging," was the description given by critic Leonard Maltin in his **Movie & Video Guide** while **The Time Out Film Guide** was more critical, saying, "A generally trivial exercise that never matches the punch of the original."

Leading UK film critic Leslie Halliwell committed the sin Crumb probably feared most, as he wrote in his **Halliwell's Filmgoer's Companion**, "Satirical animated feature by Ralph Bakshi from his comic strip for adults only" Halliwell added, po-faced, "Pretty repellent adventures in the urban underground." Reflecting his out of touch generation, he concludes, somewhat illiterately, "The contrast between the subject and the old fashioned Tom & Jerry style were striking."

Crumb for his part promptly denounced the movie, demanding his name be removed. To complete his distancing, he then killed the character off, having a spurned female ostrich slay him, Trotsky-like, with an ice pick through the skull. The story, *Fritz the Cat Superstar* appeared the same year in **The People's Comics**. Only Crumb's second post-1965 story to feature Fritz, it was also his last.

A sequel film, *The Nine Lives of Fritz the Cat*, was released in 1974 in which Fritz is now married and living on welfare with a nagging wife. Smoking pot to escape reality, he imagines himself in eight other lives, including being an aide to the President (Kissinger!), an astronaut and an orderly to Adolph Hitler. This time, as well as Crumb, Bakshi was not involved either, with the film directed by Robert Taylor. "Woefully inept" was **Time Out's** succinct summary.

THIS PAGE: Fritz, pre and post Hollywood. At first glance only the usual animation dumbing down, until you look at the hands. No tit fondling and no crotch pressing for this X-rated video sleeve.

FACING PAGE: The 96-page Life and Death of Fritz the Cat collection [Fantagraphics, 1993].

Art: Gilbert Shelton, Fabulous Furry Freak Brothers #3 [Rip Off Press, 1973].

Chapter 3:

Grass Roots

Drugs in Comix

"Dope will get you through times of no money better than money will get you through times of no dope." . . . THE FABULOUS FURRY FREAK BROTHERS

*Get ready for a big hit of Gilbert Shelton, a snort of **Cocaine Comix**, a few tokes of **Dope Comix**, **Dopin' Dan** and **Dealer McDope** as well as the latest crop: **Knockabout**, **Electric Soup** and **Northern Lightz**.*

FLOWER power brought about the age of peace, love and understanding but it was still a revolution—one fuelled by sex, rock music and in particular, drugs. The hippies' love affair with mind expanding and mood altering chemicals and plants was reflected in the comix, most obviously in **The Fabulous Furry Freak Brothers,** Gilbert Shelton's tales of a hapless and hirsute threesome of stoned wastrels who have become icons of the era.

Feds 'n' heads

Although famed fictional San Francisco denizens Fat Freddy, Freewheelin' Franklin and Phineas Phreak first hit the scene in Austin, Texas where, in 1968, Shelton featured them in a strip in his home town's underground newspaper, **The Austin Rag.** When the 28-year-old cartoonist—along with many of America's youth—hit the trail for the City by the Bay, the Freak Brothers hitched a ride along with him and later that year made their comix debut in **Feds 'n' Heads,** a one-shot from the Print Mint.

Soon they were appearing in another underground newspaper, **The LA Free Press,** where their zany attempts at scoring drugs, getting high, attempting to get laid and generally trying to bum a free ride through life reached a whole new and significantly larger audience.

With sufficient strips under his belt, in 1971 Shelton and his partners in Rip Off Press published the first issue of **The Fabulous**

Furry Freak Brothers** as a standalone collection. Mirroring the characters' laid-back attitude, it is a title that has only managed 13 issues in more than three decades but all of them have been constantly available through multiple reprintings and collected editions throughout the world. Its wide appeal, extending beyond nostalgic hippies, spliff-smoking ravers and other potheads, reaches out to regular Joes who can get into its digs at the stereotypical hippie lifestyle.

No longer an alternative, with worldwide sales in the millions, the Freak Brothers had followed **MAD Magazine, National Lampoon** and other one-time radical humour concepts to reaching iconic status and becoming household names.

In fact, Shelton's strip evoked the late '60s dropout scene so successfully that in 1972—just as he had accumulated enough material to produce a second issue—publisher Hugh Hefner approached Shelton to produce a *Fabulous Furry Freak Brothers* board game for his **Playboy** magazine.

The early popularity of the cartoonist's draft-dodging hippie heroes was further proven by their appearance in a range of early anthology comix including **Yellow Dog, Radical America Komiks, Zap Comix** and **Rip Off Comix** as well as the American magazine devoted to dope

> Hugh Hefner approached Gilbert Shelton to produce a Fabulous Furry Freak Brothers board game for his **Playboy** magazine.

ABOVE: Kitchen Sink's 1978 anthology, Dope Comix, featured no less than 14 strips, all drawn by different artists including Kim Deitch, Jay Lynch, Howard Kruse and Denis Kitchen.

LEFT: The first issue of Gilbert Shelton's Fabulous Furry Freak Brothers has proven so popular that since 1971 it has been reprinted no less than 18 times in the US alone. Other issues, like 1977's #5, have not only been kept in print but have also been represented as deluxe coffee table editions (shown).

smoking **High Times**, a leading player in the drive to reform the US's prohibitive marijuana laws.

By 1975, Shelton had completed collecting and reprinting all the material he had been producing for other titles. In an identical position to the pioneers of comicbooks when they ran out of newspaper strips to reprint but had a viable market clamouring for more, new strips had to be created for the eagerly demanded fourth issue of **The Fabulous Furry Freak Brothers.** To enable Shelton to achieve this, he brought in Dave Sheridan—and later Paul Mavrides—to help him produce the new full-length strips.

Dealer McDope

Sheridan was already responsible for another of the drug icons in Dealer McDope. Described as the quintessential marijuana merchant, the longhaired pot peddler made his debut in Rip Off Press' **Mother's Oats #1,** the first of the undergrounds devoted entirely to dope-tinged tales.

McDope appeared in all three issues of the 1969 to 1976 title with the first story, *The Doings of Dealer McDope*, lauded as an accurate portrayal of an acid trip.

Leo Paoli, an attorney who led the first significant fight to legalize marijuana in California, authored the 1972 California Marijuana Initiative to promote pot's

decriminalization. His group collected half a million signatures, and the initiative was placed on the November 1972 ballot as Proposition 19. While it lost, it garnered an impressive 34% of the vote. Such was the authenticity of Sheridan's character that Paoli chose Dealer McDope as the poster image for the entire campaign.

However Sheridan's creation is probably better known outside of California as a result of the 1972 *Official Dealer McDope's Dealing Game,* produced by Last Gasp Eco-Funnies. A complex Monopoly-style board game, it involves players actually going out and purchasing gear to stay in the game. Naturally, the winner is the one with the biggest stash, while quality is also important, with testing time factored in.

A similar but far simpler *Cluedo*-style game, *It's A Raid*, set during a Freak Brothers party, came as the inside back cover of the UK collection **Thoroughly Ripped**.

Dr Atomic

Completing a spaced-out triumvirate of stoned comix characters is Dr Atomic, a Larry Todd creation for the comix section of **The Sunday Pages,** a short-lived San Francisco underground paper. Mad scientist Dr Atomic's major profile was probably through 1974's 20-page

LEFT: As well as helping Gilbert Shelton with his new Freak Brothers strips, Dave Sheridan expanded the market for his own Dealer McDope character when Last Gasp-Eco Funnies produced his Official (!) Dealer McDope Dealing Game in 1972.

FACING PAGE: Dealer McDope also scored bigtime, upstaged only by the Freak Brothers in #1, when Rip-Off Press featured the character to star in the second and third editions of their 16 issue Underground Classics series.

RIGHT: Gilbert Shelton's portrayal of evangelist Billy Graham ("The Nation's Spiritual Counselor") reaching out to a whole new flock when he preaches in San Francisco. Now if only he'd remembered to bring his swear box...

FACING PAGE: The title says it all for this 1974 Kistone Press 20-page one-shot, Dr Atomic's Marijuana Multiplier.

oneshot **Dr Atomic's Marijuana Multiplier** [Kistone Press]. "Double Your Dollars, Triple Your Dope" the cover line ran on this outrageous how-to title which lured in its audience by promising to increase the potency of marijuana by five to six times.

More prolific than his fellow artists but still slow compared with mainstream cartoonists, Todd produced enough work for the dope-loving Doc to appear in six issues of his own title across four years, all published by Last Gasp between 1978 and 1981.

Dopin' Dan

Just as folk singer Tom Paxton immortalized the discovery in "Talking Viet Nam Pot Luck Blues", Ted Richards used comix to celebrate one of the very few plus points US Army recruits found on landing in Vietnam. Dopin' Dan was a G.I. who the **40-Year-Old Hippie** creator was unfortunate enough to introduce in **Air Pirates Funnies** #1. When the title felt the wrath of Disney and disappeared after a mere two issues, Dan was prematurely airlifted into his own title the following year.

About as regular as The **Fabulous Furry Freak Brothers** and **Mother's Oats, Dopin' Dan** didn't fare that much better than his

parent title, running to only four issues from 1972 to 1981. But the connection to Dealer McDope, Dr Atomic and the Freak Brothers was superficial because, as Richards explains, "An irony of the strip was that the storylines rarely mentioned drugs—the character's name was a satirical play on the titles of two other popular 'army' comic strips of the day: *Sad Sack* and *Beetle Bailey*."

From its 1977 first issue, Dan and the Freak Brothers also had regular strips in **Rip Off Comix.** Although the laid back G.I. bailed out in 1980 with #7, Shelton's hippies hung around for another five issues until #12 [1983].

While Shelton, Todd and Sheridan were the big names in drug comix, Crumb produced scattered strips and covers, such as **Stoned Picture Parade #1** [Apex, 1968] and there were lots of others with less high profiles.

Kenneth P Greene produced **Tooney Loons and Marijuana Melodies** in 1971 and Adam's Apple followed with Michael Krueger's **Stoned Out Funnies** a year later but invariably most underground anthology titles had some drugs-based material.

One example was Tom Veitch and Greg Irons' drug parody of Sgt Rock, a World War II hero from mainstream comics publisher DC.

Continued on p98

The Adventures of Sgt Smack and Easy Co took it to the edge in the 1972 first issue of **Deviant Slice**.

To toke or not to toke...

The San Francisco Comic Book Company appeared to join the dope trail with its **Stoned Picture Funnies** [1975]. But they only scored two out of three. It was in pictures, and it was funny but the "stoned" part of the title of this one-shot must have been a comment on the state of mind of the artists rather than their subjects, which had little to do with dope. Either that or it was a cheap marketing ploy.

While **Fabulous Furry Freak Brothers** and the like revel in the hedonistic hippie lifestyle, not all of the comix creators were publicly pro-drugs and this was reflected in their stories.

On one side, Shelton had Freewheelin' Franklin saying, "Dope will get you through times of no money better than money will get you though times of no dope," but he also had Fat Freddy warning readers of the dangers of speed (amphetamine sulphate). It was a warning that R. Crumb also issued in his two-page *Street Corner Daze* strip for **Zap** #3 [Print Mint, 1968].

In **The Great Marijuana Debate** [Krupp Comic Works, 1972], Jay Lynch examined both sides of the

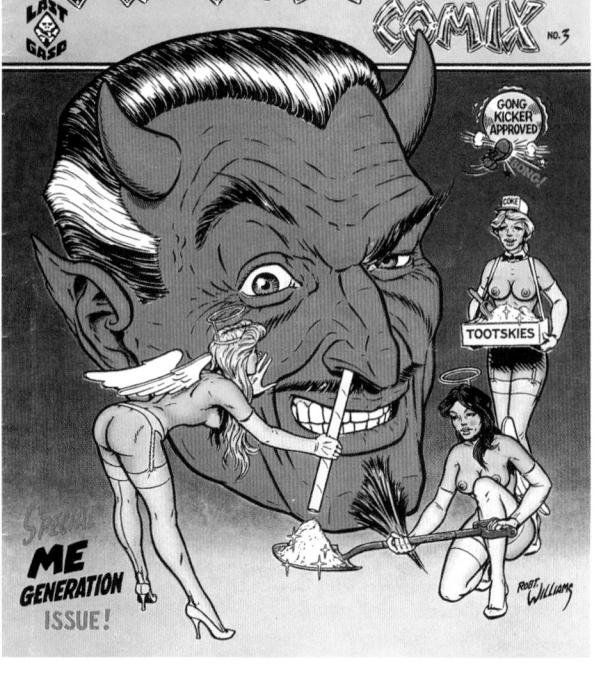

"to toke or not to toke" argument. But while the cartoonists continued to use cannabis and LSD as rich source material and for inspiration, things were starting to go to pot. The comix audience was changing the recreational drugs that it was taking.

The increasing use of heroin, speed and cocaine, as opposed to the less addictive dope and hallucinogenics favoured by peaceniks, was bringing with it a fresh set of problems and some members of the comix community were moved by this enough to help.

As early as 1972, Print Mint produced the no-nonsense **Tuff Shit Comics.** A one-shot focusing on drug abuse, it was a benefit book for a Berkeley methadone clinic.

A similar venture followed in 1980, **Are Your Highs Getting You Down?** Written and drawn by **Gay Comix** contributor Mary Wings, it featured comic strips based on the personal experiences of two women's substances abuse groups. It was circulated free of charge and funded in part by a grant from the California Arts Council. Last Gasp repackaged and republished the title in 1981.

Another credable info-comic was **Cops 'N' Dopers**. First released in 1977 by Mayflower Unlimited, this one-shot was a people's guide to the 4th Amendment or *How To Avoid A Bust.* A portion of the proceeds from the sale of this regularly

LEFT: Artist John Higgins and UK underground title Home Grown risked corporate wrath in their depiction of a toking Batman, Hulk as a peacenik, Plastic Man going out on a limb and a weirdly not out of place Dr Strange, surrounded by stars of the underground including Mr Natural, the Fabulous Furry Freak Brothers and Honeybunch Kaminski.

FACING PAGE: With #3, Last Gasp Eco-Funnies dropped their clever Cocaine Comics front cover topline of R. I. P.-snortin', but made up for it with this piece of devilish Robert Williams 1981 artwork.

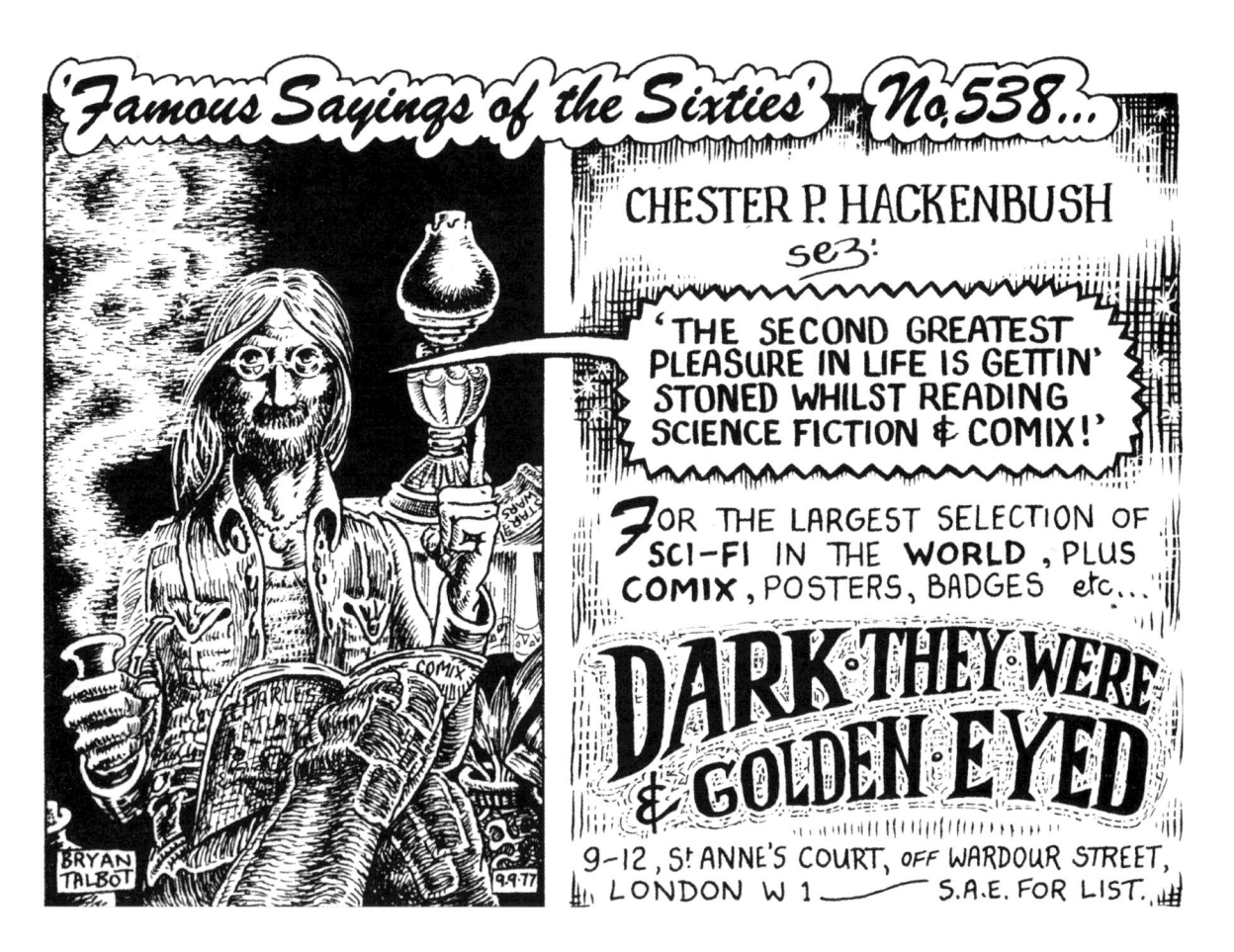

reprinted comic is donated to NORML [The National Organization for the Reform of Marijuana Laws].

Cocaine... in my brain

The move away from the softer drugs was most clearly symbolized by Last Gasp's **Cocaine Comix**. Launched in 1976, not only was it more blatantly drug-related than the company's earlier **Mother's Oats** but it also promoted a far more addictive substance.

The massive inroads made by cocaine into the drug culture were also evidenced in a two-parter issued by Kitchen Sink Press in 1984. **Harold Hedd in Hitler's Cocaine** featured Rand Holmes' horny longhair in a slapstick search for a cache of Bolivian marching powder lost during World War II. But it was a far cry from the sort of stories the Canadian cartoonist used to tell.

He had begun his harder-edged *Harold Hedd* strip in the pages of the *Georgia Straight* in 1971. Obviously influenced by Shelton's

THERE WILL NOW BE A SHORT INTERLUDE

TALBOT '77

NORMAL READING MAY NOW BE RESUMED

WILLOW PATTERN COMIX

BRAINSTORM STUDIOS

ABOVE: Home Grown was a short-lived UK underground magazine from Alchemy Publications [1977]. Across its ten issues it ran a variety of mindbending comic strips and featured early work by John Higgins, Bryan Talbot and authors Julie Burchill and Tony Parsons.

LEFT: Talbot again, with a stand-alone page illustrating the power of the weed. With a spaceman as the focus, in control of such mysteries as the Giant Heads of Easter Island and Mayan stone carvings. Heady stuff, Bryan!

FACING PAGE: Britain's first combined comix, comics and sci-fi store celebrated the underground press through its advertisements. This example, by Bryan Talbot, features the artist's psychedelic alchemist Chester P. Hackenbush, from Brainstorm [1975].

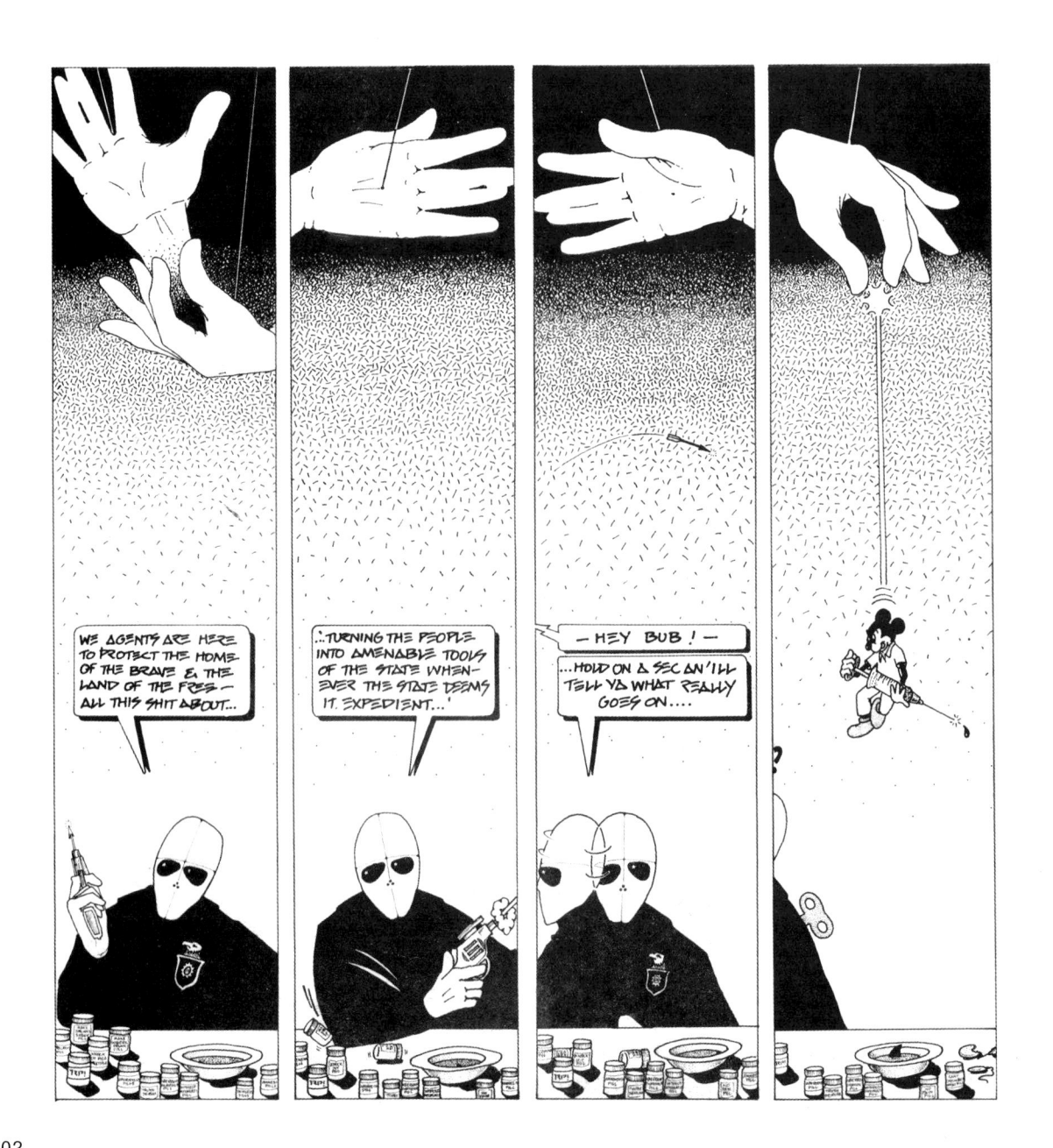

Freak Brothers and featuring a similar cast of hippie stoners, it dealt with the British Columbian drug culture and the issues arising from it. Holmes' strips glorified over the top drug usage and explicit sex. Legend has it they were as often based on actual events as they were on fictional ones.

In 1972, his weekly strips, which ran for almost a year, were collected by the *Georgia Straight* in two oversized comix.

Kitchen Sink's aptly titled **Dope Comix** was something of a throwback. Launched in 1978, well after the comix boom had peaked and even troughed, the scope of its stories went beyond dope to include all sorts of illegal substances but it mainlined on hallucinogenics. It continued through to 1981 but with only four issues published it was little more than an annual event.

US drought

Although the US market for dope comix all but died in 1981 with **Dope Comix #4**, there was still one last title which appeared to extol the virtues of drug use, but in reality was a bizarre adaptation of a World

ABOVE: A 1977 Home Grown illustration by the now-mainstream artist John Higgins, who also provided many of the title's cover visuals. LEFT: Illustrating a Michael Marten text feature on the CIA (Confusion. Intrusion. Anxiety. "They flashed their badges—they were employees of the Company"). Art by Chris Morton, 1977, also from Home Grown #2.

RIGHT: A Northern Lightz MAD Magazine-style back cover, by Mark Stafford, revealing the true source for Isaac Newton's inspiration.

FACING PAGE: Scotland's head boys produce Northern Lightz (cover to #8 by Nulsh shown), which regularly stars the McBam Clan (bottom left).

War II propaganda film. In 1993, Starhead Comix published Art Penn's **Hemp for Victory,** based on the film of the same name produced by the United States Department of Agriculture 50 years earlier.

But while American titles have fallen on fallow ground, the British have been more fertile in cultivating a perennial crop. While the 16-page one-shot **Spaced** [Sheridan Comics; 1974] hardly bloomed, the six-issue **Brainstorm Comics** [Alchemy Publications, 1975-77 with its *Journey into Delirium* strip] was a major hit. However, the sole UK comic blatantly devoted to the drug culture was H Bunch's wonderful **Dope Fiend Funnies** [1974] featuring work by a host of cartoonists including Steve Parkhouse, Edward Barker and Chris Tyler, unlike most other UK undergrounds of the time with nothing but US reprints.

Outside of Knockabout's occasional forays, notably **Acid Head Arnie**

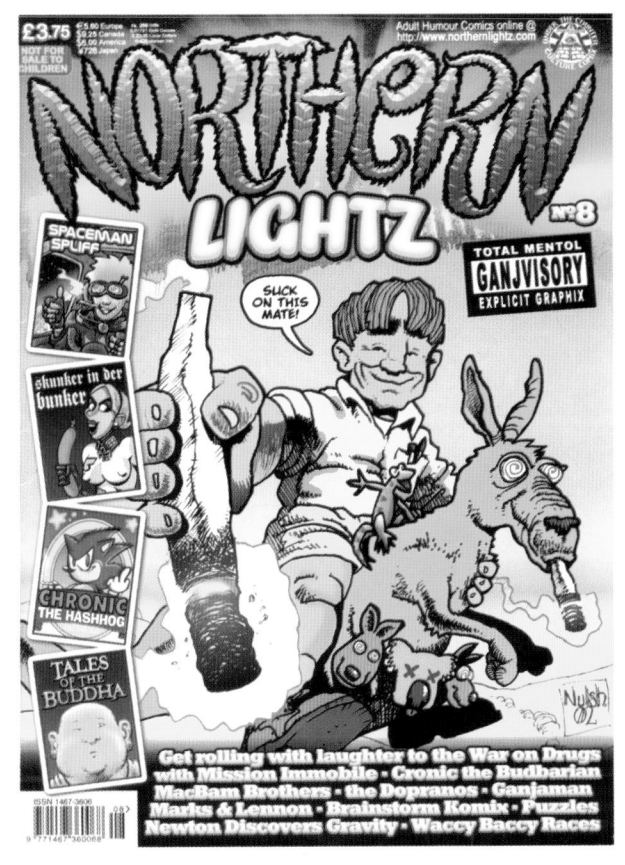

[1997] and the Crumb/Shelton reprints, it's been the Scots who have kept things moving with the 18-issue **Electric Soup** [1989-1993] and its successor, the highly impressive **Northern Lightz** (ten remarkably frequent issues and counting). They have continued a stoned tradition through such strips as *The Astounding Ganjaman, Spliff Warz, The Dopranos, Waccy Baccy Races, Great Moments in Dope History* and *Hashpuss* (there just had to be a cat in there!) plus their homage to the Fabulous Furry Freak Brothers, the title's flagship characters, Dave Alexander's Mad Mentol MacBam Clan (Shug, Pudden and Tam).

Those F***ing Cats!

Fritz... Firkin... even Fat Freddy's... There's obviously something about a cat's feisty, independent nature and "fur-q" attitude that appeals to the artists of the comix counter culture community.

WHAT have hippies got against dogs? Just about every leftover flower child you see in the street seems to have a pooch in tow, but whenever an underground artist fancied a spot of anthropomorphic antics the cat was the beast of choice. Not only that but just about all the major feline funsters had a thing about the letter F—Fat Freddy's Cat, Fritz the Cat, Firkin the Cat... Obviously Otto Mesmer's surreal 1915 cartoon series *Felix the Cat* has a lot to answer for!

Gilbert Shelton and Dave Sheriden's nameless cat-of-Fat-Freddy starred solo in numerous underground newspapers and comics as well alongside his master in **The Fabulous Furry Freak Brothers**. The lazy and belligerent cool one spent most of his days finding new ways to irritate Fat Freddy. But at night he had wild escapist adventures working undercover for the US government and engaged in surreal sagas like the *War of the Roaches*. After nine years of driving his stoner owner insane the nameless one finally got his own title in 1977.

One of Robert Crumb's most famous creations, Fritz the Cat, first 'officially' appeared in *Help!* #22 in 1965. Fritz was a cynical anti-hero

who spent his life wandering through the Sixties counter culture taking advantage of drugs and naive girls up for "free love." The 1960 creation of Charles and Robert Crumb, he appeared in numerous titles until— incensed by the fame given to his creation through two less-than-faithful feature films—the disowned and degraded feline was killed by a vengeful female ostrich with an ice pick.

Meanwhile, in the UK, Tym Manley and Hunt Emerson's **Firkin the Cat** started in the soft porn mag **Fiesta** in 1981. The surreal idea of a cat dispensing sexual wisdom (a pussy talking about doggie positions) worked surprising well, taking a tongue-in-cheek look at the vast range of bizarre carnal peccadilloes preoccupying humans. Virgin Books collected the strips in 1985 followed by Knockabout in 1989 and 2002.

And the list goes on. In the UK alone, cartoon cats include more Emerson: Puss Puss and Calculus Cat plus Alan Moore's Maxwell the Magic Cat, and a history going all the way back to James Crichton's 1937 creation, **The Dandy's** Korky the Cat. In the US, the kooky Krazy Kat Kapers set the surreal standard in 1913 while the erotic antics of Reed Waller and Kate Worley's **Omaha the Cat Dancer** added a new dimension in the 1980s.

ABOVE: The Collected Fat Freddy's Cat Volume One [Knockabout, 1983]. The cat's solo strip origin is said to be due to Shelton needing a small space filler for his Fabulous Furry Freak Brothers comics as the strips being collected were all the wrong shape.

LEFT: Hunt Emerson and Tym Manley's Firkin the Cat takes on that perennial comix nemesis, Mickey Mouse, or rather Ricky Rat.

FACING PAGE: Crumb kills off his Bakshi-bastardised cat in The Complete Crumb Comics Volume 8 [1992].

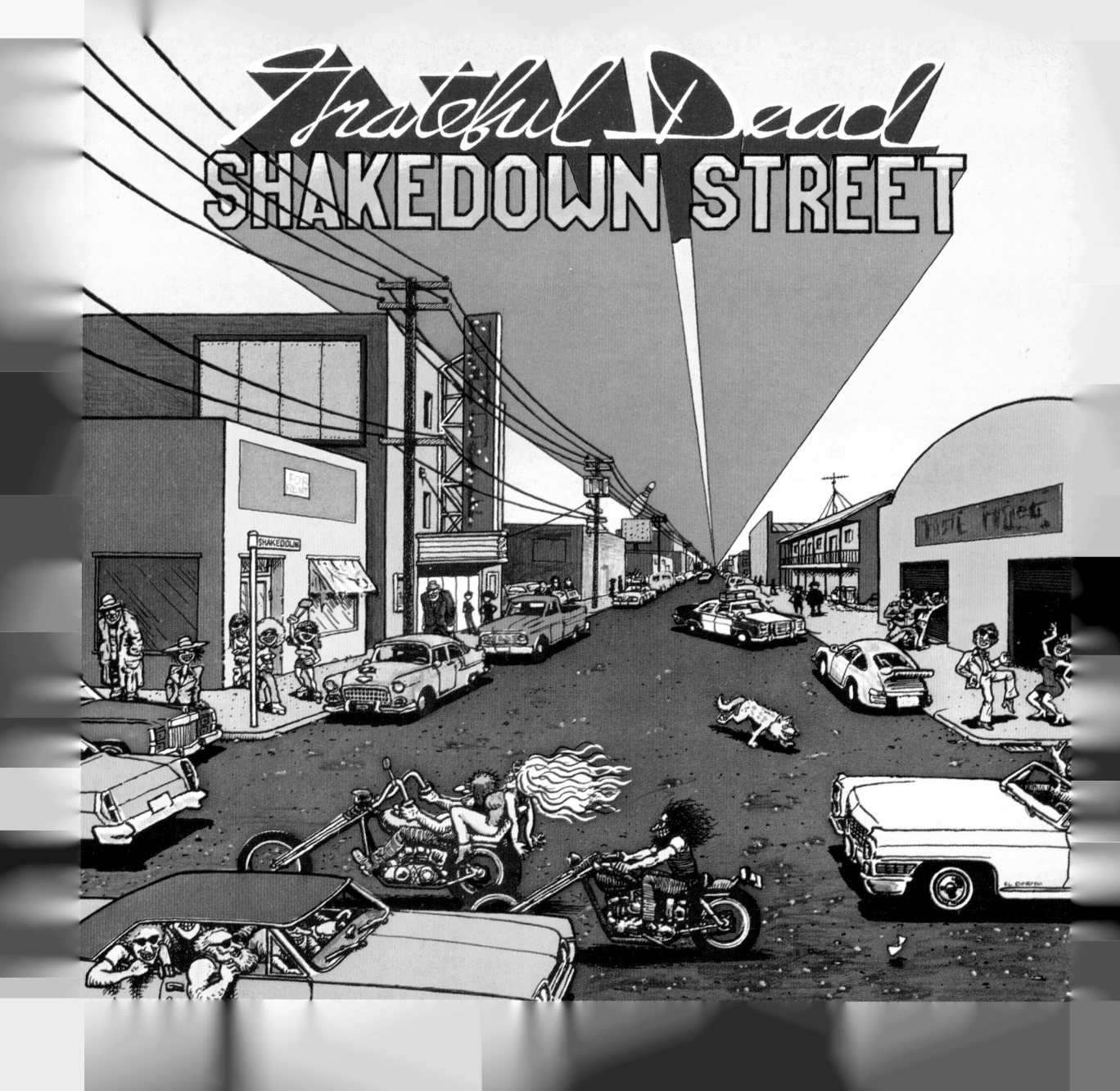

Chapter 4

Beyond the Page

Adding music to the movement

"I submitted the Appetite cover as a joke 'cause I didn't think anyone would use it." ...AXL ROSE ON ROBERT WILLIAMS' APPETITE FOR DESTRUCTION COVER ART

Some underground comix artists lived a wild, hedonistic lifestyle more reminiscent of rock stars than cartoonists—perhaps because they also supplied the artwork to a generation's anthems and festivals.

THE comix being produced by and for the self-styled children of the revolution were an aspect of the cultural sea change that remained all-but unknown to the un-hip Joe Public of the late 1960s.

More obvious were the fashions; the long hair, tie-dyes, bell bottoms and Afghan coats—and the music. Full of experimentation, with drugs, sex and politics-riddled lyrics; it was dubbed psychedelic, and travelled the world. It became known as *Electric Music for the Mind and Body*, taking the term from the title of Country Joe and the Fish's first album. With it came a new art style, one that had its genesis on the streets of San Francisco.

Rival promoters Chester "Chet" Helms and Bill Graham encouraged Haight Ashbury's Big Five artists (Wes Wilson, Alton Kelley, Rick Griffin, Stanley Mouse and Victor Moscoso) to push the boundaries with their poster art to publicise rock concerts at the legendary venues—the Fillmore Auditorium West and Family Dog's Avalon Ballroom. Becoming increasingly bold and innovative, they blended together a variety of influences including Art Nouveau, Pop Art and Op Art, creating a brand new style that **Time** magazine dubbed *Nouveau Frisco*.

They constantly strove to outdo each other while promoting local bands Jefferson Airplane, the Grateful Dead, Quicksilver Messenger Service and Big Brother and the Holding Company. "What's significant is that these posters were created with an intensity that was lived," wrote Bonnie Maclean, Bill Graham's wife and fellow poster artist.

> "...these posters were created with an intensity that was lived."
>
> *...Bonnie Maclean*

Of all the cartoonists, Rick Griffin became the longest lasting member of the poster art scene and—even after moving into comix—stayed involved until his death in 1991.

Having already illustrated album sleeves for Jack Marshall's *My Sun, the Surf Nut* [1960], the Challengers' *Lloyd Thaxton Goes Surfing with the Challengers* [1963] and *Surf's Up* [1965], Griffin arrived in the Bay Area via Los Angeles in 1966 with the Jook Savages, a loose collection of Beat writers and artists, looking for work.

His first poster was for a Jook Savages exhibition which prompted the organizers of 1967's *Pow-Wow: A Gathering of the Tribes for a Human Be-In* to ask Griffin to design a poster for the event. The Human Be-In, which starred revolutionary avatar of the mind Timothy Leary, poet spokesman for the Beat generation Allen Ginsberg plus a host of local bands, became a landmark festival of the era kicking off both the Summer of Love and Griffin's poster career.

Chet Helms liked the designs and went looking for the So Cal surfer. "He saw those two posters, found out how to contact me and asked me to draw posters for the Family Dog. So I sort of stumbled into the Bay Area and got drawn tight into this scene, just like about everything else that's happened to me in my life," Griffin explained.

With colleagues and compatriots like Moscoso, Jaxon and Irons, it was inevitable that Griffin would get involved in the nascent comix scene. Yet what started his comix career was an unexpected

RIGHT: Pow-Wow: A Gathering of Tribes for a Human Be-In. The poster that launched Griffin's career, complete with all the trademarks of his style, ranging from use of psychedelic lettering to cosmic imagery.

PREVIOUS PAGE:
Aoxomoxoa, a Grateful Dead release from June 1969, with sleeve art by Rick Griffin. The album was originally to be called Earthquake County, but was changed to its unpronounceable pallendromic name at the insistance of Griffin.

FACING PAGE: Psychedelia's Big 5 [1967]. Alton Kelley, Victor Moscoso, Rick Griffin, Wes Wilson and Stanley Mouse.

encounter with Crumb, whose *Abstract Expressionist Ultra Super Modernistic Comics* in **Zap** #1 had been inspired by a strip incorporated into one of Griffin's posters.

"I came home one day, and there was Crumb sitting on my front porch. He introduced himself. I had seen his cartoons in **Yarrowstalks** and I had seen the first commercial **Zap**, that was the one with the car on the cover and all the people sitting in the car. I had seen it and bought it and so I knew who he was. He said he was going to publish **Zap** as a periodical and he wanted me to come on board and asked if I knew any other artists who worked in the cartoon format, and I told him about Victor Moscoso, and Crumb asked me to extend an invitation to Moscoso. That's how Victor and I wound up in comics."

After attending Yale University in the early '60s, Moscoso had moved to San Francisco to study at the Art Institute, later becoming an instructor there. In the fall of 1966, he had seen some of Wes Wilson's rock posters at a dance at the Avalon Ballroom and decided, "I could make some money doing posters for these guys."

So when Griffin gave him the offer, Moscoso—the first to include

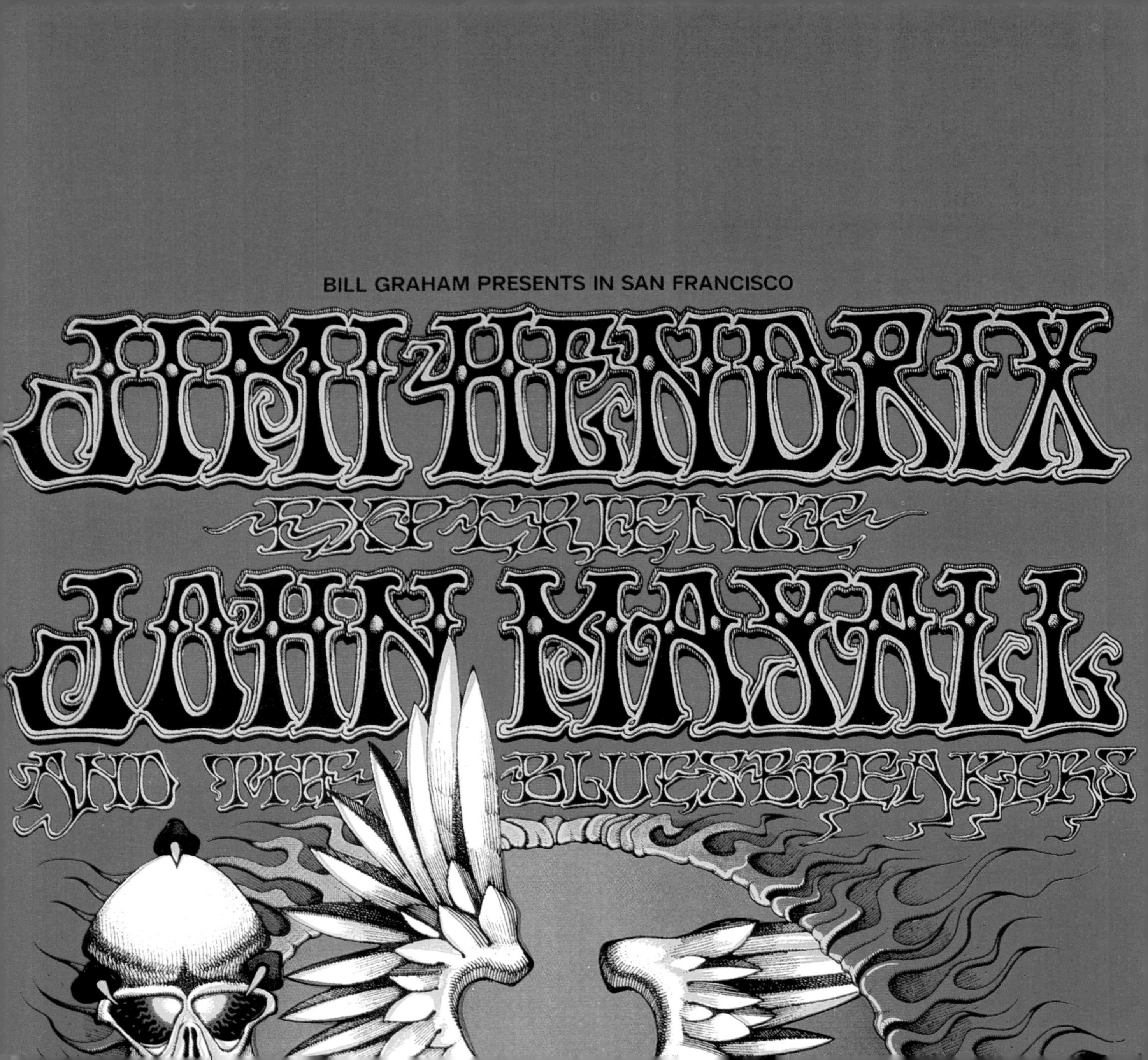

BILL GRAHAM PRESENTS IN SAN FRANCISCO
JIMI HENDRIX
EXPERIENCE
JOHN MAYALL
AND THE BLUESBREAKERS

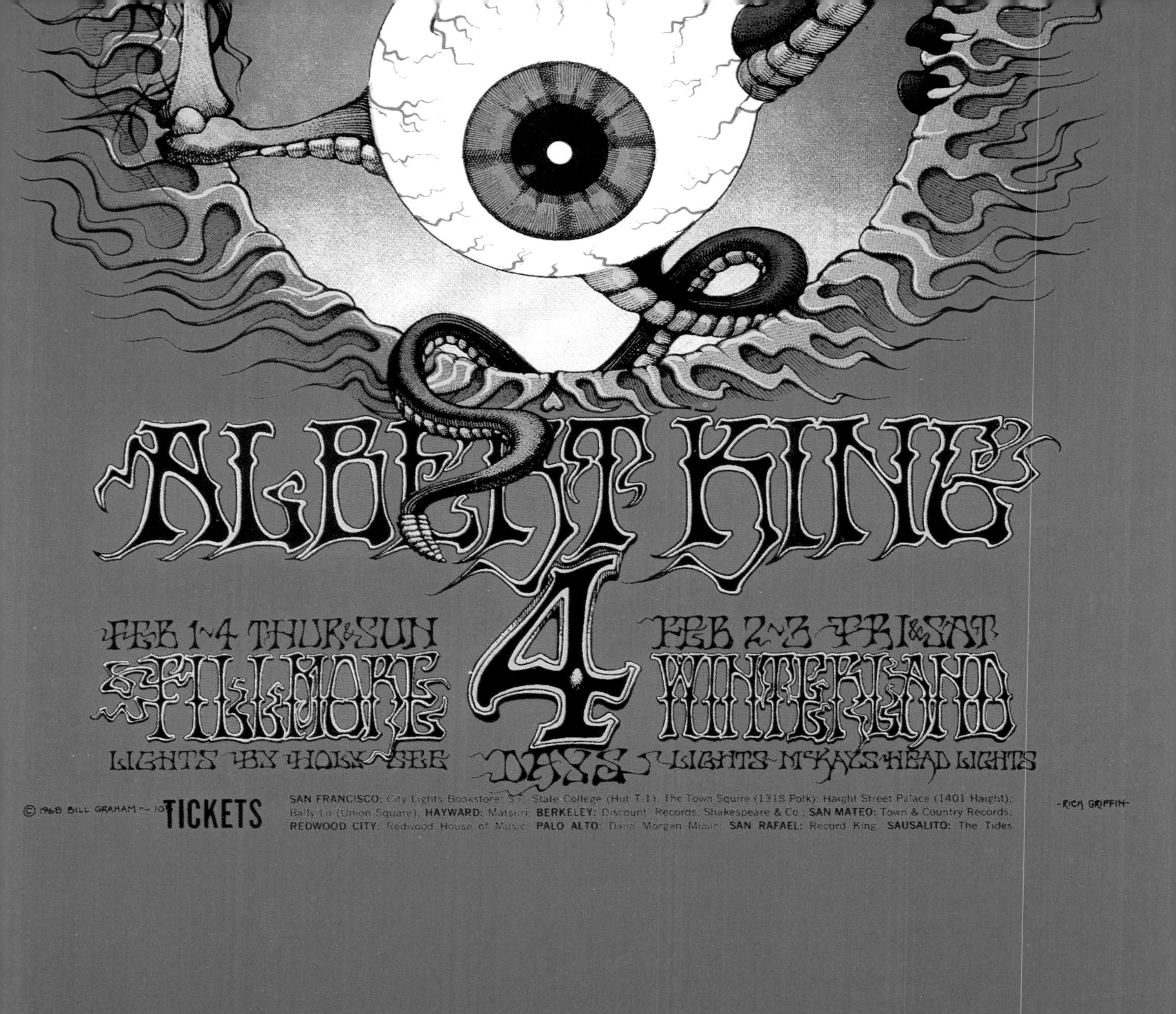

ALBERT KING
4 DAYS
FEB 1-4 THUR & SUN
FILLMORE
LIGHTS BY HOLY SEE
FEB 2-3 FRI & SAT
WINTERLAND
LIGHTS MCKAYS HEAD LIGHTS
© 1968 BILL GRAHAM ~ 10
TICKETS
SAN FRANCISCO: City Lights Bookstore; S.F. State College (Hut T-1); The Town Squire (1318 Polk); Haight Street Palace (1401 Haight); Bally Lo (Union Square); HAYWARD: Matsuri; BERKELEY: Discount Records; Shakespeare & Co.; SAN MATEO: Town & Country Records; REDWOOD CITY: Redwood House of Music; PALO ALTO: Dana Morgan Music; SAN RAFAEL: Record King; SAUSALITO: The Tides
-RICK GRIFFIN-

ABOVE: A 1974 illustration for Rolling Stone magazine by Rick Griffin, who also designed the magazine's title logo.

RIGHT: Another legendary Moscoso poster for Big Brother.

PREVIOUS PAGE: Rick Griffin's Eyeball (Bill Graham number 105) is quite possibly the most widely known visual from the '60s rock 'n' roll era. The image has achieved iconographic status worldwide having been found painted on tribal buffalo skulls in the jungles of Thailand, printed on T-shirts in the Chilean desert and tattooed on Japanese punks in Osaka. Shame he never trademarked it.

FACING PAGE: The full front and back cover image for Victor Moscoso's Color Comics [Print Mint, 1971].

photomontage, was already designing two or three posters a week. He'd also set up his own company, Neon Rose, and was taking advantage of his position in this hip new market, selling copies for a dollar each, rock posters which became enshrined on bedroom walls. Not impressed with the Crumb proposal, he said to Griffin, "Why should I do something that's going to be thrown away?"

"I became an international celebrity, or rather, I became internationally recognized," Moscoso said after his Neon imprint started shipping posters across the world. "That was far out. I never thought it would happen after my first poster came out."

Moscoso and Griffin, after teaming up for 1967's **Joint Show** with the rest of the Big Five, got together and created a series of posters

for Pinnacle Productions, promoting Janis Joplin and Big Brother, B.B. King and Pacific Gas & Electric. "We had different approaches to the posters and at the bottom were three comic panels which Rick drew," said Moscoso referring to the inspiration for a comic. "Rick had done a poster parody on **The San Francisco Chronicle**'s comic section. After seeing this poster, which was like Disney on LSD, it turned me in the direction of cartoons, as opposed to photos."

So Moscoso was won over, suddenly realizing that the newsprint approach was a cheaper, more accessible way of getting his work to a larger audience.

Two contemporaries of the comix scene, Jaxon and Greg Irons, were also involved in the San Francisco poster scene, but remained better known for their comix work.

Go west, young Greg

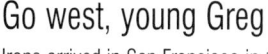

Irons arrived in San Francisco in 1967 after an LSD and speed-induced failure at a draft physical, and like the others, was looking for work. With a sketchbook collection of acid-enhanced impressions described as "bizarre conglomerates of urban decay," he initially drew a poster for the Western Front dancehall.

Irons then met Graham from the Fillmore Auditorium which resulted in an overnight, amphetamine-induced poster, and eight further commissions. He eventually produced posters promoting some of the era's most prominent groups; The Paul Butterfield Blues Band; Crosby, Stills, Nash & Young; Santana and a poster advertising a Chuck Berry concert which is considered a classic of the genre. Irons nouveau psychedelic style was also found on album sleeves for Jerry Garcia's band Old and In the Way,

"America's Heaviest Rock Band" Blue Cheer and the renamed Jefferson Starship.

Then in 1968, having the credentials, Irons headed to London to work on The Beatles' hippie trippie animated *Yellow Submarine*. He returned to San Francisco the following year and resumed drawing rock posters. But joining the exodus from the by-then floundering poster scene, Irons switched to cartoons and was soon published in **Tragi-Comix** in 1969.

Jaxon, another artist who can arguably lay claim to self-publishing the first underground comix in 1964's **God Nose (Snot Reel)**, arrived in '66 and became art director with the Family Dog for the next two years. His business acumen helped Chet Helmes subsidize the Avalon Ballroom concert operation, but combined with commitments to producing posters and handbills for The Vulcan Gas Company, Texas' original counter culture dance hall, the heavy workload began to take its toll.

"I was burnt out," recounts Jaxon. "I took some time off, went to Hawaii and smoked a lot of good dope out there—Maui Wowie—and started to carry a sketchbook again, which I hadn't done for years.

"I definitely got back into drawing there and it wasn't long afterwards that, lo and behold, here's R. Crumb down on Haight Street hawking his **Zap Comics**. It came together rapidly after that. We still had the network in place that had been distributing the posters, so when people started getting burned out on the poster trip and put their energy into comix, all the head shops were there. All the distributors and everything. It was a natural."

BILL GRAHAM PRESENTS IN SAN FRANCISCO

CROSBY·STILLS·NASH&YOUNG

BLUES IMAGE
&JOHN SEBASTIAN

THURS OCT·2   FRI·SAT OCT·3·4
at FILLMORE   WINTERLAND
WEST
MARKET & VAN NESS   POST & STEINER

·LITTLE PRINCESS 109·BROTHERHOOD·LIGHT·

TICKETS

ABOVE: A grinning Greg Irons checks out the underground comix competition.

LEFT: Crosby, Stills, Nash & Young's Fillmore West/Winterland gig poster from Irons in 1969.

FACING PAGE: Chuck Berry is immortalized for his 1969 Fillmore West appearance by Greg Irons.

119

Even over in Milwaukee Denis Kitchen was frequently drawing posters and flyers for The Velvet Whip, Furry Quim Slash and The Baroque. Music and comix had seriously begun to cross over. Artists were regularly commissioned for album sleeves, from Griffin, Corben, Shelton on Grateful Dead covers and Kitchen's Jim Spencer sleeve for his *Major Arcana* album, through to more recent work by Trina Robbins for Mary Buffet and Paul Mavrides' sleeve art for Butthole Surfers' *ElectricLarryland*. The comix crowd was suddenly being acknowledged by a wider audience, even in its own underground with William Stout's cover art to over 40 bootleg albums and more legitimately for the Firesign Theatre, an influential San Francisco-based comedy group.

But Crumb's album cover for Big Brother and the Holding Company's 1968 *Cheap Thrills* became the best known of the generation. Originally titled *Sex, Dope and Cheap Thrills*, CBS Records had been nervous about the sex and dope, but since cheap thrills didn't threaten them, it became the album's title.

The front cover was a result of Crumb meeting Dave Richards, the band's roadie, and asking to meet Big Brother's vocalist Janis Joplin (she later retorted "The 'Keep on Fuckin' guy!? I'd love to know him"). Big Brother's drummer Dave Getz then got hooked on Crumb's art and said to the roadie, "How about getting him to do an album cover for us?" Richards promised to mention it.

ABOVE LEFT: The multi-million selling Meatloaf album, Bat Out Of Hell, put Fantagor artist Richard Corben firmly in the public eye in 1977.

BELOW LEFT: The infamous back-turned-front cover for the album that made Janis Joplin into a star, Cheap Thrills.

FACING PAGE: William Stout's homage to Crumb's Big Brother cover for a bootleg Rolling Stones album.

When eventually offered the *Cheap Thrills* sleeve, Crumb agreed but with a condition; "Yeah, I'll do your album cover, the only thing is when I meet Janis I want to be able to pinch her tit." Richards forgot to check but Crumb—on a promise—drew the sleeve anyway.

According to guitarist Sam Andrew, "The woman on the *Cheap Thrills* jacket is Crumb's idealization of Janis as the ultimate hippie chick with proud, ripe buttocks and jutting nipples. He also caricatured the rest of the band, studying us as we played a gig. His impressions were originally for the back of the album. A high school yearbook layout was to be the front, but the flavour of it wasn't right. The back cover was superb though, so we just put it on the front and it worked."

Bap attack

After the album came out, the band ran into Crumb at a party. When Crumb was introduced to Janis, he just leaped in. "He grabbed her tit!" said Richards. "She just looked at him and said, 'Oh honey!' and Crumb was delighted." The following year, at the opening of the New Comix Show in Berkeley, Janis and Crumb posed for photographers, kissing each other passionately.

Crumb has since produced a mass of album sleeves, principally for jazz and blues artists, although he provided covers for the Grateful Dead. Indulging his passions for art and music, he also produces sleeve art to his own banjo recordings with the Keep on Truckin' Orchestra, the Cheap Suit Serenaders and Les Primitifs Du Futur.

The title of most infamous rock image from an underground artist has to be awarded to **Zap**'s Robert Williams. Cartoonist turned fine artist,

Williams was caught in an international controversy when he agreed to let a group of aspiring musicians use his painting, entitled *Appetite for Destruction*, for their 1987 major label debut. "I don't even want to fucking talk about Guns n' Roses, man. Let's just say I grabbed the soap on that deal," says Williams.

"Some people in San Francisco told me there's this band that wants to use my painting, I said I'm not interested and anyway I think they're making a really bad judgement call wanting to use that piece. They hounded me month after month and finally came down here and I get confronted by this guy Axl Rose. I thought he was just another gay transvestite. He comes in and I say 'OK, look through my slides and pick out something,' ya know. They wanted this particular picture and I said, 'Well, ya know that's gonna get you in a whole lot of trouble.' He replied, 'Well we want it,' and my reply was 'If you've got the guts to use that on an album cover that's bitchin'. So they did! Then overnight they're the top band in the country and I charged 'em what I'd charge any shitty little punk rock band. I didn't even know they were on a label at the time!"

"What's wrong with being sexy?"

But Williams' woes were just beginning, "Then it hit me. Feminism. These feminists, oh Christ! I was on MTV two or three times defending this album cover, which I originally advised them not to use... Six or seven feminist groups are boycotting all the record stores that carry the album, closing 'em down... Then some woman comes to my defence in Berkeley, and all the feminists start finding all the trash on this poor lady and putting it in the newspapers to make her life miserable, and on and on and on..."

"When you consider the climate of Hollywood where we were all living," recounted lead guitarist Slash, "that painting would have been one of the least shocking things going on. We'd seen some pretty hectic shit and we just didn't feel the picture fell into that category. To us it was just a picture that looked cool."

"I could've retired on the T-shirt sales alone!"

The sentiment was reiterated by vocalist Rose. "Robert Williams is a great artist and I just happened to particularly like that cover. I submitted the *Appetite* cover as a joke, 'cause I didn't think anyone would use it... I just really liked it and tossed it in. I couldn't believe they really wanted to use it."

But the whole affair left Williams with a bitter taste, "So the gist of this story is that Axl and Slash came to me again for a second cover for *Appetite*... and I turned 'em down. I felt like I'd been sodomized. They paid this little pissy ass amount of money 'cause I thought they were nobody and they then sold 14 million goddamn records! And I'm not even talking about the T-shirt sales... I could've retired on the T-shirt sales alone! So, ya see, there was one idiot in the whole program and that was me. Everyone says sue their ass off, but I'm a responsible individual and if I made the mistake I just have to bear it," a poorer but wiser Williams admitted.

RIGHT: Boycotted in the States and banned in Europe, the original Guns n' Roses album cover artwork to Appetite for Destruction [1987]. The art has become Robert Williams' most famous piece.

FACING PAGE: The photograph that shows the glee upon both Joplin's and Crumb's faces as they meet at a party at the New Comix Show in Berkeley in 1968. They then made out for the cameras.

Chapter 5

Publish and be Damned

Getting the work out there

"Bob and Peggy Rita hated comix, but loved the money. They tolerated the comix because of the money" ...VICTOR MOSCOSO ON THE PRINT MINT PUBLISHERS

The Politix of Comix

As comix grew out of the 1960s political and cultural malaise they reflected the issues of those times, casting a jaundiced yet humorous eye on society and the hypocrisy in its youth culture.

POLITICAL subjects were popular targets for the underground. Titles like **Radical America Komics** (1969) which featured work by Gilbert Shelton and **Corporate Crime Comics** [1977] with Irons, Deitch and Robbins art savagely attacked Corporate America at a time long before ethical business practices were introduced. Stories on the Karen Silkwood murder and the nuclear industry whistleblower filled these indignant comix while the Vietnam War and protests against the draft were the targets of Foolbert Sturgeon's **Jesus Meets the Armed Services** [1970]. Other movements covered included anarchism, the civil rights struggle, Women's Lib and Gay Liberation.

like Manuel "Spain" Rodriguez. His stories ranged from historical, about Stalin and World War I, to autobiographical tales, of biker clubs and Chicago's 1968 riots.

Spain created the character he would be most famous for, Trashman, in 1968 in New York's **East Village Other**. His protagonist was a blue-collar champion of the radical left, defending impoverished masses against the tyranny of fascist military forces of the rich and powerful, embodying Spain's own views, once summed up as "Marxism of a sufficient libertarian bent to enable him to contribute to **Anarchy Comics**".

Published by Last Gasp, **Anarchy Comics** [1978] ran strips by Paul Mavrides, Melinda

Almost every cause created its own comicbook from marijuana legalization and Black Power to anti-abortion and anti-war. Add to this an interest in the spiritual value of taking drugs and of "free love" and, simplistically speaking, a thriving comix movement against traditional values evolved.

But this counter culture didn't create itself out of thin air. It took people with a unique vision and the drive to change things, people

Gebbie and others "inspired by or based on anarchist ideas and history in the belief that the true terrorists are governments and corporations who hold us hostage with their armaments, militaries, and intelligence activities".

With the feminist movement's rise, women cartoonists began self-publishing and providing what the comix industry was lacking: a strong, female perspective. **It Ain't Me, Babe** [1970]

championed women's liberation as the first all-women title.

The range of feminist comics grew and, by 1973, women's comics were pervasive and proud with titles like **Tits and Clits, Pandora's Box, Wimmen's Comix, Abortion Eve** and **Come Out Comix** being sexually outspoken; featuring menstruation, vibrators, abortions, lesbianism and sexual politics.

For its part, the book world took advantage of the outspoken comix artists, employing them to illustrate a range of paperbacks for Writers & Readers and UK publisher Icon/Totem. Ownership disputes aside, two wonderful lines of *For Beginners* and *Introducing* books were created, including R. Crumb's **Kafka for Beginners**, Oscar Zarate's **Freud for Beginners** and legendary Mexican artist Rius's **Introducing Marx**.

Mention must also be made of Bolivar Publishing's 1976 entry into the copyright-fraught melee through the wonderful **Introduction to Chile** by *Ogoth & Ugly Boot*'s Chris Welch.

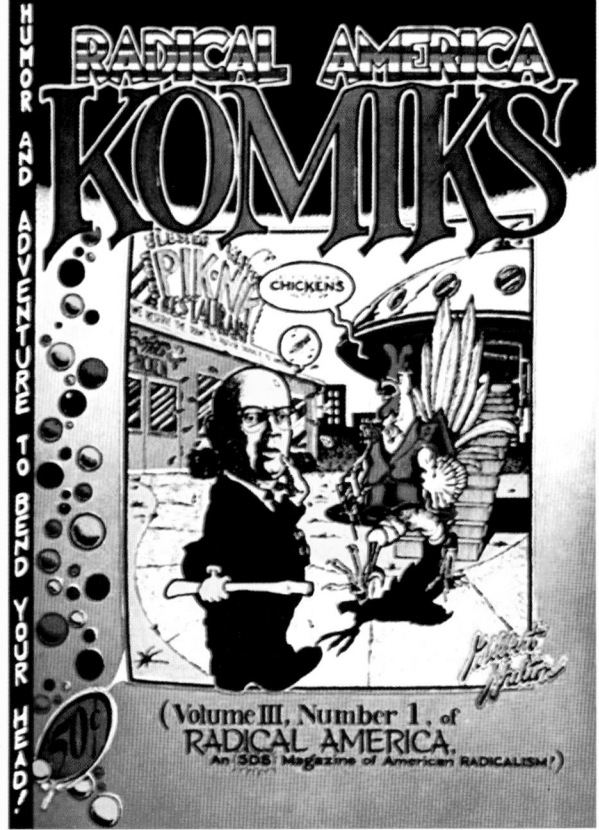

Inspiration is all very well—but once you've got the masterpiece completed, who prints it? Who distributes it? And if you overcome those obstacles, what are the possible consequences?

TO many of the cartoonists of the '60s, the siren song of the Summer of Love called irresistibly to them to produce their own comicbooks. Many had been fans of the more traditional comics—particularly the EC work of Harvey Kurtzman—and remained in love with the format. But they found the content, at the time subject to rigid scrutiny by the unremitting Comics Code Authority, to be tepid and unpalatable.

Most of them had found some success and recognition with comic strips in the sudden flurry of underground newspapers, such as **Yarrowstalks** and **The East Village Other,** which featured a high proportion of comics among their trippy visuals. The artists wanted to produce comicbooks that were contemporary, reflecting their own lives and times, but still as inspiring as their own childhood favourites had been to them.

Creativity was the keynote; business sense fell a very long way behind. Artists were thrilled by the comix format, because of its flexibility, accessibility and the comparatively inexpensive production costs. All they needed was luck, good timing and somebody like printer Charlie Plymell to get his head together. "We were having nude parties and we had complimentary tickets to the Janis Joplin and Big Brother concert, but we were too stoned to get there," Plymell admits. "We had pre-war equipment that wasn't really capable of a printing job like **Zap Comix**. I would have to make the Multilith dance and sing. But it was the lack of

> ## "...Mutants of the Metropolis, a book so unique that no one bought it, assuring our demise."
> ### ...Michael Moore, publisher

technology which caused most of the waste in run of what was supposed to be 5,000 copies...my guess is around 1,500 copies."

But however many they would finally get, the sheer bulk of them presented the artists/publishers with a problem they hadn't previously considered; how were they going to get their brainchildren into the hands of the (hopefully) eagerly waiting public?

There was no way of assessing demand before publication; the early artists and collectives just had to guess at print runs and hope for the best. If a title was a success, and sold out, it could always be reprinted, but a misjudgment would leave unsold copies on their hands.

Michael Moore, founder of the Los Angeles Comic Book Company comments, "Our first book was **LA Comics** #1 and consisted primarily of Los Angeles artists. We later went on to publish **Mickey Rat**, **Weird Fantasies** (arguably the first color underground comix; priced at 50 cents it was the first nail in our financial coffin), **LA Comics** #2 and lastly **Mutants of the Metropolis**, a book so unique that no one bought it, assuring our demise. Bill [Spicer] still has a garage full of them to this day."

A large part of the guesswork, or at least the consequences of guessing badly, was removed from the shoulders of several artists when they struck a bargain with Don Schenker, owner of The Print Mint in Berkeley, California. He offered Victor Moscoso, Rick Griffin

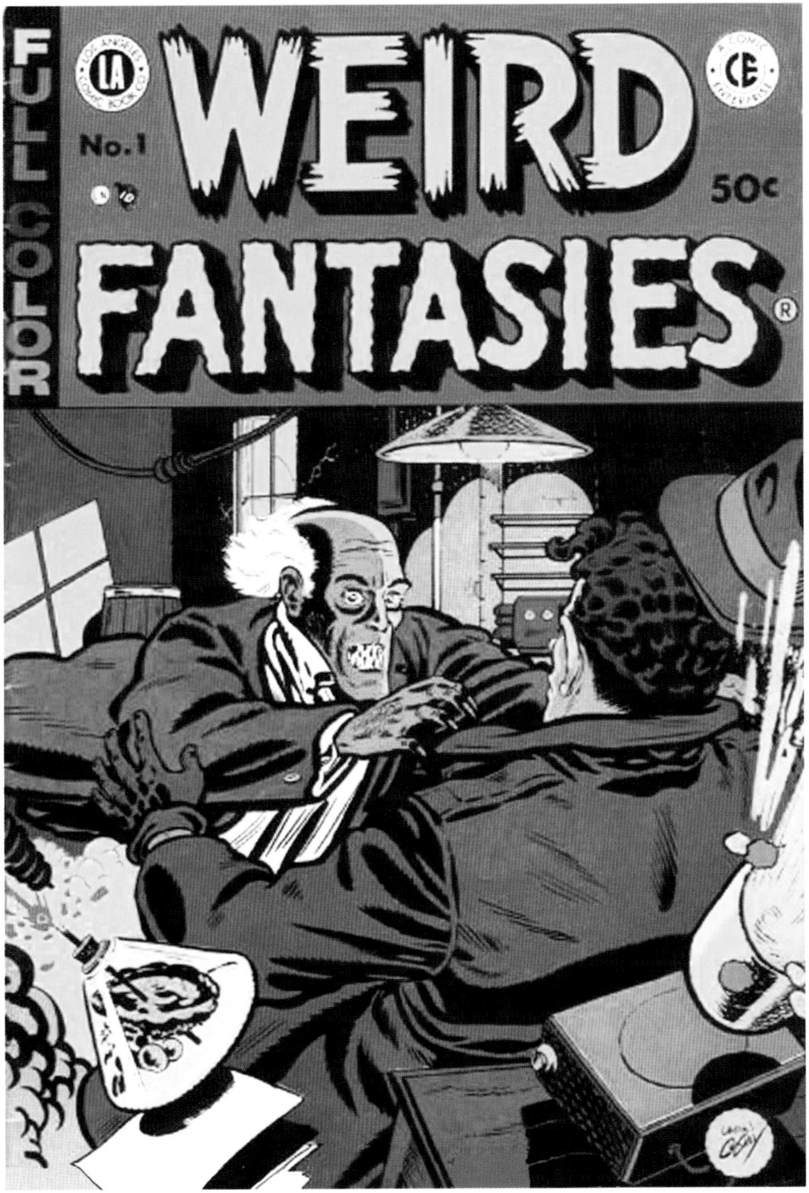

ABOVE: The final nail in Moore's coffin, Mutants of the Metropolis [1972].

LEFT: Another EC homage, in the shape of the full colour Weird Fantasies #1 [1972]. A false start for colour comix, publisher Michael Moore called it, "The first nail in our financial coffin."

Although its sales peaked in the early seventies, Zap Comics kept going at the rate of about one new issue every three years up until the present. The long wait for new issues sometimes gives cause to great publishing celebrations, such as the three-day exhibition-opening party and media frenzy at Jacaeber Kastor's PSYCHEDELIC SOLUTION Gallery on St. Mark's Place in New York City in the summer of 1990, where a crowd of thousands of curious art lovers lined up outside trying to squeeze in, forming a queue that stretched around the block. In summer 1994, the appearance of Zap N° 13 was the excuse for a big opening party at Billy Shire's LA LUZ DE JESUS Gallery on Melrose Avenue in Los Angeles; Robert and Suzanne Williams arrived in their chopped '32 Ford three-window coupe powered by a 350 Chevy engine with a nine-inch Ford rear end.

Poet Allen Ginsberg was able to force his way into the packed Psychedelic Solution Gallery to meet the Zapsters in New York because it was "his neighborhood." LEFT TO RIGHT: Victor Moscoso, Robert Crumb, Allen Ginsberg, Gilbert Shelton, Robert Williams.

PHOTO © 1991 BOB GRUEN

And now, it seems, Zap Comics has come to a crossroads in its life, set off by an internal disagreement in the editorial hierarchy.* Crumb wants to let the series die; Moscoso has been going to great lengths to keep the thing going. The other artists are divided between these two points of view. I myself have mixed feelings on the subject, I used to enjoy drawing little cartoon characters with big noses performing outrageous deeds, but since I no longer have any funny ideas I have gone into semi-retirement and now spend most of my time on my country estate with my wife Lora, tending the garden.
   Tomorrow I am taking our neighbor the Count on a SNIPE HUNT.

* see various interpretations of said event in this issue.

by GILBERT SHELTON
AMATEUR CARTOONIST & DILETTANTE BON VIVEUR
"I WAS THERE, SO I PROBABLY DON'T REMEMBER IT."

RIGHT: Allen Ginsberg joins in the Zap 13 finally on sale party, squeezed between Moscoso and Crumb, plus Shelton and Williams [top]. While Crumb and Moscoso argued over continuing Zap, Shelton split to France [below].

FACING PAGE: Turn on, tune in and drop in for a stash of comix. As The Print Mint soon discovered, owning a store means never having to buy wallpaper.

and other underground artists a deal where he paid for the printing and the film. Copyright remained with the artists, and after all expenses were paid, profit was split between Schenker and the artists. Through his contacts in the poster shops and the head shops, Schenker got the comics distributed, removing a large part of the risk from underground publishing.

After Schenker sold the Print Mint to Bob and Peggy Rita also in Berkeley, the Ritas continued with the comics publishing, though some artists maintained that they were less sympathetic to comix than Schenker had been. As Victor Moscoso recollects, "Don Schenker owned the Print Mint prior to Bob and Peggy. He sold it to them, which I'm sorry about, because they didn't appreciate comics in the same way that Don did. In fact Bob and Peggy Rita hated comix, but loved the money. They tolerated the comics because of the money. I wish Don Schenker had stayed on."

If the Ritas had, according to Moscoso, no appreciation of comix, they were nevertheless shrewd businesspeople and parlayed The Print Mint's initial involvement with underground publishing into a

THIS PAGE: Crumb wondered why Charlie Plymell split after Zap #1. This might be his reason. "A lack of technology caused most of the waste of what was supposed to be 5,000 copies. My guess is around 1,500 copies... my wife says less. But most everyone was on acid or pot and was so excited to see the finished copy, and since there was little money and barter involved, I don't know who counted."

thriving concern, their involvement lasting to the mid-'80s. Bob Beerbohm after Bob Rita's death in 1995, commented, "The Print Mint was the first company to sell directly to stores on a national basis… The Print Mint's initial print runs for all their books ran from 20,000 to 100,000 an issue, numbers that many of today's publishers would be highly envious to attain. Between 1968 and 1978, they sold over 5,000,000 comicbooks, all creator-owned with royalties to every one who created them. If a book sold well, they reprinted it again and again and continued to pay royalties on each succeeding edition."

The Print Mint also appears to have established the pattern for underground comix distribution in the USA, placing them in the poster shops and head shops throughout California. Browsing customers, drawn in by the psychedelic posters that were in vogue at the time, remembered comicbooks from their childhood and were intrigued by the new freedom of expression offered in this reincarnation of the traditional medium. At 50 cents or less, the comix were an affordable impulse buy and their popularity grew.

Where California led, the rest of the world followed. Michael Moore of the Los Angeles Comic Book Company: "Distribution was (and still is) the crucial factor in publishing. In those days comix were sold in what were known as headshops. For instance, the Free Press Bookstores in Los Angeles were really headshops selling drug paraphernalia surrounded by the protective cover of book selling. Instead of outright sales to distributors in other cities, the LA Comic Book Company would swap equal values of comix (i.e. 500 copies of **Mickey Rat** for 500 copies of **Zap** Comics) and then I would go out and sell these traded comix to the various headshops between Santa Barbara and San Diego."

Unreliable and labour-intensive, the distribution network nevertheless gradually developed, and once the underground scene began to have a few recognizable 'stars' (Robert Crumb, the Fabulous Furry Freak Brothers, Vaughn Bode), avenues opened for

RIGHT: The man who got things moving, Print Mint's Bob Schenker. Through his contacts in the poster shops and head shops, he got the comics distributed without needing a baby carriage.

BELOW: An early comix outlet, the head shop Potpourri. Rock poster artist Bob Masse produced its exterior mural in 1969.

more experimental fare. Nevertheless, most of the comicbook companies were perilously underfinanced, counting on the profits from a previous title or project to finance the next. One misjudgement could bring the entire operation down. But out of the initial experimentation, several figures emerged as pioneering publishers, removing the burdens from the artist, but facing unexpected hazards themselves along the way.

Ripping off the competition

One of the successes of the early underground, and a company which still operates today, is Rip Off Press. It began in January 1969, when four hippies from Texas—Gilbert Shelton, Jack Jackson, Dave Moriarty and Fred Todd—uprooted themselves to San Francisco, bought a printing press and set off on a plan to change the world.

Shelton's *Wonder Wart-Hog* had already scored a minor hit in the University of Texas' humour magazine and later sales to **Drag Cartoons**, and his *Fabulous Furry Freak Brothers* had premiered in **Feds 'n' Heads Comix** the previous year. Jackson had self-published

God Nose in 1964 and was keen to get his work back into print. Todd had been working as a computer technician and was thought to provide the business expertise that the others lacked. And Moriarty, according to the Rip Off website, is credited with "the megalomania needed to convince the group that four guys who knew nothing about printing should buy the press and set up shop."

Whether it was megalomania, synergy or dumb luck, they set up their press in a huge space on an upper floor of Mowry's Opera House, a building in which another printer, Don Donahue, was already producing comix for Print Mint and Apex Novelties. From their stated intention to rip off a larger share of the profits for cartoonists—the new company was dubbed "Rip Off Press."

Mowry's was severely damaged in a fire a few months after the company started, and the Rip Off crew eventually relocated, after a series of dilapidated short-lets, to the corner of 17th and Missouri, where they remained for the next 15 years. After the commercial printing business wound down in 1972, Jackson and Moriaty returned to Texas, leaving Shelton and Todd to run the business.

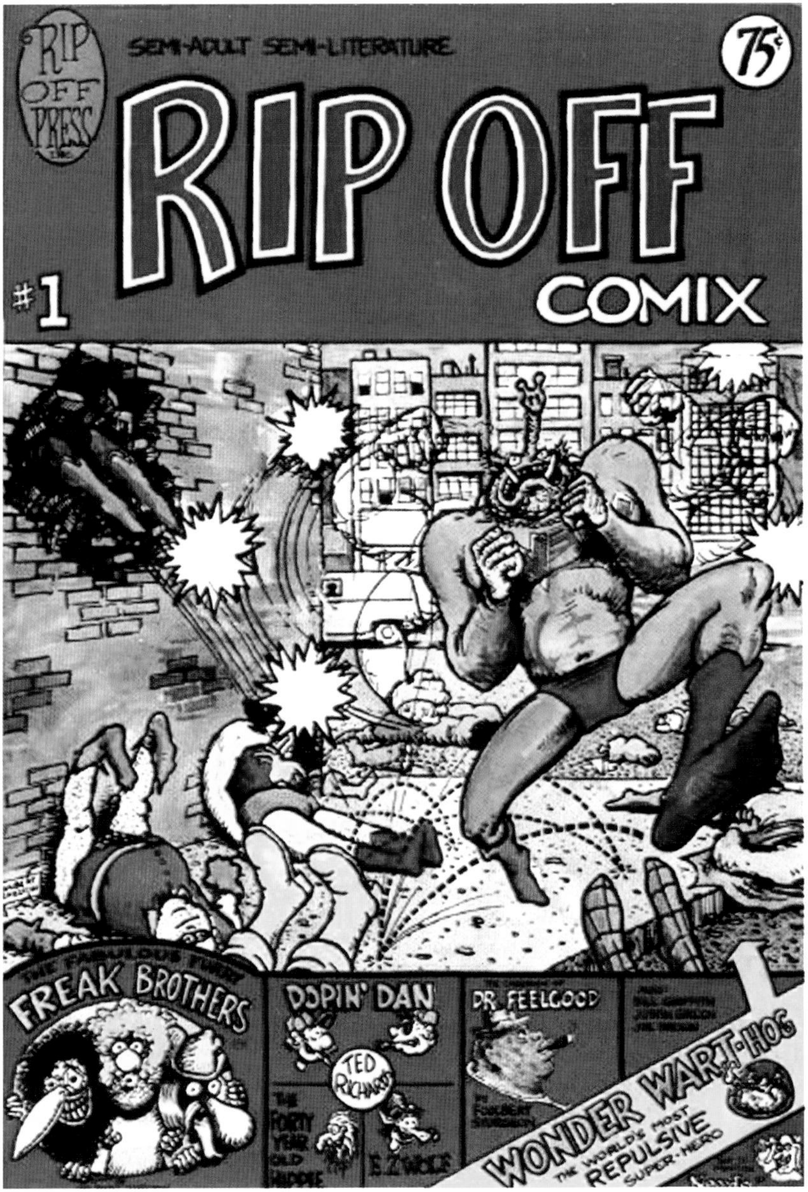

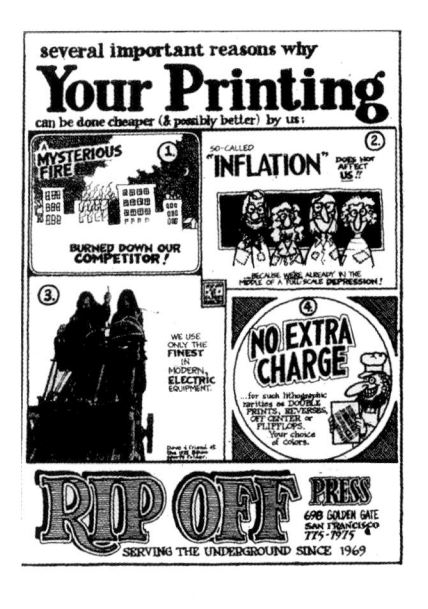

ABOVE: House advertisement for Rip Off Press' printing services.

THIS PAGE: Rip Off's first star studded anthology, featuring Wonder Wart-Hog, Dopin' Dan, The Forty Year Old Hippie, E Z Wolf, Dr Feelgood and the Fabulous Furry Freak Brothers. Damn good for 75c.

FACING PAGE: A young Gilbert Shelton [1973] alongside an equally young Jaxon; and Fred Todd admiring a lifesize Wonder Wart-Hog.

Cornerstone of the business was Shelton's **Fabulous Furry Freak Brothers**, first collected in 1971 after appearing for a few years in the **LA Free Press**. The Freak Brothers struck a chord with the readers, and have continued to sell ad infinitum, remaining in print for more than 30 years, endlessly re-collected and re-presented to the demanding public—although some uncivil critics maintain that the

Freak's core readership simply don't notice that they're buying the same thing over and over again!

Other firsts for Rip Off were the debut of Larry Gonick's critically and academically-acclaimed **Cartoon History of the Universe** series, which later sold many thousands of copies in mass-market paperbacks, and inspired several other pseudo-educational series in the same vein, and the first solo comicbook of Bill Griffith's **Zippy the Pinhead**, since 1986 the star of an internationally-syndicated newspaper strip.

The company's latter half of the Seventies was taken up by the offer of a quarter-million-dollar movie deal for the Freak Brothers, to be made by Universal. The film was never made, but the stresses of endless negotiations, compromises, and meeting with media representatives caused Shelton to move to Europe, embittered and disillusioned by the entire process.

Shortly thereafter, a crisis point for the company was caused by the election of Republican President Ronald Reagan who, in his "Say No To Drugs" phase, abruptly set about dismantling the network of head shops that distributed undergrounds.

In 1985, the last of the original Rip Off partners, Fred Todd, moved to smaller quarters and started working the firm in tandem with his wife Kathe, but a year later the warehouse housing most of the company's inventory was burnt out. The Todds relocated to Auburn, north-east of Sacramento, and have hung on there since, grimly riding out the vicissitudes of the industry. Throughout it all, Rip Off Press has adhered to its earliest policy of ensuring that comix

LEFT: In publishing terms, probably the entire comix industry's most successful character, Zippy the Pinhead.

FACING PAGE: Gilbert Shelton's peek inside the Rip Off Press offices.

QUALITY PUBLISHING SINCE 1969

creators retained ownership of their creations, a practice still not necessarily the rule in publishing, even among alternative publishers.

Kitchen Sink, and finally sank

Starting his professional career in 1968 as a self-published underground cartoonist in his native Milwaukee, Denis Kitchen rapidly discovered that his business and organizational gifts outstripped his not inconsiderable artistic skill. Starting with one title, 1969's **Mom's Homemade Comix**, he formed a "hippie empire" comprised of a record label, a head shop, a commercial art studio, plus mail order, distribution and his publishing imprint, Kitchen Sink Press.

He also co-founded two alternative weekly newspapers, but for 30 years his primary focus was on publishing comicbooks and cartoon collections.

Among the classic underground anthologies he produced were **Snarf**, **Dope Comix**, **Bizarre Sex**, **Gay Comix** and **Twisted Sisters**, but by the late 1970s and 1980s, Kitchen's interests had become more mainstream and assimilationist than the other founders of underground comix. Kitchen Sink acquired a reputation for prestige, high-quality hardcover and paperback collections and repackagings of comics creators' work, both mainstream (**The Spirit, Li'l Abner, Batman** and **Superman**) and alternative (Crumb, Waller & Worley, Charles Burns, Moore & Campbell).

Throughout he remained committed to freedom of speech and opposed to censorship. So much so that in 1986 Kitchen founded the Comic Book Legal Defense Fund as a non-profit corporation dedicated to defending the industry's First Amendment rights. The need for this arose in the wake of a number of prosecutions of comics retailers for selling adult-themed material. Such busts were often made by lazy law enforcement officials as 'easy arrests,' since most comics retailers are too poor to mount an elaborate defense and the majority of judges and juries still adhere, through ignorance, to the old cliché belief that comics are for children. Kitchen continues to serve as President of the CBLDF today.

Despite Kitchen Sink's high profile and the respect and stature it won in the comics community, an apparently infelicitous choice of investor resulted in Kitchen being dismissed from his own company in December 1998. The investor group that had purchased a majority interest refused to invest new capital, in view of the then decline in comics-related publishing. In 1994—when they came on board—comics industry sales were around a billion dollars, but by 1998 this figure had declined to $400 million, with comics stores in the USA having diminished from 6,500 in the early '90s to under 4,000. This was worsened by fewer of the remaining outlets being willing to risk their purchasing power on anything other than mainstream comics and merchandise.

RIGHT: Kitchen's Bijou Funnies hosted ten top name strips each in its 8-issue run [1972-73], with its final edition in colour, attacking the new law allowing local communities to ban material considered obscene.

FACING PAGE: King of his Milwaukee-based hippie empire, Denis Kitchen.

RIGHT AND ABOVE: Despite the best possible lineup of artists, Last Gasp's Slow Death Funnies stopped being so funny after the first issue took so long to sell, and continued for another 10 issues simply as Slow Death.

FACING PAGE: Last Gasp's Ron Turner, still Gasping after 30 years.

An announcement in April 1999 by the company's chief financial officer stated that Kitchen Sink Press had been "exhausted of assets, and is no longer able to make good on debts to creators and vendors."

After the dissolution of Kitchen Sink, Kitchen became a partner with Judith Hansen in Kitchen & Hansen Agency Inc, acting as representatives for comics artists and writers. The Denis Kitchen Art Agency continues to sell original art for clients such as Will Eisner and the Harvey Kurtzman estate and publishes a small number of books under the new imprint of Denis Kitchen Publishing Co. He has even considered going back to his roots. At the time of his dismissal from Kitchen Sink, he observed, "I've been a publisher for 28 years, but I've been a reluctant businessman. I would like to go back to being an artist."

Big lungs

Ron Turner's Last Gasp, still trading today, began at a year-end party in the Berkeley Hills almost 30 years ago, when someone handed the very stoned graduate psychology student a copy of **Zap Comix**, and inadvertently rekindled his forgotten love of comicbooks.

"I remember reading it and remarking how close it came to the heightened mind-experience one got when stoned. It brought back all my love of comics, but in an adult form that I could appreciate. I went into the back room and started reading the damn thing over and over."

Shortly afterwards, Turner moved to Berkeley and became involved with some people who had started the first ecology centre in the USA. Hoping to raise funds for the centre, as well as to increase ecological awareness, he borrowed $2,500 from a friend and published the first issue of **Slow Death Funnies** as a benefit book, including Robert Crumb, Gilbert Shelton and Greg Irons as contributors.

"I can't remember now who came up with the name Last Gasp. It was either me or Gary Arlington [of the San Francisco Comic Book Co]. We originally needed a name for the Ecology Centre comicbook —one of us suggested **Slow Death Funnies** and the other suggested **Last Gasp Comix & Stories**. When I needed a name for the company I just used the runner-up name, so I'm always indebted to Gary for his insight into naming comicbooks."

Slow Death by name...

Slow Death Funnies #1 came out on the first Earth Day, April 15 1970, and was received enthusiastically at campuses all over the Bay Area.

Unfortunately, when Turner arrived at the Ecology Centre with the 20,000 copies that they had agreed to take, they were less than enthusiastic. In the few months it had taken to put the benefit book together, the old staff had been replaced. "They looked at me and said, 'What's this for?' When I explained to them they said, 'Well, we'll take ten copies.' I said, 'Well, that's nice but I've got 20,000!'"

Armed with this mass of the seemingly appropriately named **Slow Death** #1, he began travelling back and forth across the country selling and giving away comix, running the business out of his garage. However, Last Gasp soon began distributing titles published by other companies simply because Turner was receiving them in payment for his own publications. This barter system was to form the nucleus of the distribution business that Last Gasp still operates to this day.

Among the pioneering steps taken by Last Gasp was to publish the first feminist comicbook, in partnership with Trina Robbins, **It Ain't Me Babe**. Its success inspired Robbins to co-found the Wimmen's Comix collective, which published 14 issues of its eponymous anthology plus **Skull Comix**, which brought the virtually unknown Rich Corben to the public eye.

The Wimmen's Comix collective also published several groundbreaking comix in the autobiographical-confessional genre including the darkly humorous **Binky Brown Meets the Holy Virgin Mary** by Justin Green [1972], a title which has become an

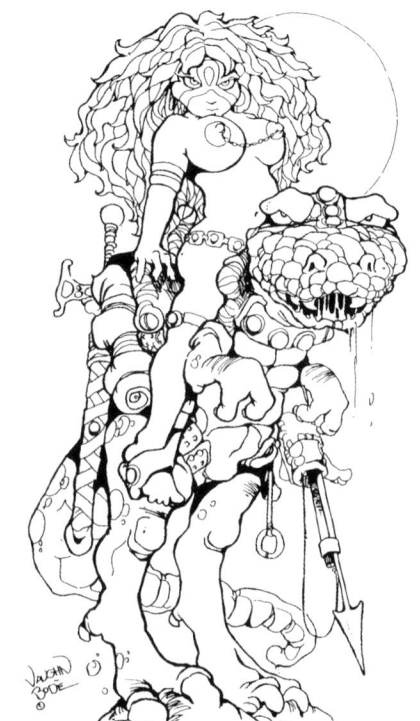

acknowledged inspiration to many artists now producing biography style work, including Art Spiegelman and Robert Crumb.

Police raids

Of course, after the hassle of getting the work printed, then distributed, the reactions of the public frequently have unexpected consequences. One of the earliest incidences of undergrounds falling foul of the law was **Zap** #4, particularly the Robert Crumb-produced strip *Joe Blow*, featuring Dad, Mom, Junior and Sis in a very graphic satire of the—in this case—literally incestuous all-American family. Or as Moscoso had the misfortune to be quoted saying, "You can cut off a guy's penis and devour it, you can even chop people up into little pieces, but you can't have sex with your children."

The police raided the City Lights bookstore in San Francisco, and in New York **Zap** #4 was prohibited from being sold over the counter. Nevertheless, after paying a fine the City Lights' proprietor, poet Lawrence Ferlinghetti, continued to sell that and subsequent issues, without incident. Predictably, the attention caused **Zap**'s reputation and sales to rise.

Zap #3, with its centrefold of Donald and Daisy Duck engaging in oral sex somehow escaped the wrath of the Walt Disney Corporation, but the **Air Pirates** underground comic attracted the full fury of the Mouse's owners, becoming a cause celebre in the underground comics world. *[See feature, page 56.]*

VAUGHN BODÉ'S EROTICA

ABOVE: With an enforced downturn in comix distribution in the early 1970s, few creators were 'big name' enough to have their titles stocked. Along with Crumb and Shelton, Vaughn Bode (pictured) achieved bankable status.

LEFT: Reprinting Bode's Cavalier strips, the Last Gasp 1983 hardcover, published in paperback in 1996 by Fantagraphics Books (volumes 1-3).

FACING PAGE: Bode's girl on dinosaur print [UK, 1976].

Another publication that attracted the attention of the police and the judiciary was feminist comic anthology **Tits & Clits**, launched in 1972. Two women cartoonists, Joyce Farmer and Lyn Chevely, outraged by the violent, bloody and misogynistic scenes in **Zap Comix**, set out to self-publish comix just as outrageous as **Zap**, but from a woman's perspective, and focusing primarily on sex rather than violence. As the title grew it attracted other contributors including Lee Mars and Roberta Gregory.

"Prevailing Community Standards"

Bearing in mind the subject matter, and wanting 'equal exposure' with Robert Crumb's **Big Ass**, they felt an equally outrageous title would

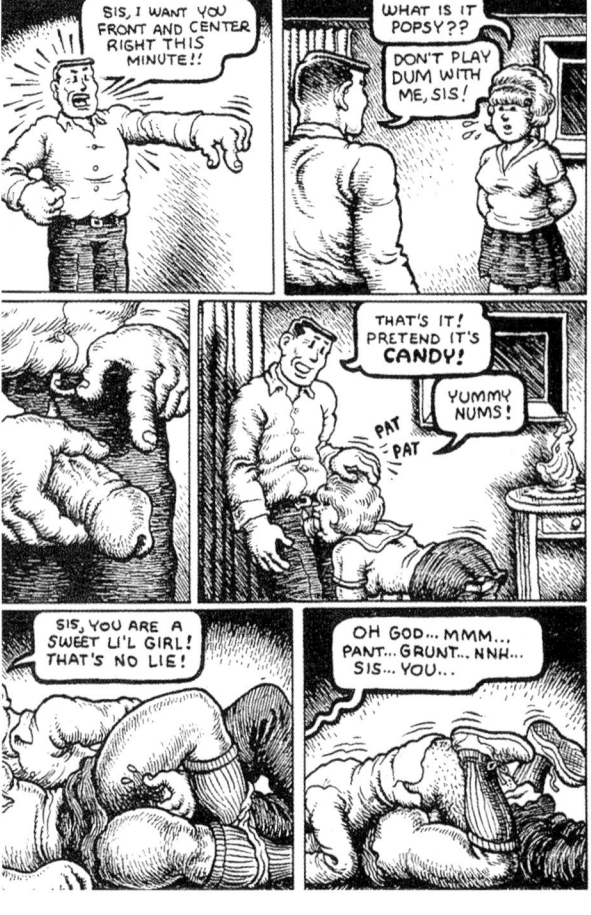

have a strong effect. **Tits & Clits** as a title proved to be both their triumph and their downfall. Although not a 'sexy' comic in the ordinary sense—it dealt realistically with sexual complications including masturbation, birth control and menstruation, but shot through with a mordant sense of self-mockery—the title alone was an attention-grabber, and sold to feminists, curious bystanders, and the furtively horny alike. However, it also attracted the wrong sort of attention.

Following Supreme Court legislation that publications could be ruled obscene if they offended "prevailing community standards," the head shops and underground comix with their subversive statements became easy targets for the police and a title like **Tits & Clits** scored high on their 'to do' list. Following a purchase by an undercover policeman at an Orange County bookstore called, ironically, Fahrenheit 451, the bookstore owners were arrested and Farmer and Chively were sought by the police. They hid their stash of copies, all 40,000, with friends.

Faced with the possibility of a year's imprisonment and fines of $10 per copy, plus loss of their homes, livelihoods and custody of their children, the women spent almost two years fearful of arrest and incarceration. In 1974, the District Attorney's office announced that it would not prosecute the case further, primarily due to intervention by the American Civil Liberties Union. Farmer and Chively rallied and published **Tits & Clits** #2 in 1976, followed eventually by seven other issues. But the news of their case, and of similarly threatened cases, had narrowed the market. Many bookstore owners were unwilling to risk prosecution and arrest for such a low-profit item and by the late '70s, except for a few solid-gold sellers (Crumb, **The Freak Brothers**), the audience for undergrounds could seldom find any.

Not that it now needed any help, but a further nail in the coffin of small print run undergrounds was the massive hike in paper costs.

ABOVE: Poor City Lights, they got busted in the '50s over Ginsberg and Ferlinghetti poetry, then in the '60s along comes Crumb's Joe Blow and it happens again.

FACING PAGE: The strip that startled everybody, Crumb's Joe Blow [Zap #4]. S Clay Wilson: "I talked Crumb (a repressed Catholic choirboy) into drawing 'dirty'… that is drawing anything that occurred to him, without censorship or concern for an imagined audience. He took my advice and did so with relish."

Passed on to publishers, this meant that all but the largest could no longer afford to put out titles at competitive cover prices.

Farmer and Chively continued to work in the industry, but like many others were creativity inhibited by the events they had been through. Joyce Farmer said in 1988, "Deep inside me, fear still censors my brain before my fingers can begin a pirouette."

Perhaps the most unusual and pervasive aspect of underground publishing is that essentially the same battles need to be fought over

and over again, as, with titles remaining in print, new cases arise every year of comix being seized, censored and destroyed.

This applies not only to the USA—where the response has been the founding of the Comic Book Legal Defense Fund—but particularly to international distribution, where Customs authorities have broad discretionary powers and no discernible guidelines or restraints and are free to destroy other people's property with virtual impunity.

In England, in April 1985, Judge Harold Branson ordered approximately 550 copies of issues 1, 2 and 4 of **Tits & Clits** to be destroyed, together with Melinda Gebbie's **Fresca Zizis** and other 'obscene' comix imported from America.

In 1995, Knockabout fought successfully against the seizure of works by Robert Crumb, Phoebe Gloeckner and others, confiscated on import. Some of the items in question had been in print for over 25 years at the time of the dispute, and reprinted in mass-market editions in mainstream bookshops all over the United Kingdom. All Knockabout won in that case was the right to the return of their own property, with no compensation for lost sales or large legal bills. But that remains the outstanding victory in a long line of seizures and hearings disputed by Knockabout.

In 2001 the Little Sister's Art and Book Emporium in Vancouver became the victim of an arbitrary seizure—the most recent of many—of underground and alternative comix brought over from the US. The trouble between Little Sister's and Canada Customs had started years earlier and culminated in 2000 with the ruling that Customs had not only unreasonably delayed and held much of Little Sister's imported merchandise, but also did it through "systematic targeting" of materials bound for the store. It turned out, however, to be a hollow victory as they were back in court the following year. Rather than accepting it, a defence fund was organized with two benefit books **What's Wrong?** and **What Right?** being published to raise funds for the battle. Two books because one was X-rated and

LEFT AND FACING PAGE: One bastion of bias where sexism appears not to be on the agenda is with inter-national Customs officers. Comics produced by women have as tough a time when exported as anything else. Last Gasp's Fresca Zizis by Melinda Gebbie [left] fails to travel well, as does Pandora's Box [facing page] from those brave women who also brought you Tits & Clits.

the other an all-age title. As owner Robin Fisher explained, "I want little old ladies to read it; I want 8-year-old boys to read it; I want everybody to read it and not get hung up on anything in it."

Canada already had a reputation for censorship. **Freak Brothers** was banned for years because of a law prohibiting any mention to marijuana that was not critical. While that law was overturned, it appears not to have made its customs officials any more liberal.

Another case involving Canadian customs occured recently when Fantagraphics Books mailed a copy of their excellent 2002 Patrick Rosenkranz hardcover **Rebel Visions** across the border to **Moondog** creator George Metzger. Instead of the book, he received official notification it had been seized as it contained "sex with mutilation, bestiality and incest." With a subtitle of *The Underground Comix Revolution 1963-1975* and after 30 years of meticulous research, it would have been difficult for Rosenkranz to write more than a pamphlet without mentioning any of the above. Fortunately, Metzger appealed the ruling, resulting in an email withdrawing the sanction.

Despite mainy people's groundbreaking efforts, the underground comics' struggle for freedom of speech and expression, in defiance of oppression and censorship, is sadly one that does not have an end in sight. Forget Superman's "Never-ending battle for Truth, Justice, and the American Way." The true never-ending conflict is the war against the ignorant and censorious, which—it appears—will sadly remain with us for generations to come.

RIGHT: Of the Published and be Damned contenders, the winners have to be the Air Pirates. On Disney, O'Neill said, "We called them out. Why have a fight if no one comes." Pictured right is the rebel crew, Gary Hallgren, Dan O'Neill, Shary Flenniken and Ted Richards, attempting to raise legal fees.

FACING PAGE: O'Neill gets a few tips from king rebel Harvey Kurtzman [top left]. Spruced up to face Disney lawyers, O'Neill in 1971 [top right]. And she seems such a sweet girl, Pirate Flenniken [bottom left].

Unbelievably, after the case was settled, O'Neill was hired by New York's Disney merchandising art department [bottom right].

We're cool too, Daddy-o!

By the 1970s mainstream comics were in turmoil. None sold enough for full cover racking and mixed bundles supplied always included unsellable also-rans. New York needed a new gimmick.

SALES were plummeting as newsstands rejected the plethora of cheap and gaudy juvenile escapism. The Walt Disney of comicbooks, Stan Lee, knew something drastic had to be done as he saw sales drop to 25%—only one in four of the comics being printed was actually earning Marvel money. He felt the solution would be in a line of magazine-sized comics, with higher cover prices and a more mature look. If they could be sold to the trade by title rather than mixed bundles, like regular magazines, they'd get better positioning and better sales. Hey, it worked for **MAD**, so why not for Marvel?

Trying to muscle in on Jim Warren's successful magazine-sized black and white horror comics, **Eerie**, **Creepy** and **Vampirella**, Lee launched his own line of horror mags in 1973 with **Dracula Lives**, **Monsters Unleashed**, **Vampire Tales** and **Tales of the Zombie**. Sales looked good so he cashed in on a few other trends the following year with the large format **Deadly Hands of Kung Fu**, **Planet of the Apes** and a magazine version of his surprise barbarian comic success in **Savage Sword of**

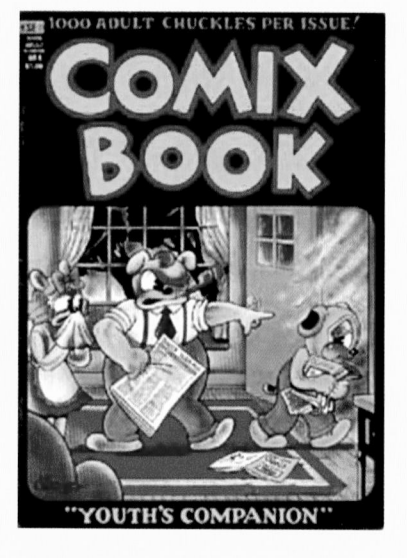

Conan. Being in black and white, these had relatively low production costs compared to full colour comics, but because of their size, they were tagged at almost three times the cover price of Marvel's regular titles. Plus with their format giving them better racking, they attracted an older audience. On a roll, he cast his net wider and spotted… underground comix!

Lee obviously thought, here were these spaced out cartoonists denied outlets beyond head shops and Marvel could give them national exposure. Who knows, used to small print runs they should be pretty cheap too! So Smilin' Stan easily persuaded a starving Denis Kitchen to work for Marvel in 1974.

Lee told him he wanted to capitalize on the "cutting-edge style" of the underground cartoonists. "Stan knew underground comix had been big, but I don't think he had any idea the whole industry was on the rocks," explained Kitchen. "He wanted to tap into the energy of the underground without ruining Marvel's clean-cut reputation. We discussed creating a hybrid magazine."

LEFT: From issue #1, Kitchen's comic strip editorial for Comix Book. As the cover line announced, "It's new! It's strange! It's subterranean!" Well, two out of three isn't bad, but "subterranean"?

FACING PAGE: The cover to Comix Book #4 [1975], Denis Kitchen's first non-Marvel issue.

Equally eager to broaden underground comix exposure and earn a decent wage himself, Kitchen agreed to create and edit a Marvel underground comic, again in the large black and white format, but without too much emphasis on sex or drugs. About as sanitized as a Disney version of *Reservoir Dogs*.

Kitchen's own company was rescued by Marvel's money and he also won unprecedented concessions for the new title. Lee agreed to return all artwork, to run no advertising and even to allow artists to keep their copyrights—all policies completely unheard of in mainstream comics publishing at that time.

The result was a mess. **Comix Book** wasn't underground, it was too wholesome. As Lee commented, "Being Marvel we couldn't get raunchy enough." Neither was it a Marvel comic, it was too whacky. Distributors and retailers were confused by this "adult" kids comic. And there was no advertising revenue.

Sales on the first issue were a nightmare so Lee quickly killed it, but by then the third issue had hit newsstands. Kitchen, working ahead for the printers, also had the next two issues well under way. Not wanting to let down the writers and artists, after a year of negotiation, Kitchen's own company was allowed to publish the final two issues, albeit scaled down, printing 5,000 copies instead of Marvel's 200,000. So ended the mainstream market's attempt to go underground. Except for Jim Warren.

The "International" Rich Corben

Renowned for guarding his turf, the **Creepy, Eerie, Vampirella** publisher wasn't too happy about Marvel's move into his virtual monopoly of horror magazines. So it's pretty safe to assume it was more than a coincidence that when Marvel launched **Comix Book**, Warren was responding with **Comix International**.

It had the same magazine format and the same newsstand distribution route, but as Warren had been experimenting with colour printing, he made this his first all-colour magazine. Known equally for his ability to run a tight ship, he offset the increased print costs by making it a cover-to-cover reprint.

Darling of the underground horror comix world and best known for his 1970-72 **Fantagor** series from Last Gasp, Rich Corben had been producing 8-page colour strips for the middle of Warren's black and white magazines for the previous year or so. These were promptly gathered up behind instant cover art made up of a collection of interior shots, to form Warren's own overground underground comicbook.

But it proved hardly any more successful than Marvel's attempt, being cancelled at issue 5 [1977], by which time the underground revolution had faded into little more than a '60s fad.

While the "Stick to what you're best at" motto leaps to mind, the mainstream experiment wasn't a total failure. Although Warren's **Comix International** did little except boost Corben's profile (his bank account certainly can't have benefitted much), Marvel's all-new experiment provided a well timed if short-term income for some of the underground's then-struggling almost-

greats (noticeable by the absence of any of the pioneers).

Kitchen does admit that he forgot to invite Zippy's Bill Griffiths to contribute. "That pissed him off. And there were other artists like Crumb who absolutely would not work for Marvel in any way, and from all that **Arcade** was born."

Most remarkably, despite Spiegelman refusing to contribute to **Comix Book** because he objected to some material in the first issue, the title did provide a mass audience for his future Pulitzer Prize-winning *Maus* by reprinting his initial Holocaust-themed 1972 **Funny Aminals** #1 three-pager in **Comix Book** #2.

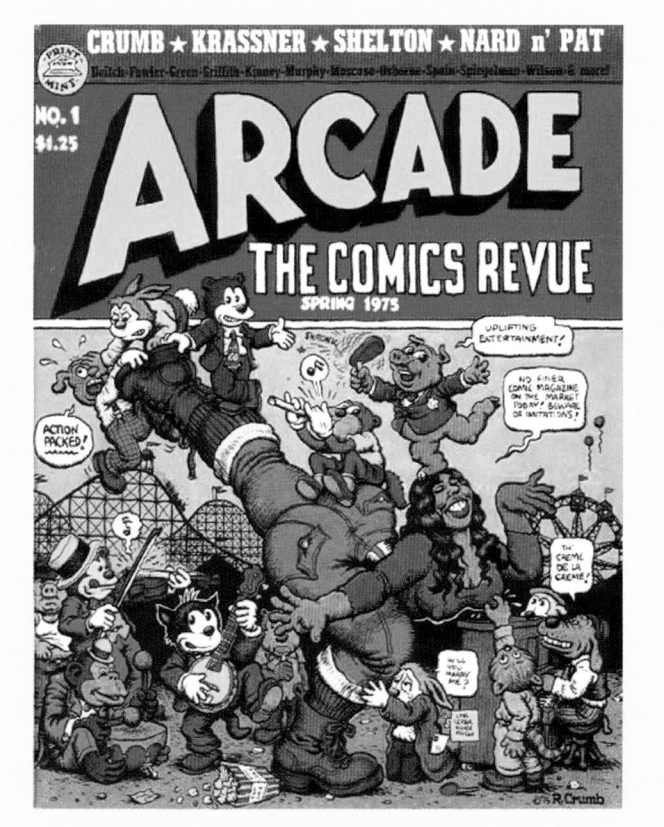

RIGHT: While almost all of the big guns steered clear of Marvel's 1974 underground anthology, they leaped on board for the following year's "real thing" from Print Mint. Arcade, The Comics Review launched in Spring, 1975 with work by Shelton, Crumb, Spain, Moscoso, Griffith, Lynch and Noomin. Comix Book contributors Spiegelman, Deitch and Green also welcomed the rescue ship.

FACING PAGE: Squaring up, the two over-ground underground titles: Marvel's Comix Book and Warren's Comix International.

Art: Melinda Gebbie, Wimmen's Comix #7 [Last Gasp, 1976].

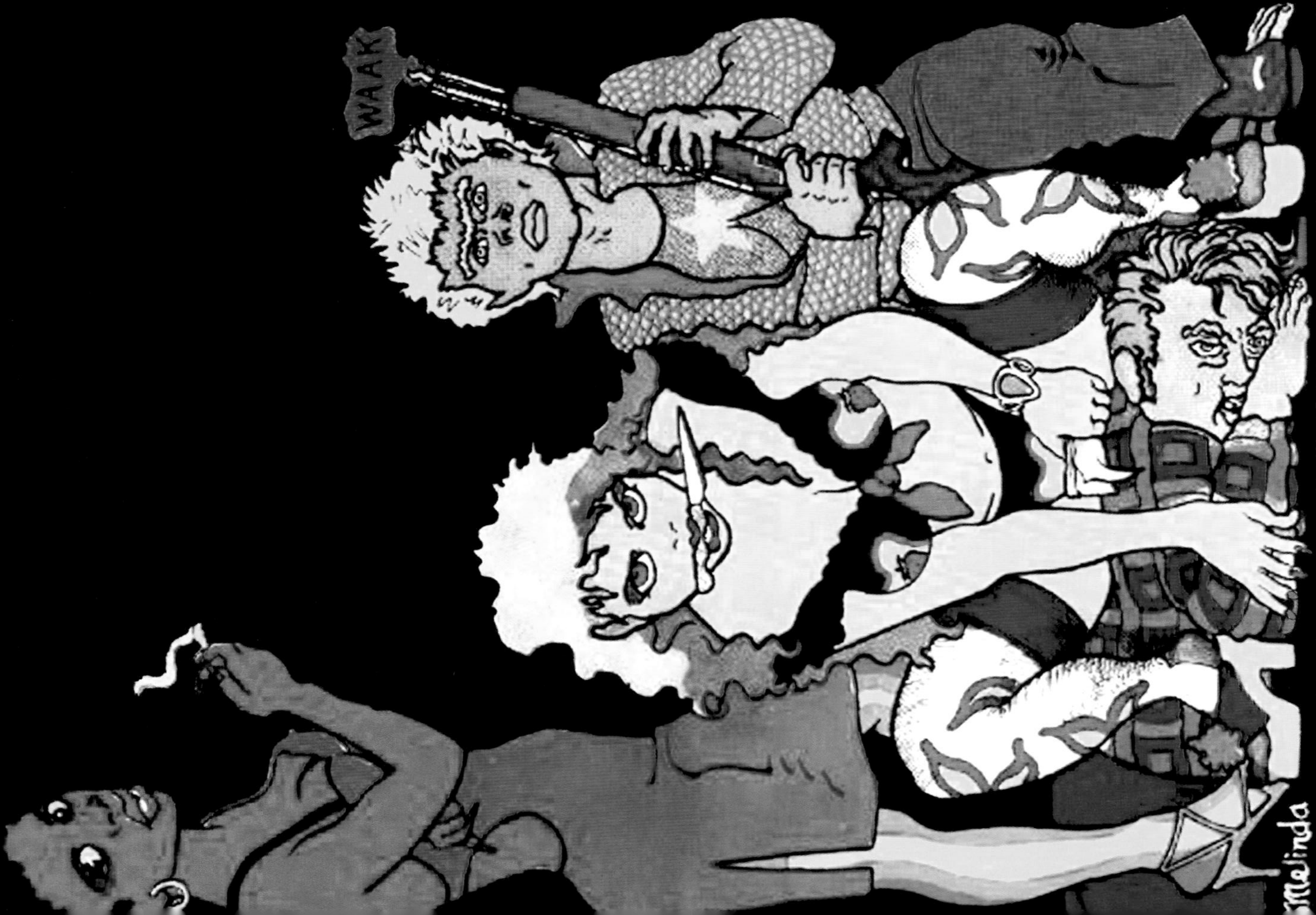

Chapter 6:

Girls On Top

Wimmen's comix

"We found the entire comix scene to be a closed Boy's Only club with no room for women." ...TRINA ROBBINS ON SAN FRANCISCO, 1970

Full of sexual exploitation, the underground's sordid comix tales of female use and drug-fuelled abuse were created by men for men. Disgusted by the mysogyny, sisters decided to do it for themselves...

THE first women to work in underground comix seem to have arrived by way of underground newspapers. The comix movement was still young when Nancy Kalish, using the pseudonym Panzika, drew her comic **Gentle's Tripout** for the New York City underground newspaper, **The East Village Other**, in 1965. On the other side of the country, Los Angeles hippie and art school dropout Trina Robbins saw the comic strip.

Like so many other hippies and college students, she'd been turned onto comics by a combination of the new Marvel Comics renaissance in superhero comics and the hip, campy Batman TV series. Under the influence of the two, she had tried drawing her own superhero comics, which didn't work at all for her. Seeing the extremely psychedelic **Gentle's Tripout,** she realized that there was another way to draw comics.

> ...comix from this period don't necessarily make much sense to the un-stoned, but they are pretty to look at.

In 1966, Robbins moved to New York's Lower East Side and began contributing her own psychedelic comix to **The East Village Other**. Viewed from a perspective of almost 40 years later, Panzika's and Robbins' comix from this period don't necessarily make much sense to the un-stoned, but they are pretty to look at.

Sharon Rudahl, a student at New York's Cooper Union art school, saw Robbins' **The East Village Other** comix in 1967. Not satisfied with the fine art program taught at Cooper Union, she realized that there could be another outlet for talented artists in the new form of underground comix.

In 1968, cartoonist Vaughn Bode, inspired by such tabloid comix anthologies as **Yarrowstalks** out of the Midwest and San Francisco's **Yellow Dog**, convinced **The East Village Other** to publish their own tabloid comix anthology, **Gothic Blimp Works**. It included the work of three women cartoonists, Robbins, Kalish, and Willy Mendes. At the same time, Kay Rudin, who had come to California from Ohio, was contributing strips to **Yellow Dog.**

By 1970, Robbins and Mendes had moved to San Francisco—then considered the underground comix Mecca—wanting to join the growing comix community. As Robbins recalls, "Unfortunately it proved not to be a Mecca for us. We found the entire comix scene to be a closed Boy's Club, with no room for women."

Since none of the men invited her into their books, Robbins found work in underground newspapers, drawing illustrations and comix for **The Berkeley Tribe** and **San Francisco Good Times**. The women's liberation movement was in full swing, and Robbins, disgusted by the misogyny of the all-male underground, reacted by joining the staff of **It Ain't Me, Babe,** the West Coast's first Women's Liberation newspaper, drawing the continued misadventures of Belinda Berkeley.

Number 1

ADULTS ONLY

50¢

WIMMEN'S COMIX

GASP!

EXCEPT FOR BEING FAT, UGLY, PIMPLE FACED, BAD-TEMPERED AND SELFISH, YOU'D THINK HE'D SEE I'M A MUCH BETTER CHOICE!

INSIDE THIS ISSUE
SEX, REVELATION, PSYCHOTIC ADVENTURE AND MORE...

ABOVE: Trina Robbins (1972) with daughter Casey. Photo by Patrick Rosenkranz.

LEFT: Wimmen's Comics #1 [1970]. The title ran to #17 [1991]. Contributor Lee Binswanger recalls, "The group lost its impetus after #17 in 1991, I think because the publishers we talked to were hard pressed to pay more than $50 a page. As many of the group was older, they were unwilling to work for such crappy pay. We should have gone back to Last Gasp, but didn't. I'm not sure why."

The not particularly subtle strip was a comix version of feminism 101, in which Robbins detailed her heroine's gradual feminising process, culminating in her leaving her "male chauvenist pig" husband and joining Women's Liberation.

Along with the newspaper's collective, she produced **It Ain't Me, Babe Comix** [Last Gasp, 1970], the world's first all-woman written and drawn comicbook. Mendes contributed a story and the back cover, while Robbins drew the front cover and two interior stories.

Other contributors were Nancy Kalish, Meredith Kurtzman, Michelle Brand, Lisa Lyons and a strip was produced collectively by the staff of the newspaper. The themes of their stories could not have differed more from the male comix of the time, which tended to feature gleeful renditions of rape and mutilation. The women in the pages of **It Ain't Me, Babe** drew and wrote about what they knew, from tales of the Goddess to rants against street harassment and fantasies of office drudges being stuck in the secretarial pool.

ABOVE: The 1970 oneshot, All Girl Thrills. Print Mint's Don Donahue described it as the worst comic he ever saw.

LEFT: Trina Robbins' Speed Queen, Yellow Dog #20 [1971].

FACING PAGE: Wimmen's Comics #9 and #16. Lee Binswanger: "The Wimmen's Comix group in the '80s was speckled with newcomers and the dynamic of the entire group was probably less political than in the '70s. The group stopped for a long time after #7; people just weren't getting along."

Lee Marrs, who in 1969 had arrived in the San Francisco Bay Area from Washington, DC, had formed The Alternative Features Service (AFS), along with Mal Warwick and John Berger.

AFS distributed news, features and comix to college and underground papers. A friend showed her his comix collection in 1970, and Marrs got the same idea other women cartoonists had: you could do this stuff in comicbooks, as well as newspapers! She took examples of her art to Last Gasp publisher Ron Turner only to be told,

"Too bad, the women's book is filled." She responded, "There's only one women's book?" She went home and started work on what would become **Pudge, Girl Blimp**.

In Seattle in 1970, Shary Flenniken, already drawing for the underground Seattle newspaper, **Sabot**, attended a party given by people she refers to as "revolutionaries" and found a pile of underground comix by the likes of S. Clay Wilson and Gilbert Shelton. She thought, "Hey, if they can do this crap, so can I!".

MEREDITH

HURRICANE NANCY

ABOVE: Yellow Dog #4 ("published as weekly as possible") was one of few early titles open to women cartoonists. Following 12 tabloid issues it shrank to comix format for a further 13.

LEFT: Star*Reach's Pudge, Girl Blimp #3 by artist/animator Lee Marrs, the ex-Little Orphan Annie art assistant who went on to The Complete Fart and Other Body Emissions [1977] before freelance commissions for DC Comics (including Viking Glory and Faultlines).

FACING PAGE: From It Ain't Me Babe [1970], the all-girl cartoon creators. Trina Robbins (sitting, with baby Casey) surrounded by Michelle Brand, Willy Mendes, Lisa Lyons, Meredith Kurtzman and Nancy Kalish and friends.

She moved to a communal house in Berkeley, California where the Air Pirates were in the habit of visiting, hanging out, and "eating all the organic eggs." Soon she started hanging out at their San Francisco house, eventually moving in with them. Advised by Air Pirates leader Dan O'Neill to create one outstanding character, she came up with Trots and Bonnie in a style inspired by early 20th century cartoonist H.T.Webster. The clever little girl and her even smarter dog first appeared in an Air Pirates comic book in 1971.

Meanwhile, Rudahl had moved to Madison, Wisconsin, and joined the staff of the underground newspaper, **Takeover**. While Rudahl was drawing political cartoons for **Takeover**, Robbins and Mendes spent the next two years producing their own comics: **Girl Fight** (Robbins), **All Girl Thrills** (Robbins, Mendes and Jewelie Goodvibes) and **Illuminations** (Mendes).

By 1972, **It Ain't Me, Babe Comix** had gone into a second printing. Ron Turner asked his employees Pattie Moodian and Terre Richards to

ABOVE: The Wimmen's Comix Collective in 1975. From left to right, standing: Becky Wilson, Trina Robbins, Shelby Sampson, Ron Turner (publisher), Barb Brown, Dot Bucher. Sitting: Melinda Gebbie, Lee Marrs.

LEFT: Shary Flenniken's pensive summary of dealing with underground comix editors.

FACING PAGE: Print Mint's all-Trina Robbins' Girl Fight Comics #2 [of 2, 1974] and the Lyn Chevely/Joyce Farmer Abortion Eve oneshot [1973] featuring a discussion about the legality of abortions and what to expect, plus "head trips before and after."

put out the word to other women cartoonists that he was ready to publish another feminist comic. Lee Marrs, visiting Turner with samples of her work on **Pudge, Girl Blimp,** was told about the women getting together to produce their own comic.

Rudahl, who had moved to San Francisco, was working at the underground newspaper **Good Times** when Robbins met her there

and told her about the new book that was forming.

All in all, eleven women showed up for the first meeting of the **Wimmen's Comix** Collective. Rudahl, Robbins, Marrs, Richards, Moodian, Michelle Brand, Lora Fountain, Shelby Sampson, Aline Kominsky, Karen Marie Haskell and Janet Wolfe Stanley all had work in the book's first issue. Not all of the "founding mothers" contributed to future issues, but there was always a core of at least eight women to put the book together in San Francisco.

They developed a rotating editorship, so that every member got the chance of editing at least one issue, and any contributor who could attend meetings had a say in the book's development. Having experienced exclusion, the **Wimmen's Comix** Collective made every attempt to be inclusive. With each issue they gained new contributors from the USA and eventually, England and Europe.

Chin Lively's Tits & Clits

While the **Wimmen's Comix** Collective was busy putting together their first issue, they were unaware that, on the other side of the same state, two women were compiling their own feminist comic.

Southern Californians Joyce Farmer and Lyn Chevely (using the pseudonym Chin Lively) self-published **Tits & Clits**, devoted mainly to the subject of female sexuality, as their reaction to the sexist treatment of women in male-dominated comix. Farmer's and Chevely's comic book beat **Wimmen's Comix** to the stands by three weeks, making it the second ever all-woman comix anthology.

Comix like **It Ain't Me, Babe, Wimmen's Comix** and **Tits & Clits** were forums for women cartoonists to communicate previously taboo subjects that mattered to them and to their readers, but which the male cartoonists wouldn't touch with a ten foot pole: sexual harassment, abortion, single motherhood and sexism.

But not lesbianism—until 1973, when art student Mary Wings picked up a copy of **Wimmen's Comix** and was outraged by what

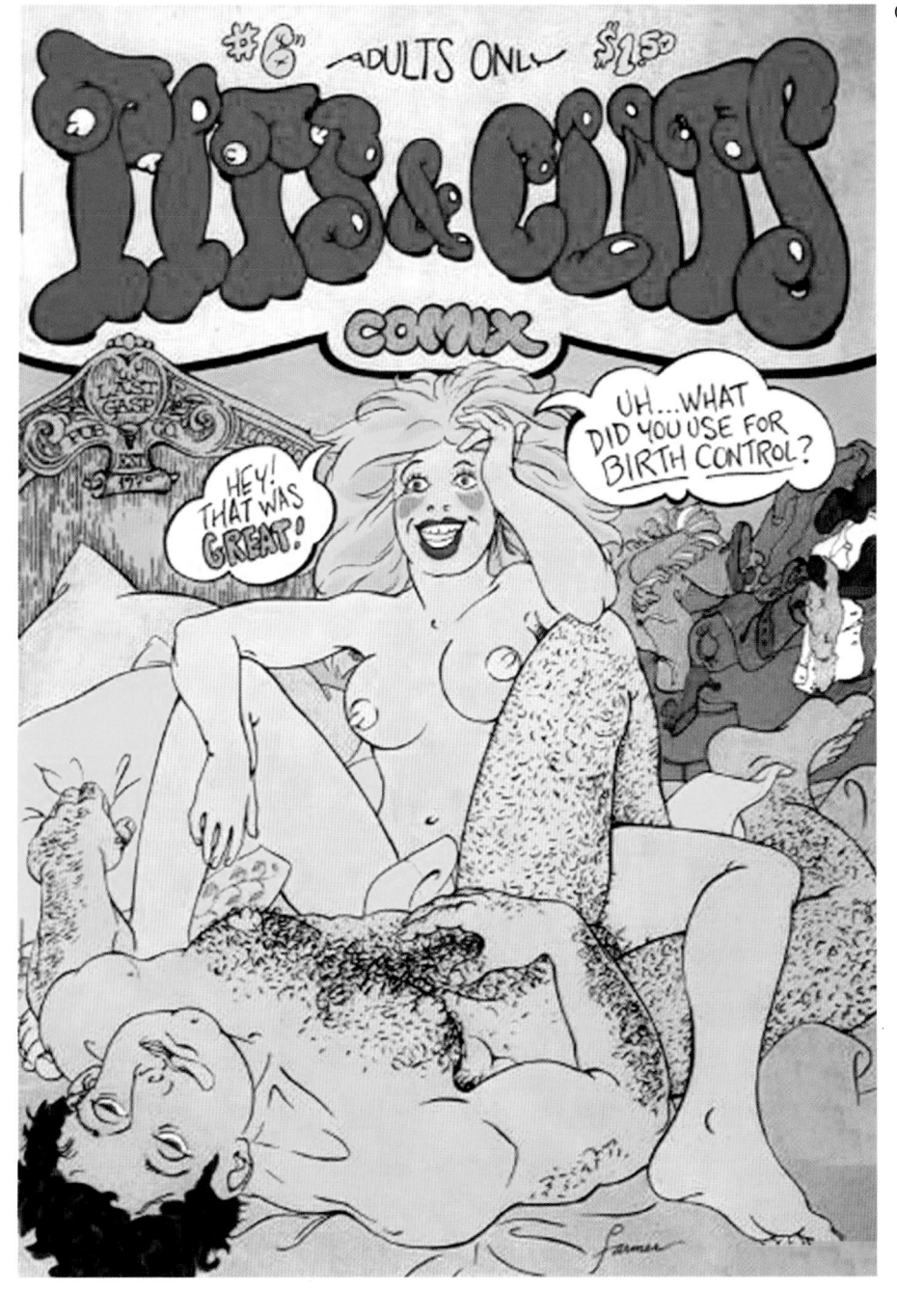

FACING PAGE AND LEFT:
Tits & Clits—Lyn Chevely
and Joyce Farmer's self-
published response to the
sexist macho comix of the
time—lasted seven issues
[1976-87] as an anthology for
women cartoonists. Last
Gasp-Eco Funnies published
the final four issues.

ABOVE: Mary Wings' Are Your Highs Getting You Down? [1981, Last Gasp]. Part-funded by a California Art Council grant, it was a docucomic oneshot on personal experiences of the two women's substances abuse groups at the Pacific Center, Berkeley.

RIGHT: Trina Robbins' cover art for The Print Mint's final issue of Yellow Dog #25 [1973].

FACING PAGE: Aline Kominksy reveals "The Origins of the Bunch," Weirdo 10 [Last Gasp-Eco Funnies, 1984].

she saw as a purely heterosexual overview. Her answer was to print the first lesbian comic, **Come Out Comix**, on an offset press in the back room of a woman's karate centre. Wings produced two other comics, **Dyke Shorts** and **Are Your Highs Getting You Down?**, a comic about drug addiction, before turning to writing. Today she's known as a mystery writer, with seven books to her credit.

That same year, Marrs, who had just published **Pudge, Girl Blimp #1**, met Melinda Gebbie at a small press convention and invited her into **Wimmen's Comix**, and Flenniken sold her first *Trots and Bonnie* strips to **National Lampoon**. By 1978, she had joined **Lampoon**'s editorial staff.

In 1974, Roberta Gregory reacted to the all straight-girl **Wimmen's Comix** by submitting her lesbian love story, *A Modern Romance*. The collective, which had never purposely left out lesbians—they simply had never received any submissions by lesbians!—accepted the clever and beautifully drawn story. By 1976, Gregory's self-published **Dynamite Damsels** became the second lesbian comic ever printed.

Within a decade, American women underground cartoonists had grown from a low of two to an unprecedented number. Many other women who appeared in the pages of **Wimmen's Comix**—among them Rudahl, Kominsky, Gebbie, Krystine Kryttre, Dori Seda, and Mary Fleener—were publishing their own solo books by the 1980s.

Wimmen's Comix lasted 20 years, producing its last issue in 1992. It remains the longest-lasting women's comics anthology.

Kitchen fantasies

The battle between the women's and the men's view of sex in comix came to a head in 1976, when Kitchen Sink publisher Denis Kitchen asked Robbins to edit a women's comic for him. Feeling that at last this was a chance for women to express their views on sexuality, she created **Wet Satin**, subtitled *Women's Erotic Fantasies*.

On the cover, Robbins drew a woman in high heeled boots and a flight suit, provocatively eating a banana while reading a copy of **A Streetcar Named Desire**. Her nose buried in the book, she skateboards down the sidewalk, missing the object of her "desire," Marlon Brando as Stanley Kowalski, who stands in a doorway as she skates past.

The interior featured a lot of turn-around-is-fair-play stories, such as *Ain't Life Grand?* by Petchesky (Margery Peters) in which women use a man as a sex object, and Robbins' satire on Eric Stanton-type bondage comics, *Rawhide Revenge*. It also featured frankly sexual stories, like Lee Marrs' gentle *Flight of Fancy* in which a woman fantasizes sex with a bird-man, and Joey Epstein's blatant all-night threesome, *Night of Dynamite*.

The trouble started when Kitchen Sink's printer refused to print the book, claiming it was pornography. It had to be printed in San Francisco. In her editorial for **Wet Satin** #2, 1978, Robbins described the situation: "Our publisher had a printer who refused

Continued on p172

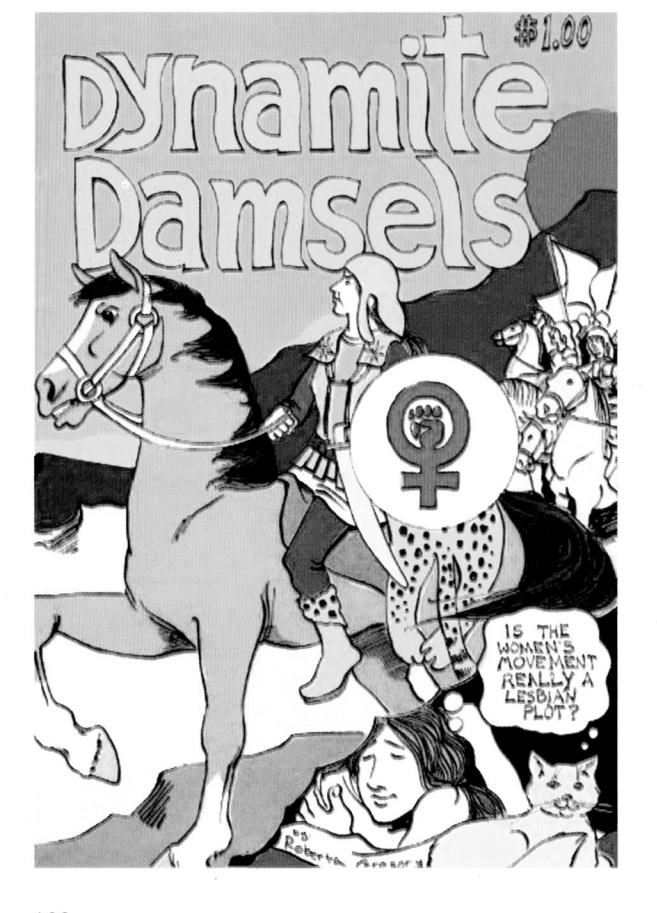

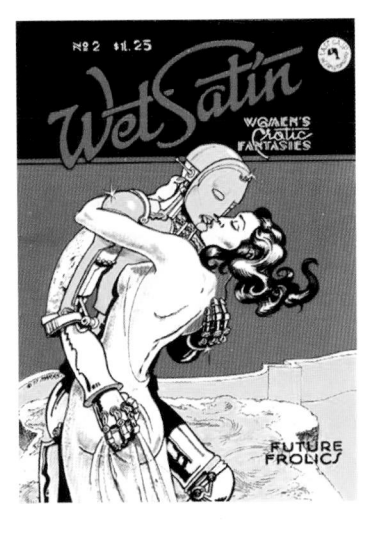

THIS PAGE: Wet Satin was the Trina Robbins edited anthology of women's erotic fantasies, commissioned by Kitchen Sink in 1976. Following Kitchen's problems in printing it, the title switched to friendly rival Last Gasp for the second issue.

FACING PAGE: In 1976, Roberta Gregory was among the first women to self-publish a comic book, Dynamite Damsels. It starred Frieda the Feminist, and was based on Gregory's real-life experiences in the feminist and lesbian movements. Mary Wings produced her own lesbian comic, Dyke Shorts in 1978, a follow-up to her previous year's Come Out Comix.

OVERLEAF: An excerpt from Aline & R. Crumb's Arline 'n' Bob, That Thing in The Back Bedroom, [Weirdo #9, 1983].

to touch **Wet Satin**, calling it pornographic. This man had printed all of Krupp's underground comics, including **Bizarre Sex**. (Check this one out at your local comic book store and see for yourself! One cover was so objectionable that it had to be covered with white paper!) When asked why he drew the line on **Wet Satin** #1, he answered that the predominantly male comics were all satires, but that **Wet Satin** #1 was serious, and therefore pornographic.

Yet **Screw**—by no means a feminist journal—said in a review, "The humor in **Wet Satin** is another welcome change from other undergrounds... what might have been a tedious and boring look into sexual psyche of 'liberated' women, turns out to be a series of clever, satirical and entertaining cartoon strips."

Wet Satin #2 included Lee Marrs' cover, depicting a woman and a robot making love on a giant peanut butter sandwich, plus Mary

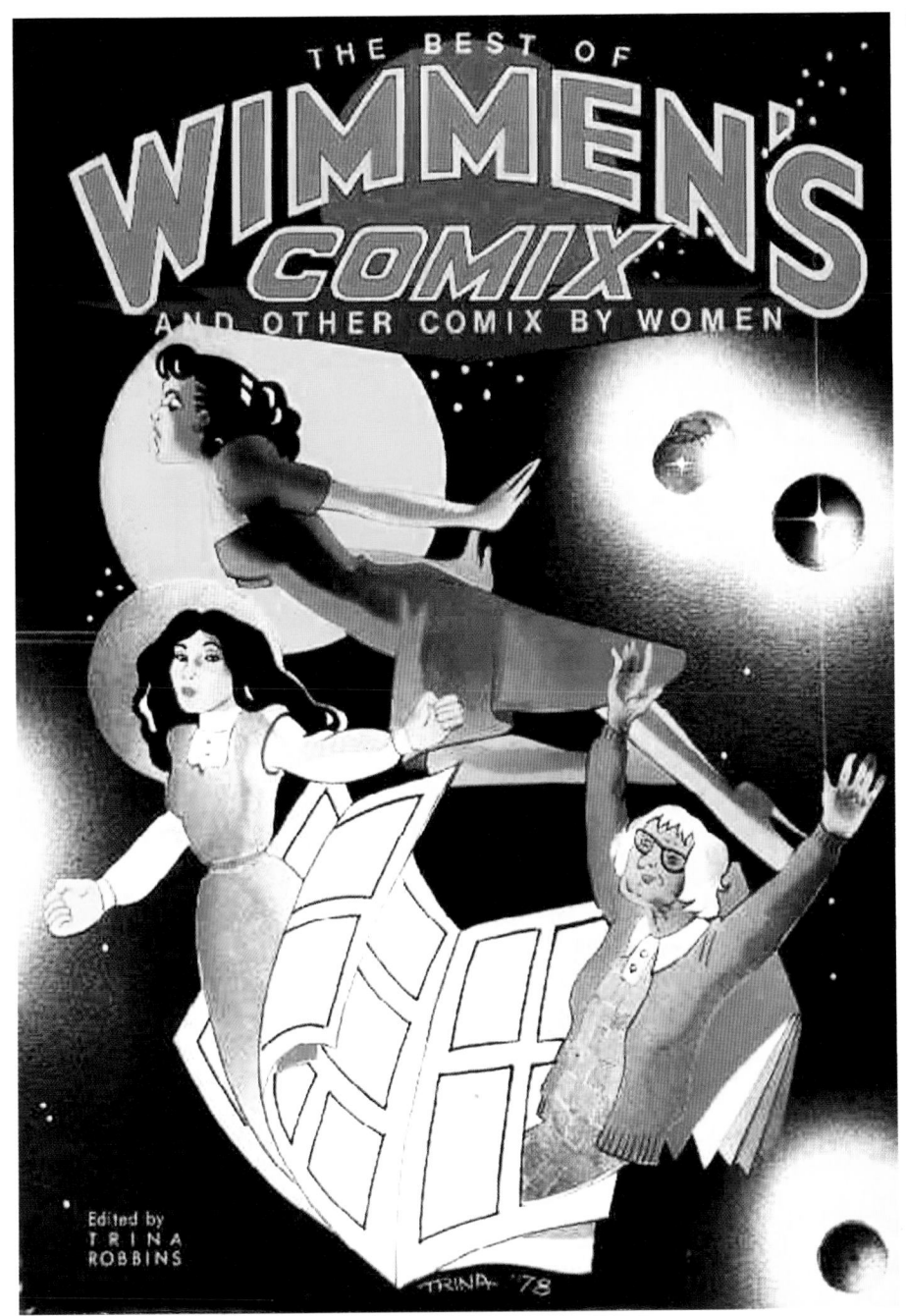

LEFT: Hassle Free Press (now better known as Knockabout) produced a UK large format collection, The Best of Wimmen's Comix in 1979. Cover art by editor Trina Robbins.

FACING PAGE: A recent arrival, but one of the most popular yet. Not only is she the star of Roberta Gregory's Naughty Bits [Fantagraphics, 1991 to date], but Bitchy Bitch also has her own newspaper strip, syndicated to a number of remaining alternative newspapers including The New York Press and the Seattle Weekly.

Wilshire's first underground strip *Those Beautiful Babes in Their Bain de Soleil* and Joey Epstein's castration satire *Nifty Ways to Cleave Your Lover*, which predated Lorena Bobbitt by about 15 years.

Not surprisingly, the same printer again refused to print it. This time Ron Turner worked out a co-operative agreement with Kitchen, in which Last Gasp published the book, and provided Kitchen Sink with comics for distribution. Robbins ended her editorial: "As for the printer, I leave you to draw your own conclusions."

Brit grrrls

1978 was also the year that UK women entered the underground comix scene with **Heroine**, the first British women's comicbook. In

Birmingham, Suzy Varty was the only woman in the Arts Lab Comics Collective, which had produced five issues of **Street Comics**. She also belonged to a woman's art group which was working on a postal art event called Feministo. As part of the event, they produced a magazine which the Arts Lab published, leading to the collective asking Varty to produce an all-woman comic. In an e-mail to Robbins, Varty writes, "...inspired by your good self (you stayed with me in 1977, as I recall) and undaunted by the lack of visible women cartoonists, I attempted to put together **Heroine**."

Varty succeeded in her attempt, with a crew of all-women contributors, and one man: Varty, Robbins, Sue Ash, Lyn Foulkes, Julia Wakesfield, Kate Walker, Meg Amsden, Judy Watson, Paula Williams, and Borin Van Loon. She took the comic to the 1978 Birmingham National Women's Liberation Conference, where, "It was highly thought of as art from the women's movement."

Varty opened the comix door for UK women, and Sheba Feminist Publishers followed across the threshold a year later with their book, **Sourcream**. It included comics by Lesley Ruda, Jo Nesbitt, Liz Mackie and Christine Roche. A second issue, which came out in 1981, featured no less than 13 women, including Viv Quinlan, Fanny Tribble, Rosalind Scott and Janis Goodman.

Carol Bennett's Fanny

As a result of books like **Heroine** and **Sourcream**, the amount of women emerging into the UK comix scene enabled Carol Bennett of Knockabout Comics to found the British Women's Comic Collective in 1991, with **Fanny** as their flagship title. So far, at least eight comic anthologies have been published under the Fanny logo, including the anti-war book **Ceasefire**, and the lesbian anthology **Dyke's Delight**.

Although UK comix are still male-dominated, female cartoonists continue to infuse the industry with a healthy dose of humour and feminism.

LEFT: Robert Crumb started Weirdo as editor, then quit after a couple of years. Peter Bagge did the same. So Aline Kaminsky-Crumb edited the last nine issues. Her husband continued to supply cover art, her first being modelled after Cosmopolitan.

FACING PAGE: Mary Wings' original biographical 1974 oneshot, which she wrote, drew and published, with a little help from the Portland Women's Resource Centre.

Zippy the Pinhead

The underground sea-change that revelled in the permissive society, psychedelic music and tie-dye also gave birth to an American presidential candidate—albeit the strangest ever.

THE star of his own nationally syndicated newspaper strip since 1980, Zippy is a microcephalic clown based in part on the sideshow 'pinheads' who appeared in *Freaks*, Tod Browning's classic 1932 horror movie.

In addition to the uncommon shape of their heads, microcephalics are known for their childlike personalities and rapid-fire speech. Zippy creator Bill Griffith: "Their scrambled attention spans struck me as a metaphor for the way we get our doses of reality these days. The kind of fractured, short term information overload that we're all exposed to every day."

The cartoonist was also inspired by old posters of *Zip the What-Is-It*, a microcephalic in the Barnum & Bailey sideshow from 1864 to 1926. He created his first pinheaded character for **Real Pulp Comix** #1 [Print Mint, 1970] when he was asked to draw an offbeat romance story for the title. Editor Roger Brand suggested, "Why don't you make the characters really strange, not normal people at all. Just pick some very bizarre people?"

The result was *I Gave my Heart to a Pinhead but He made a Fool out of Me*, a five-pager about a love triangle involving a male and a female pinhead and a normal woman. The male—named Danny but called Zippy by the female pinhead—came back six months later in the second issue of Griffith's own Print Mint title, **Tales of the Toad**. "What happened, ultimately, was that Mr Toad became Zippy's sidekick. By 1974/75 Zippy was in the driver's seat," explained Griffiths, who also drew Zippy strips for such titles as **Arcade** and **Rip Off Comix**.

In 1975 Griffith discovered an amazing coincidence. He had been named William Henry Jackson after his great-grandfather, while *Zip the What-Is-It* was born William Henry Jackson in 1842. Realizing his fate was cast, in 1976 Griffith began a weekly *Zippy* strip. Initially appearing only in the underground paper **The Berkeley Barb**, it was later syndicated nationally by Rip Off Press beginning Zippy's move towards stardom.

Inspirating the Coneheads characters who Dan Ackroyd introduced on *Saturday Night Live* in 1978 and featured in their own 1993 movie, Zippy headlined Rip Off Press's **Zippy Stories** [3 issues; 1977-78] and Last Gasp's **Yow Comics** [2 issues; 1978-80]. He also featured regularly in **National Lampoon** and **High Times** with strips running in both from 1977 to 1984.

He was also becoming a merchandizing success. With his face on T-shirts, posters and related paraphenalia, Zippy—whose "Are we having fun yet?" catch phrase appears in **Bartlett's Familiar Quotations**— made a move into politics. Running as an

independent presidential candidate in 1980, the year Griffith took over syndication of his strip, Zippy stood against Regan/Bush and Carter/Mondale. The publicity stunt worked wonders reaping him massive media exposure.

In 1985 Griffiths contributed *Zippy* six days a week to the **San Francisco Examiner**, a bastion of Establishment liberalism. The next year he was approached by syndication giant King Features although the person handling the purchase had an ulterior motive. "He told me he took it because to him *Zippy* was like a ticking time bomb on the doorstep of King Features. Plus he was a big fan. So he was indulging his taste and thumbing his nose at his boss as he left," said Griffiths.

With the strip now appearing daily in over 200 newspapers, Griffiths has given the world such Zippyisms as "If you can't say something nice, say something surreal," "I hope my sensitive female side is wearing sensible leather pumps," "I think I'm having a mid-week crisis," and "Zombies rule Belgium".

Chapter 7:

Anarchy in the UK

Blimey, it's the limeys

"I think there is an underground these days. The question is, what is underground? Political or stylistic?" ...HUNT EMERSON

America's underground comix scene was burgeoning with talented cartoonists from very early on. But it took the Brits a little longer to catch on to the underground revolution and the possibilities of new alternative comics. When they did, the end product was positively unique.

INVARIABLY early UK undergrounds were content to reprint American strips by the usual suspects, Robert Crumb, Gilbert Shelton, Spain et al. The first homegrown showcases for the American alternative lifestyle appeared in titles such as the underground London newspaper **IT (International Times)** and the infamous **Oz** magazine. Inevitably, the appearance of these strips began to influence the up and coming UK artists.

Outside of existing publications picking up comix to cheaply bolster their editorial content, by 1968 American material also began appearing as complete UK reprints, sitting alongside imported editions and finding an eager hippie Brit readership ready to devour the West Coast "freak" comix.

While the American material was becoming more widespread, it wasn't until 1970 that the first truly British underground comic, **Cyclops**, appeared. Created by a comix-loving group of freelance artists and contributors to **IT** and led by Graham Keen, **Cyclops** reprinted strips by Spain and Shelton as well as adding new material from UK creators including Ray Lowry, Martin Sharp and Edward Barker. Barker proved to be an important cartoonist as he would become co-responsible for one of the UK's most nefarious comix, **Nasty Tales**.

Damning it with faint praise, **Cyclops** was probably ahead of its time. Ungainly with its tabloid-sized newspaper format folded in half for racking with standard-sized magazines (**Andy Warhol's Interview-**style) and with its avant-garde content—ranging from adapting William Burroughs to *Flash Gordon* to *Captain Dopefreak*—**Cyclops** failed to find a solid market and collapsed after a mere four issues.

Unfazed by **Cyclops**' demise, Edward Barker and **IT** co-founders Paul Lewis and Mick Farren launched **Nasty Tales** in 1971. Intended as a sister publication in order to fund the constantly-ailing **IT**, **Nasty Tales**' format was similar to the USA's **Zap**.

Once again using a mix of US reprints and new material (with Barker, Malcolm Livingston and Chris Welch providing the home grown), **Nasty Tales** managed a more respectable run than **Cyclops**,

> "Among comic strips and comic books, this **[Nasty Tales]** is rather better than most and a good deal less insidious in its effect upon public taste than **Superman**."
> *...Germaine Greer*

JULY

CYCLOPS

No 1

BURP

William Burroughs
Malcolm McNeill
Raymond Lowry
Edweird Etc.

3/-

LEFT: Graham Keen was a man with a vision. A longtime fan of comics and comix, his dream was to publish a title which could showcase all his favourite strips and creators. Sadly, not enough readers shared his dream. Cyclops folded at issue 4.

IS IT FOR THE PUBLIC GOOD?

YES!

WHAT WOULD YOU FEEL WAS THE POTENTIAL READERSHIP FOR A MAGAZINE LIKE NASTY TALES

PEOPLE WHO ARE ATTRACTED BY THE TITLE 'NASTY TALES'. IT WOULD ONLY BE COMPREHESABLE TO ADULTS

PEOPLE WHO USE MARIJUANA MIGHT BE BROUGHT TO THINK IN A DIFFERENT WAY ABOUT THEIR ACTIVITIES WHEN IT IS PRESENTED TO THEM IN THIS WAY. THAT MUST SURELY BE TO THE PUBLIC GOOD.

COUNSEL: DOES A SEXUAL THEME RUN THROUGH **CRUMB'S** WORK?.
PERRY: YES..... PAGE 50 WOULD HAVE TO BE FAR MORE SHOCKING TO MAKE THE MESSAGE CLEARER I HAVE SEEN FAR MORE HORRIFIC ORGY DRAWINGS THAN THIS ONE IN AMERICAN HORROR COMICS!!
PROSECUTION: WOULD YOU PUT FORWARD PROPOGANDA CARTOONS AS SOMETHING OF ARTISTIC MERIT?"
PERRY: YES THEY DO HAVE LASTING MERIT.

PERRY: ...THESE ARTIST OF THE **FURRY FREAK BROTHERS** IS EXTREMELY CLEVER. **DIRTY DOG** IS USING THE FORMAT OF THE ANTHROPOMORPHIC **DISNEY** STYLE ANIMALS. THIS IS A NICE TWIST ON THE STYLE OF CARTOON IT IS PARODYING. THESE ARE NOT CONVENTIONAL CHARACTERS THEY ARE DRUG ADDICTS. IT IS NOT TAKING THE NORMALLY ACCEPTED AND PERHAPS BLINKERED ATTITUDE TO THESE ISSUES BUT IS BROADENING. IT.. I WOULD NOT AGREE THAT IT COULD BE DESCRIBED AS 'MINDLESS AND DISGUSTING'."

lasting seven issues before coming to the attention of the police and being put on trial in January 1973.

It's a set-up, man

An eight year-old had managed to buy a copy of the adult comic at a local newsagent and his mother complained to the police. Obviously a woman on a mission, it was later revealed she had put her son up to it. The law moved in and raided the **Nasty Tales** office—much to the

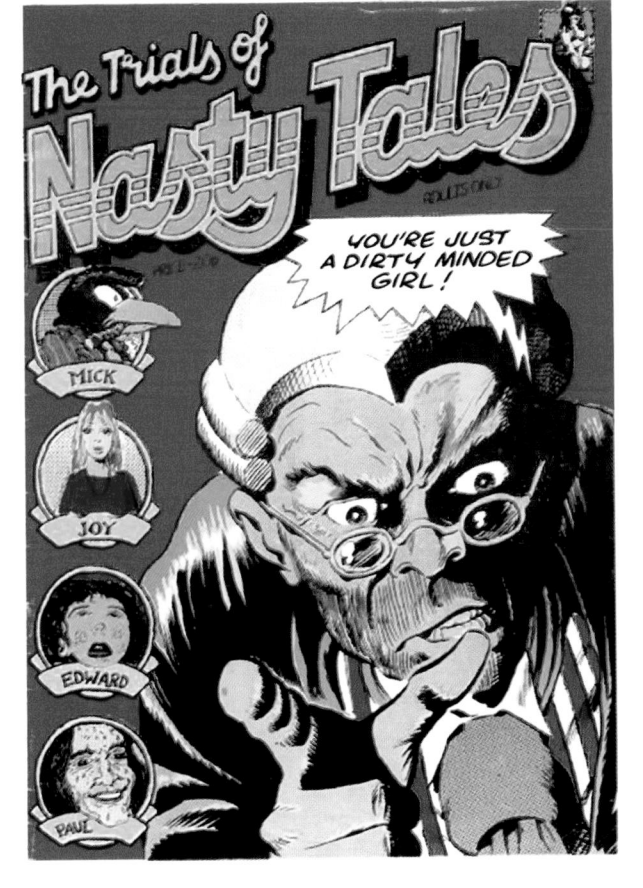

bemusement of Joy Farren, who was the only one present. The bust was a success, as they hauled away several boxes of office copies of the comic. Four defendants, Paul Lewis, Mick Farren, Edward Barker and Joy Farren were later charged with "Possessing an obscene article for gain, namely 275 copies of **Nasty Tales** No 1."

The main focus of the trial was on a reprinting of the notorious Crumb strip, *Grand Opening Of The Great Intercontinental Fuck-in and Orgy Riot.* The defence team called up such luminary witnesses as Germaine Greer who boldly stated, "Among comic strips and comicbooks this is rather better than most and a good deal less insidious in its effect upon public taste than **Superman**."

The jury was out for four and a half hours and returned a majority verdict (10-2) of Not Guilty. It was the first obscenity trial of a comicbook in British history, costing the taxpayer £15,000, according to London's **The Times** newspaper.

If you've got it, flaunt it!

Boosted by their success in the courts and in conjunction with Felix Dennis' H Bunch Associates, the **Nasty Tales** team released a comic publishing the actual court hearings in **The Trials of Nasty Tales** [1973].

Artists contributing their sometimes realistic sometimes bizarre styles to convert the transcripts into comic form included Edward Barker, Chris Welch, George Snow, Martin Sudden and Dave Gibbons.

Shortly after **Nasty Tales** was launched, and following **IT**'s lead, **Oz** magazine decided to create its own spin-off, **Cozmic Comics**, in 1972 .

Continued on p187

LEFT: The celebratory Trials of Nasty Tales [1973], with cover art taken from Dave Gibbons' clean-cut contribution to the anthology (see over for excerpt).

FACING PAGE: A montage of styles used to illustrate leading feminist Germaine Greer's testimony (top) and that of prominent author and film critic George Perry.

NASTY TALES IS DIRECTED TOWARDS YOUNG PEOPLE -- WHAT YOU MIGHT PERHAPS CALL HIPPIES. IT IS UNDERGROUND IN THE SENSE OF ALTERNATIVE SOCIETY MIGHT BE A BETTER DESCRIPTION. THE WHOLE THING OF SETTING UP A DIFFERENT FORM OF LIFE STYLE...

ENCOURAGING PEOPLE TO LIVE OFF THE LAND, TO LIVE IN COMMUNES, TO HAVE A BETTER DIET, TO BE BETTER HUMAN BEINGS!

I SAY, I SAY, I SAY!

HOW CAN YOU LIVE OFF THE LAND UNDERGROUND?*

* JOKE -ED.

THERE WAS GENERAL LAUGHTER...

HA H

HEE H

THERE ARE LOTS OF PEOPLE WHO ARE UNHAPPY ABOUT SEX AND FEEL GUILTY ABOUT IT. ALL THAT NASTY TALES DOES IS SOMETIMES POKE A LITTLE FUN AT IT ...

IT IS IN NO WAY ADVOCATING UNUSUAL SEX ...

Art: Dave Gibbons, The Trials of Nasty Tales [1973].

This was primarily as a fund raiser for recent court fees. Like **Nasty Tales**, **Oz** was no stranger to legal battles, having had an extremely high profile court case itself in 1971. **Oz** was formed by Australian Richard Neville, Jim Anderson and the "freak with a briefcase" Felix Dennis, the magazine's business manager.

When the three invited minors to edit their Adults Only magazine— the infamous 'School Kids' issue—it didn't sell particularly well, and had been dismissed as a failed experiment when, months later, the obscene publications squad burst into the **Oz** office in Holland Park, locked doors, disconnected phones and began carting away 'evidence.'

Summoned to appear at London's Old Bailey, where England's most significant crimes are heard, Neville, Dennis and Anderson were accused of having "conspired with certain other young persons to produce a magazine which would corrupt the morals of children and other young persons" and was intended to "arouse and implant in the minds of those young people lustful and perverted desires."

The **Oz** defendants' lawyer was John Mortimer (author of **Rumpole of the Bailey** novels), and the trial was marked by farce and humour. It would last six weeks and become Britain's longest obscenity trial.

Like the **Nasty Tales** trial, the focus was on the content of the cartoons. In **Oz** the legal action was over a montage that featured the children's character Rupert the Bear, whose head was stuck on top of some Robert Crumb cartoons (again!) so that it appeared Rupert was having rampant sex and wielding a huge penis.

Bizarrely, the **Oz** defendants were subjected to forced haircuts, giving a clue as to their real crimes. As Charles Shaar Murray, one of

RIGHT: Martin Sudden's rendition of a key point in the defence's closing statement.

FACING PAGE: Not the best defence witness for Nasty Tales, a stoned Edward Barker takes the stand.

the original **Oz** School Kid editors, wrote in **The Guardian** newspaper 30 years later, "This was a cultural war disguised as an obscenity trial." Jonathon Green agreed in his book **All Dressed Up**, "The Establishment did not like **Oz** or the counter culture that it represented—when Neville naively, injudiciously, combined 'children' with the usual irritants of sex and drugs and rock, they saw their chance."

It was all about the old reactionary past, represented by Judge Michael Argyle, against the new generation of hippies and counter culture. Supporters of **Oz** demonstrated outside the Court and marches were held across London, even burning a picture of Argyle.

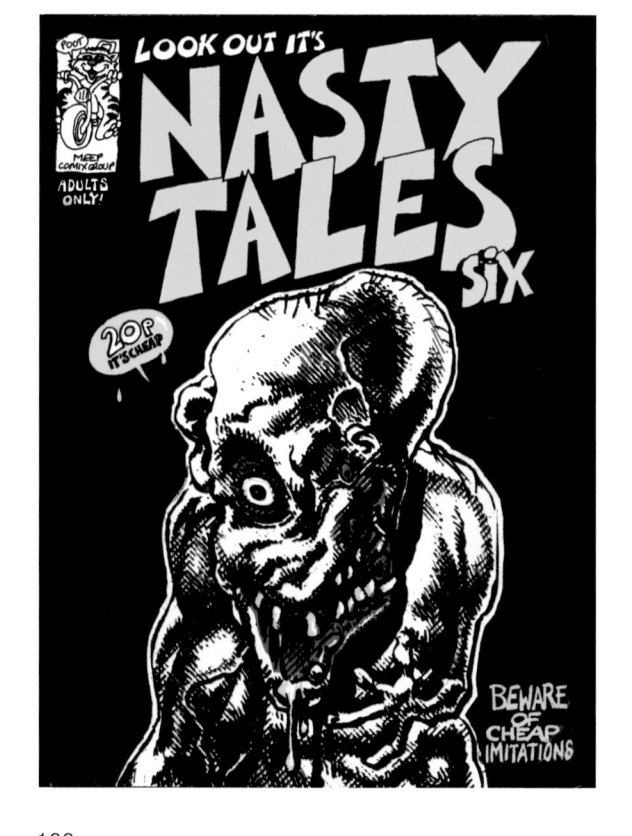

Controversy erupted when the sentences were handed down—15 months and deportation for Neville, 12 months for Anderson and just nine months for Dennis because, according to Argyle, he was "very much less intelligent than his fellow defendants."

Illustrating Argyle's amazing ability to be so wildly inaccurate at character assessment, surely a major handicap for a high court judge, it should be pointed out that Dennis went on to become one of Britain's most powerful magazine magnates and the country's 56th richest man.

But Judge Argyle had so thoroughly misrepresented the defendants and their case—dismissing highly respected and credible witnesses as "*so-called* defence experts"—that the conviction was overruled on appeal. Neville and Anderson nevertheless left the country soon afterwards. The reactionary Argyle retired in 1988 for a gentler pursuit, that of taking up a campaign for the return of the death penalty in the UK.

Cozmic Comics

After the trial Felix Dennis tried to raise extra funds through **Cozmic Comics**. It was, like so many, a collection of US reprints with some new UK material. However, it soon spun off 20 oneshots with British-created comix like Joe Petagno's **It's Only Rock 'n' Roll Comix**, Chris Welch's **Ogoth and Ugly Boot** and Mike Weller's **The Firm**. Young and eager artists including Dave Gibbons and Brian Bolland did their early work here, before becoming major props in mainstream super-hero comics, with Gibbons drawing the seminal **Watchmen** and Bolland responsible for breaking Batgirl's back in **Batman: The Killing Joke**.

In 1974 Bolland self-published a comic, "50 copies of something called **Suddenly at 2 o'Clock in the Morning**, containing my highly politically incorrect *Little Nympho in Slumberland*—a spoof of Winsor McCay's *Little Nemo in Slumberland*, obviously. It didn't seem offensive at the time, but later I got a lot of stick about that strip from feminists, quite rightly."

ABOVE: 1973's May offering from Cozmic, Zip Comics #1. Behind a Rand Holmes cover, this oneshot features all homegrown material by Edward Barker, Dave Gibbons and a range of talented Brits.

LEFT: Elevated to their own title by Cozmic Comics, the Chris Welch-drawn biker heroes face the multiple horrors of a post-Apocalypse London [1973].

FACING PAGE: 1972's Nasty Tales #6, a bumper issue with reprints of "The Legion of Charlies" (part 2) plus a Rich (Gore) Corben strip and frame enlargement for the cover. It also includes Crumb's "A Gurl" and Sheridan's horror strip "The Answer." New material from Edward and the Farren/Rowley and Welch "Ogoth and the Sky Women" were featured too.

189

Giving the work wider exposure, **Graphixus** [1978], a British underground anthology title edited by Mal Burns, reprinted *Little Nympho* with new covers by Bolland. Other British comics artists who worked on **Graphixus** and have since gained higher profiles included Garry (Marvelman) Leach and John (Hellblazer) Higgins. But, like so many British attempts, **Graphixus** was short-lived, lasting only five and a half issues (a 5b) although Burns found another publisher and went on to co-edit another breakthrough title, **Pssst!**. However, despite its

slicker production values, with full colour glossy pages, and its national newsstand distribution, it failed to survive its launch year, folding with issue 10 [October, 1982].

Felix Dennis' **Cozmic Comics** lasted three years, until 1975, outliving its parent title **Oz** which ended in 1973. However, 1975 did see a pivotal new comic continue the underground tradition. Entitled **Brainstorm Comix,** it would become one of the most influential and successful British underground comics ever.

Talbot's journey into delirium

Brainstorm was the creation of artist Bryan Talbot and publisher Lee Harris. Harris ran a head shop in London's antiques and hippies magnet Portobello Road called Alchemy, "…selling anything associated with alternative culture at the time. I dispensed balms from the East, exotic herbal highs in large jars, perfumed oils, incense. I thought of myself as some sort of 'medicine head'."

A 20 year-old Talbot made friends with Harris in 1973 and after the artist had been to visit Felix Dennis at **Cozmic Comics** Harris agreed to publish Talbot's work. "I was in London to submit a strip to **Cozmic Comics,**" recalls Talbot. "The strip was accepted, but they never produced another issue, never paid me and I never saw the artwork again." The strip was a forerunner to *Chester P Hackenbush, The Psychedelic Alchemist* who would become a crucial figure in British underground comix. Asked about the unusual name, Talbot admits to having swiped it from his friend Chester West and Groucho Marx's Dr. Hackenbush from the film *A Day at The Races*.

"The first story was little more than a picture book for trippers," said Talbot. "I'd been studying classic book illustrators such as Arthur Rackham and was trying to produce a synthesis of their styles and US underground styles… And yes, I was trying to be a smart arse."

Brainstorm tapped so well into the hippie trippy zeitgeist that it was selling 12,000 copies per issue at its height. But like all undergrounds,

RUPERT FINDS GIPSY GRANNY

MY CURIOSITY IS AROUSED... I'LL JUST TAKE A PEEK AN' THEN SPLIT!

TEE HEE

1 " It looks just like a ball to me," " Open it and see."

LEFT: Oz's Unholy Trio, the men behind the infamous 1970 Schoolkids Issue—Jim Anderson, Richard Neville and Felix Dennis.

BELOW: The women in front of the infamous Schoolkids issue. Edited by under 16s for over 18s, this brought the three publishers before the bench for sentencing.

FACING PAGE: Schoolkid humour from Oz 28. Rupert Bear, that British institution of 'innocent delightfulness,' with his face superimposed on a lewd R. Crumb sketch. Other drawings included Rupert charging towards granny with a massive erection. The court was not amused.

192

successful or otherwise, cash flow was the perennial problem that closed down **Brainstorm** after six issues in 1977.

Hunt Emerson and Ar:Zak Comix

The '70s also saw the formation of the Birmingham Arts Lab, "A loose collective of creative people working together with no pretensions or 'stars' among them," Emerson recalls. The Arts Lab (using a publishing identity of Ar:Zak) grew to become one of the country's leading alternative centres for the arts and Emerson, along with Paul Fisher, David Holton and Martin Reading, was at its heart. "There was lots of avant garde theatre, cinema and music. It was very odd."

He was initially lured there as an artist, rather than as a cartoonist, and helped run the printing press. He briefly left but was pulled back by Reading, to help design promotional material for the cinema. The press was supposed to be profit making, "But it never worked like that." Emerson and others somehow convinced the Arts Lab that they could make money producing comics. Some of Emerson's earliest work produced there included **Large Cow Comix** and **Outer Space Comix** (both written by Brian Hills) plus **The Adventures Of Mr. Spoonbiscuit** and **Pholk Comix** [all created in 1974]. These were small digest-format comix, with **Pholk** mixing two themes, adapting traditional English songs into comic strips.

Much to his astonishment, Emerson's frenetic surreal swirl of lines coupled with his skill as a storyteller, a humourist and a cartoonist soon earned him a place at the very top of the underground movement. To this day he continues to express surprise about his status, saying with his trademark embarrassed chortle, "I've become a part of history."

Having independently established themselves in the underground scene Chris Welch and Hunt Emerson then joined forces to create the Konvention of Alternative Komix or KAK, Britain's first-such event. It took place in 1976 in Birmingham and was intended to galvanize the

UK underground movement. Its success ensured a follow-up the next year, but sadly it was the last one as other commitments took priority.

In 1976 Emerson also contributed and edited **Street Comix,** the Art Lab's biggest comic title. The first issue was actually a giveaway with a non-comics publication, **Street Poems**, but then appeared in its own right from issue 2. **Street Comix** saw many cartoonists pass through its pages including UK national newspaper **The Guardian's** multi-award winning contributor Steve Bell, plus the ubiquitous Bryan Talbot, co-creator of *League of Extraordinary Gentlemen* Kev O'Neil (at the time with children's comics publisher IPC Magazines) and Suzy Varty, the most prolific of the UK's female underground creators. **Street Comix** lasted six issues until 1978. Emerson left the Arts Lab the following year and teamed up with what would become Britain's most successful underground publisher, Knockabout Comics.

Near myths

Meanwhile, out of Edinburgh came Rob King's **Near Myths** [1978], the first British "ground-level" comic. A bridge from the early underground titles to the modern day UK mainstream, it could be considered a forerunner to the highly influential **Warrior** [1982] which introduced the US to the work of a host of top name creators (Alan Moore, Steve Dillon, et al) and characters such as *V for Vendetta* and *Marvelman*, plus psychotic cyborg *Axel Pressbutton*, who had begun life in an underground strip by Alan Moore (under the pseudonym of Kurt Vile) for alternative music mags **Dark Star** and **Sounds**, before being reprinted in **Rip-Off Comix** #8 [1981]. Moore, now celebrated as one of the greatest ever comics writers, actually began his career as a cartoonist with yet more cat comix through his *Maxwell the Magic Cat* strip under another nom de plume (Jill de Ray) for his local newspaper **The Northants Post** [1979-83].

But when **Near Myths** launched, it was the closest thing the UK had to the French trippy sci-fi comic **Metal Hurlant** [1975] and their savagely political **A Suivre** [1978].

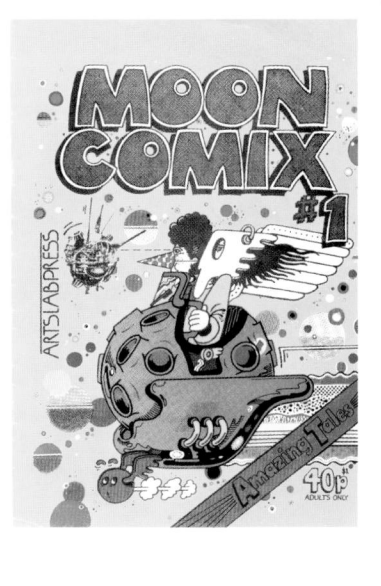

ABOVE: Birmingham's Arts Lab Press produced a range of comix under the Ar:Zak imprint. The David Noon edited Moon Comix #1 [1977] included early Hunt Emerson work ("The Wooden Hose of Troy starring Helen Highwater") and Noon's own cover-starring Zolbo. 1978's Moon Comix #3 is of special interest, containing a never-reprinted out of continuity Luther Arkwright strip (Chapter III) co-starring Mick Farren and Chris Welch's Cozmic creations, Ogoth and Ugly Boot.

LEFT: Bryan Talbot cover art to Brainstorm #2 (1976) starring his psychedelic alchemist Chester P. Hackenbush.

FACING PAGE: An excerpt from a 1994 Suzie Varty comic strip for the Brighton based GirlFrenzy #4 ("Articles, strips and no make-up tips").

Near Myths was also important for introducing Bryan Talbot's seminal *The Adventures Of Luther Arkwright.*

It was the place where comics' bette noir, Grant Morrison, cut his storytelling teeth. Still at school, the Scot created *Gideon Stargrave* for #2 (a dandy super-spy heavily influenced by Michael Morcock's Jerry Cornelius novels—as was Talbot's Arkwright, to whom he bears a strong resemblance). Stargrave featured throughout Morrison's work, most notably 20 years later in his DC/Vertigo opus, **The Invisibles**. But the writer still cringes about his early material, "Pretty embarrassing stuff—the work of a 17 year old who doesn't get out of the house."

Other contributors to **Near Myths** included Graham Manley and Tony O'Donnell, both of whom went on—bizarrely—to work for the ultra-conservative Scottish **Beano** and **Dandy** publishers, DC Thomson. **Near Myths** closed in 1980 after five issues, and is now a rare collectable as in 1983 the publisher's entire stock of back issues was pulped.

Taking the Pssst!

Two years after **Near Myths**' demise, Serge Boissevain's **Pssst!** magazine appeared. Preceded by an innovative pre-launch London nightclub party, that Boissevain invited artists to attend with their portfolios, it became clear this was to be something very different.

Across its 10 issues of wildly eclectic content, it was a title worthy of the cliche of being "ahead of its time." Boissevain, a wacky French philanthropist, aimed to create a European-style title containing a mixture of adventure, humour and experimental strips. Contributors attracted by the publisher's flair and non-conformity included underground mainstays John Higgins and Mike Matthews plus Dave

RIGHT: Spotlighting Luther Arkwright, Bryan Talbot's cover art to Near Myths #3 [1978].

FACING PAGE: Grant Morrison's "pretty embarrassing stuff," Gideon Stargrave.

Thorpe, Angus McKie, Shakey Kane, John Watkiss and Paul Gravett. It also became the new home for Luther Arkwright [#2-10], its only serial. Beginning with reworked **Near Myths** reprints, Boissevain later published the first volume of the novel in 1982.

Further underlining Boissevain's unique approach, Gravett—who later managed the prestigious Cartoon Art Trust with Prince Philip as its patron—took the **Pssst!** double-decker bus on a promotional tour around the UK in "the coldest winter in years." While the bus was parked on an Ipswich local government lot, several visiting employees

were shocked at the "semi-salacious" art. The **Pssst!** team was informed they were no longer welcome and hounded out of town.

Ultimately **Pssst!** failed because it was too experimental. However it was the forerunner of many comics magazines and blazed the trail for titles like **Escape**, **Heartbreak Hotel** and the Tank Girl-starring **Deadline**.

At the start of the '80s, many frustrated comics creators were producing their own small self-published titles, but without focus. So in 1981 Paul Gravett, then **Pssst!'s** promotions and traffic manager, set up a mail order distribution company, Fast Fiction, consolidating these disparate talents into one cohesive voice. Dubbed "The Man at the Crossroads" by **From Hell** artist Eddie Campbell, Gravett was, and still is, one of the key figures in British comics.

Along with writer/artist Phil Elliott, Gravett would set up stalls at comic marts around London, promoting individual creators' titles. It became a huge success, selling work as diverse as Glenn Dakin's self-published strips and **Barefoot Gen**, one of the first Japanese mangas to be translated into English. Gravett and Elliott soon started publishing their own showcase anthology, also called **Fast Fiction**. Early contributors included Campbell, Elliot and Ian Wieczorek.

There's no escape

Gravett cranked his publishing ventures up a notch when in 1983 he and partner Peter Stanbury launched **Escape** magazine. "Our models for **Escape** were looking as much in Europe as the US," he recalled. "There is no denying the fundamental example set by Spiegelman and Mouly's **RAW**," he added, "bridging the US underground with its European counterparts."

Escape raised the profile of many artists, including Eddie Campbell, Paul Johnson and Rian Hughes, who ironically ended up at AOL Time-Warner's DC Comics. **Escape** had become an essential outlet for new talent and a well-deserved success. So much so that its final nine issues "did a **RAW**" and were published by Britain's kings of graphic

novels, Titan Books. **Escape** lasted 19 issues, until 1989, spawning two key graphic novels, **London's Dark** by James Robinson (now a Hollywood screenwriter) and Paul Johnson plus **Violent Cases** by the then-unknown team of Neil (**Sandman**) Gaiman and Dave (**Cages**) McKean.

Escape's success meant Gravett relinquishing Fast Fiction to Phil Elliott, then Ed Pinsent, another comic creator. It shut in the early '90s, but not before bringing the small press scene together and inspiring Pete Ashton's BugPowder and Slab-O-Concrete's own distribution.

INTERVIEWS
SERGE CLERC IN A HURRY AND BANTER WITH BIFF

While **Escape** was vital to the growth of the UK alternative, it was rarely controversial. A Manchester based publisher, however, was already well-known to the police before they began producing their **Lord Horror** and **Meng & Ecker** comics in 1989.

Savoy Books: bad to the bone

The company was formed by David Britton and Michael Butterworth in 1976 and to say that their publishing tastes were wide-ranging would

be a gross understatement. Publishing obscure writers and reprinting abstruse classics, from Henry Treece to Jack Trevor Story and Charles Platt, Savoy continually and deliberately courted controversy. When James Anderton became Chief Constable of the Greater Manchester Police (also in 1976) a 15-year feud started, with the police raiding Savoy's premises over 50 times, often with sledge hammers.

More than any other comix publisher in the UK, Savoy can truly lay claim to the title "underground", both in content and mentality. They published one of the first UK-originated graphic novels in 1976, James Cawthorn's **Stormbringer**, an adaptation of Michael Moorcock's **Elric of Melnibone** fantasy novel and had a healthy relationship with New English Library (NEL) distributing an average of 25,000 copies of their first 21 titles. Then, in 1981, continual police harassment and the collapse of NEL forced them into liquidation, but they continued trading under other Savoy names.

Britton then wrote the **Lord Horror** novel [1989] for Savoy, a story about a sadistic and erudite Nazi loosely based on the World War II Nazi collaborator "Lord Haw Haw." Several weeks after its publication it was seized along with the comics. Police raids continued up to October 1997 when Customs officials took over with the seizure of material being returned from the US in April 1999. Britton was jailed in 1993 for four months, serving two. This was his second sentence for publishing "seditious material."

The charge leveled at the **Lord Horror** novel was eventually overturned, but Savoy soon lost the 'Battle of the Comics'. Without a jury trial, July 1996 saw 4,000 **Lord Horror** and **Meng & Ecker** titles deemed obscene and destroyed by the police; the first time this had

LEFT: Savoy's Meng & Ecker #9. Art: Kris Guido.

FACING PAGE: Escape #1's impressive line-up included Serge Clerc, Hunt Emerson, Myra Hancock, Rian Hughes and Phil Elliott (cover).

happened in relation to comicbooks. All previous hearings had been given jury trials that had overturned whatever restrictive measures the authorities sought to impose. Savoy wasn't that lucky.

Presiding at the trial of **Lord Horror** and **Meng & Ecker** in July 1992, Judge Gerard Humphries revealed his obvious bias against comic readers in his summation, stating, "It is luridly bound and it is more likely than novels, etc, to attract attention from the less literate."

Unabashed, Savoy continued the comicbook exploits of Lord Horror in the Kris Guidio drawn **Hard Core Horror** 1-4, "seamlessly mixing eroticism and elegance with ultraviolence and sadism."

Issue 5 was illustrated by long-time Savoy collaborator John Coulthart, whose bleak and rigid depictions of death camp architecture were both disturbing and intricate. Following 15 issues, with the last eight using the subtitle of *Reverbstorm*, readers have been promised, "The series will conclude in spectacular fashion with 40 pages of painted/digital artwork combining Cubist / Expressionist influences with elements from all the previous issues. Wild images at the apex of the *ricorso*. A fitting end to a series like no other."

The repugnant **Meng & Ecker** comic, a spin-off from **Lord Horror**, recounted the misadventures of the mutant twins of Dr Josef Mengele. Gross and depraved, the stories had the twins wreaking absolute havoc and carnage, while indulging in impossible sexual exploits and throwing out nihilistic and wildly non-PC one-liners.

Heavy handed irony has been Savoy's main weapon against the status quo, but often it has come across as totally gratuitous, leading a 1996 appeals court judge to comment that their publications were likely to upset right-thinking people.

Toilet humour

"Right thinking people" were also in for a shock when, in Newcastle in 1979, a uniquely British phenomenon was born to proud parents Simon and Chris Donald. The teenage Geordie brothers self-published 150 copies of a small comic. Their baby was called **Viz** and would become not only the best-selling comic in the UK ever, tipping 1.25 million per issue, but also the best selling magazine, alongside commercial giants the BBC's **Radio Times** and IPC's **Woman**.

Taking the Punk ethos of energy, aggression, DIY and an "up yours, mate" attitude, **Viz** turned British comics on their head. Its roots were firmly planted in the tradition of children's weekly comics **The Beano** and **The Dandy** but whereas the Dundee-based publishing giant DC Thomson had the mildy anarchic Roger the Dodger, Minnie the Minx and the Bash Street Kids, **Viz** went for the adult jugular

LEFT: Before quite frankly becoming the saviour of Marvel Comics' X-Men, "Frank Quitely" drew for the Scottish underground title Electric Soup, revelling in showing his two-colour love of veteran Scots comics artist Dudley D. Watkins.

FACING PAGE: In their ninth issue, Savoy's Meng & Ecker delight in testing out an old guillotine on a museum curator. Art by Kris Guido (1994).

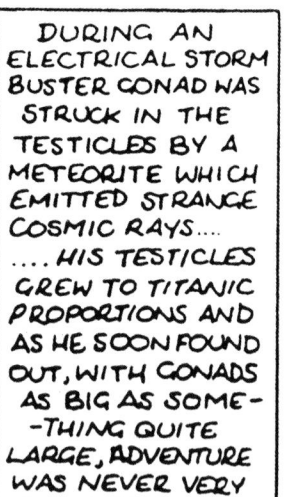

with *Nobby's Piles, Sid the Sexist* and *The Fat Slags.* No story was too ludicrous or too offensive.

The strips were based on a familiar visual formula with over 20 pictures per page and almost every strip a single pager. This was a look that the whole of Britain had grown up with since the 1940s and was a masterstroke. It allowed adults to have a damn good laugh while simultaneously wallowing in nostalgia and reading a fart and fanny-packed *Benny Hill Show* kind of story.

Word of mouth spread as the circulation grew through pubs and student union bars in universities across the country. The price and print quality went up and the Donalds brought in Simon Thorp and Graham Dury to help out. By the mid-eighties **Viz** was selling 4,000 in the North East of England.

New characters like *Finbarr Saunders and his Double Entendres* and *Buster Gonad and his Unfeasibly Large Testicles* were added and in 1985, despite or because of its outrageous content, **Viz** finally achieved national distribution through Virgin record shops. One Virgin employee was so impressed with the magazine he left to set up a publishing company to run it. John Brown recalled, "From the moment I saw it I knew that it had the potential to be huge—comedy and sex are the two biggest general interest subjects in the world."

Over the next five years **Viz**'s sales grew to a staggering 500,000 an issue as it quickly became a national institution, simultaneously receiving plaudits and pariah-hood. The majority of readers were male twenty-somethings but **Viz** boasted the largest female readership of any comic at 75,000 (a mere 15% of the total sales). Yet, despite **Viz**'s continued growth there were accusations of stagnation as the formula began to run dry, something the editorial team boasted about, with such cover lines as "48 pages packed with all your favourite joke."

But new characters were soon added including *Millie Tant,* an ugly feminist and politically correct extremist—everything **Viz** was not!

Regardless of its offensive nature, **Viz** always avoided any serious attacks on politics, and so was never regarded by the authorities as a subversive threat in the way that **Nasty Tales**, **Oz** and **Lord Horror** were.

continues on p206

LEFT: Headlining Hitler, France and Princess Di, nobody escapes the caustic humour of Viz.

FACING PAGE: An excerpt from one of the Donald Brothers 20-panel pages, featuring a star of the Viz firmament, Buster Gonad.

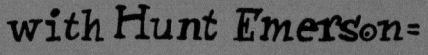

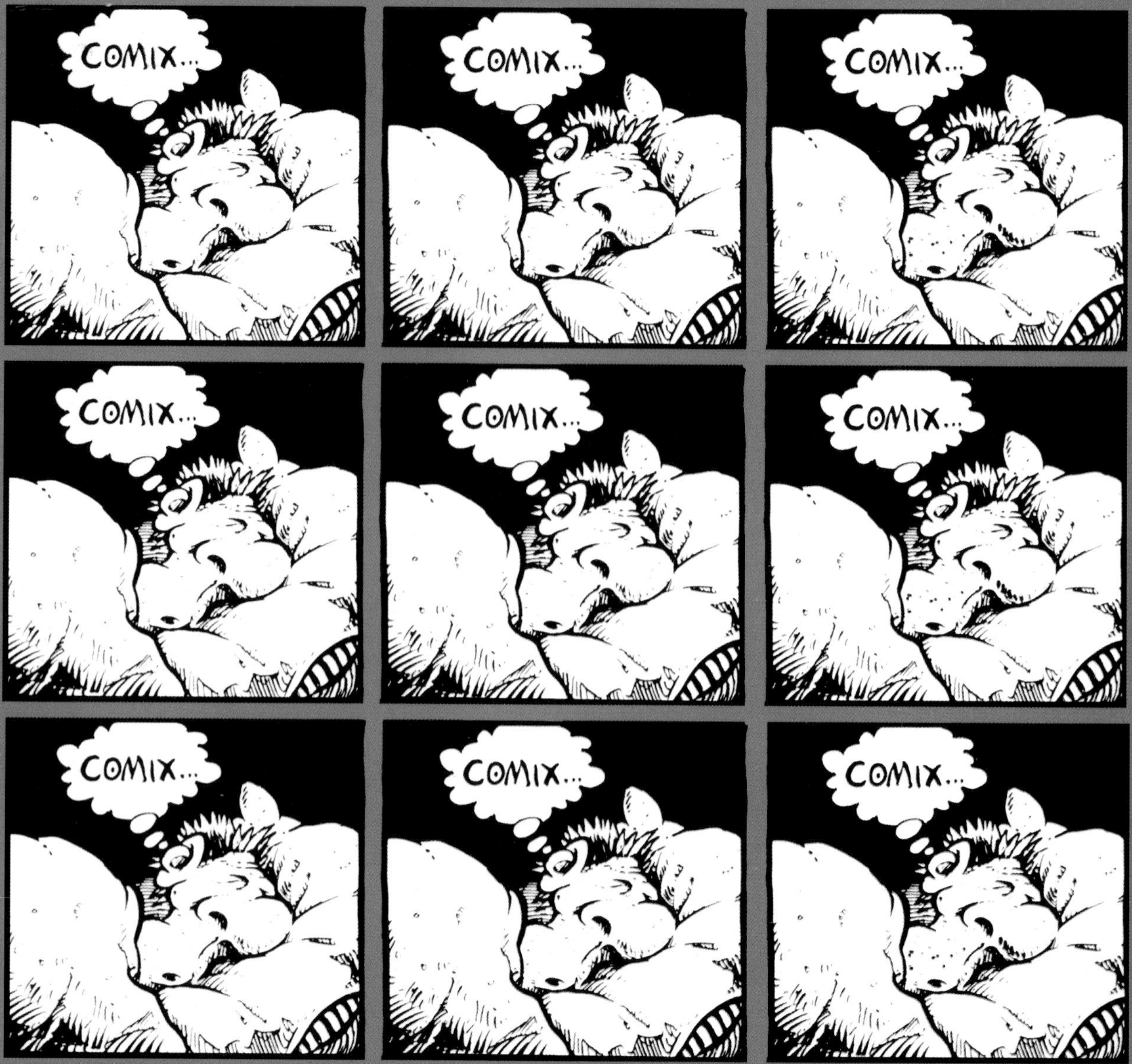

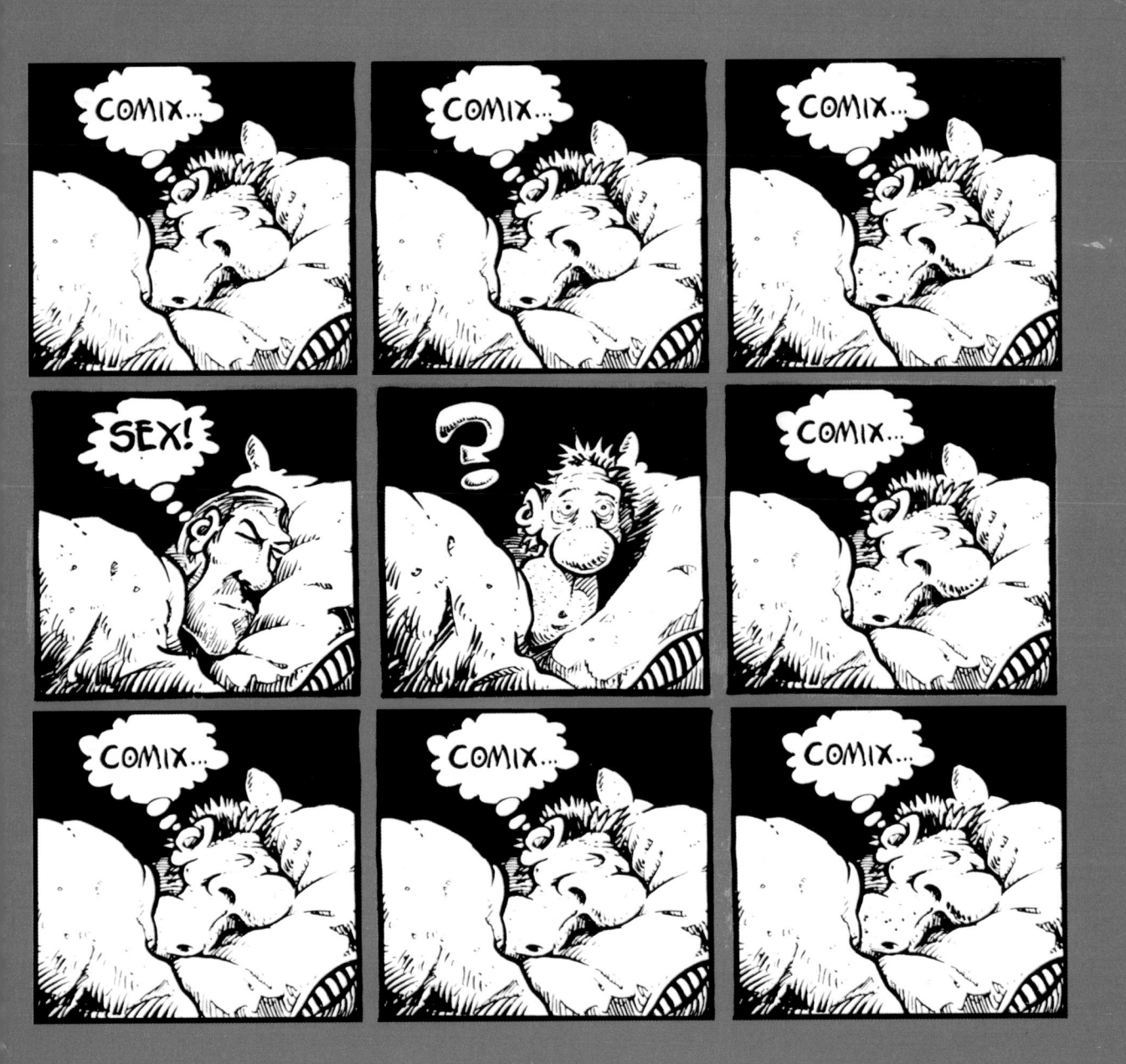

With such a huge success it was inevitable that pretenders to the **Viz** throne would try to copy the formula and in the late Eighties/early Nineties a slew of titles appeared, including the pithily-titled **Zit, Poot, Gas, Smut** and many more. Most failed after a few issues but a few were moderately successful, filling the gap between issues of the phenomenal bimonthly, among them **Oink** [1988], **Brain Damage** [1988] and **Talking Turkey** [1991].

Today **Viz**'s sales are slightly less than the dizzying heights they reached in the Eighties but after several TV cartoon spin-offs and numerous annuals and merchandise, it has achieved something few undergrounds even aspire to, having assured itself a place in its nation's heart forever.

Knockabout

Despite all the work by creators, editors and publishers over the years, the true guardians of UK underground comics are undoubtedly Knockabout's Tony and Carol Bennett. More than any other publisher they have been the most constant and prolific importer, distributor and producer of counter-culture titles.

In the late '70s a friend of Hunt Emerson's, Carol, was running a head shop, Japetus, in Birmingham, where Emerson was first exposed to the American undergrounds. Tony Bennett had a long history in book publishing and distribution—primarily in poetry and "arty" titles—and supplied books to Japetus. Tony and Carol eventually

moved to London, married and formed a subdivision of their perhaps too ironically titled company, Hassle Free Press.

Acquiring the reprint and distribution rights to **The Fabulous Furry Freak Brothers** from Gilbert Shelton, the husband and wife team renamed their company Knockabout Comics in 1980 and launched their anthology title of the same name. "I'd lost touch with Tony and Carol for a few years," recalled Emerson, "Then they rang up and asked if I'd like to contribute to **Knockabout** and I was delighted!"

The Knockabout anthologies featured a wealth of talent ranging from such US cartoonists as Justin Green and Kim Deitch to UK artists Graham "Pokketz" Higgins and Savage Pencil. But the shining star was always Emerson.

Knockabout Comics would become Emerson's most prolific publisher over the next 23 years, releasing 20 of his comics and large format albums including zany yet faithful adaptations of **Lady Chatterley's Lover** and **The Rime of the Ancient Mariner** plus his own **Casanova's Last Stand**.

In the 1980s Knockabout imported **Weirdo** magazine and others including R. Crumb's huge volume of work. In a savvy move, and aware that some of Crumb's work may be deemed indecent by the fascistically strict laws concerning comics, they brought over single copies of each issue.

Only when Knockabout had successfully obtained the written assurances from Her Majesty's Customs & Excise that the titles were

'OBSCENE' ISSUE! $2.00

KNOCKABOUT Comics

CENSORED

CENSORED

CENSORED

ADULTS ONLY!

OUTRAGEOUS TALES FROM THE Old Testament

HUMAN SACRIFICE

Wrath of GOD

Deadly Tent Pegs

MURDER

ENORMOUS BOILS

JUDGES, KINGS and PROPHETS

THIS PAGE: Emerson also produced cover art and an interior strip for the benefit issue, Knockabout Comics #4 (left) and the "Wrath of God" strip for their Outrageous Tales from the Old Testament [1987, above].

FACING PAGE: Hunt Emerson finds a cheap model to pose for a cover caricature, himself. Knockabout's large format anthology, Seven Deadly Sins [1989] featured work by Alan Moore, Neil Gaiman, Kim Deitch, Bryan Talbot, Mike Matthews and Dave Gibbons as well as Emerson.

Name Dropping

*I RECOGNISE THE **FAECES** – I JUST CAN'T PUT A **NAME** TO IT!*

Some Like It Hot

FOOOM!

*GOT TO LAY OFF THAT **VINDALOO**!*

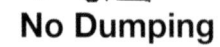

RIGHT: Alan Grant, John Wagner and Simon Bisley—bastions of such comics legends as Batman and Judge Dredd—set up Bad Press in 1997 to produce their own underground title, Shit the Dog.

Despite the UK news trade being happy to profit from a proliferation of sex and violence titles, they refused to handle Shit the Dog (!).

Legal counsel for one distributor, which handles the sex 'n' soccer daily, The Sport, advised them it would be deemed bad taste and indefensible in court.

Self-distributed and self-syndicated, their Shit went down the pan after four steaming issues.

No Dumping

CONSTIPATION!

acceptable did they import the bulk of their stock, thus avoiding the risk of any potentially costly seizures. Despite this, the archaic UK obscenity laws and Customs officials have been constant thorns in the company's side. Countless times Knockabout has been taken to court by the Crown Prosecution Service. Remarkably Knockabout has won every single case, but at great cost.

In 1984 they were tried for importing and distributing drug-related material (with strips by recidivists Crumb and Shelton). In order to pay for their legal fees they released the **Knockabout Trial Special**. Contributions came from a range of comics notables including Steve Bell, Biff, Brian Bolland, Duncan Campbell, Phil Elliot, Hunt Emerson, Dave Gibbons, Steve Gibson, Cliff Harper, Lee Harris, David Hine, Mike Matthews, Alan Moore, George Szostek, Bryan Talbot, Suzy Varty and Chris Welch.

1995 saw Terry Zwigoff's Crumb film released in the UK and naturally Knockabout wanted to promote their new Crumb book at the same time, but **My Trouble with Women** had already sold out. However their US distributor, Last Gasp, still had stock so Knockabout asked for copies to be sent back quickly to the UK.

Customs seized the returning books at Heathrow Airport under Section 42 of the Customs Consolidation Act (CCA) of 1876, yes 1876. The compilation was made up of Crumb's earlier imported work, of which every single item had previously been passed by Customs. However this arbitrary and objective Act of Law enables any Customs Officer to seize any publication which he or she considers "indecent or obscene" regardless of whether it was earlier certified acceptable for import, regardless of whether it was published in Britain or elsewhere, and regardless of whether it could be seized under the Obscene Publications Act of 1959. Now that's power.

The authorities knew they couldn't prosecute **My Troubles with Women** under the Obscene Publications Act as they would have to convince a jury that the book had "a tendency to corrupt and deprave," which would have been impossible. Whether people liked Crumb's work or not, there would be no problem establishing that it had artistic merit. With the artist's deliberate grungy and unflattering style, it could never be deemed pornographic.

In fact, HM Customs & Excise actually only objected to three drawings out of the book's total of 760. So, under the CCA, they confiscated Crumb's **My Trouble with Women** on the whim of a single Customs Officer, subject only to the confirmation of a magistrate who in practice must rely on the officer's evidence.

The **My Trouble with Women** case was the most high profile of many brought against imported comics under Section 42 with various fund-raising stunts staged—including one with the author of this book parachuting for the cause. While more money was offered for a jump without the chute, a four figure sum was still raised.

The case was tried in January 1996 and again Knockabout won, much to the huge embarrassment of the new head of Heathrow's Customs office and her entourage of seven suited and booted officials and legal eagles, up against a motley crew of ageing hippies.

Not only was Knockabout constantly in and out of court in the Nineties, but so were the specialist retailers who stocked comix. In 1993, London's Gosh Comics was unexpectedly raided by twelve burly Customs Officers who took eight hours to search through the stock for offences... using an alphabetical checklist which began with 'erection' and ended with 'urination'. Presumably 'anal' and 'zoophilia' were quite acceptable.

> ...they confiscated Crumb's **My Trouble With Women** on the whim of a single Customs officer...

The owner of the store, Josh Palmano, compromised and rather than face a lengthy legal battle agreed the stock could be destroyed in exchange for the prosecution being dropped. Among the work seized and later burned was **Peter Pank** by Spanish artist Max, an irreverent but relatively innocuous punk version of Peter Pan published by Knockabout. Despite **Peter Pank** being a UK title—making it nothing to do with HM Customs—thanks to an outdated law the authorities could have stated that according to the dreaded Customs Consolidation Act if illegally imported matter was stored together with home-grown produce the whole lot would be liable to confiscation. Yes, the Act covers both

BELOW: Killed by Hollywood "fixing", Alan Martin & Jamie (Gorillaz) Hewlett's Tank Girl had been the star of the UK alternative press, appearing monthly in almost every issue of Deadline [1988-95].

comics and foodstuffs. So merely by being racked alongside imported comics, titles could become 'tainted.' Which may explain why copies of **Wonder Woman** and **Tarzan** were also seized!

A skinhead thalidomide

The 1990s off-the-wall titles included Dix's **She Ate My Porridge**, Simon Henwood's **Johnny Pumpin** and black culture comix Marceeah, Wayne Massop's **Sphinx** and Bobby Joseph's **Skank** and its successor **Black Eye**. While **Skank** sank paying Olympic Gold Medallist Lindford Christie £15,000 because of their Lunchbox Christie strip, one true life comic couldn't even find a publisher willing to print it in the first place.

Londoners Pete Milligan and Brendan McCarthy grew up during the skinhead decade of the 1970s and with colourist Carol Swain produced **Skin**, a 48-page colour comic about an old friend, an aggressive rebel suffering from phocomelia, or "seal limbs." The humour and violence was such it was turned down first by a colour separation house, who refused to handle the art, and then by everybody approached, even publishers of the wildly sexist **Viz** and the darkly fascistic **Judge Dredd**.

Finally Tundra—an idealistic vanity publishing company set up by **Teenage Mutant Ninja Turtles** co-creator Kevin Eastman—took the book on, mere months before closing. Ironically, while Eastman and partner Peter Laird's heroes in a halfshell had started from nothing and ended making them millions, Tundra had started with millions and, within three years, ended with nothing. Except an eclectic publishing legacy including John Wagner and Alan Grant's schizoid Scot **The Bogie Man** (televised starring Robbie Coltraine), Ed Hillyer's **Skidmarks** and **Cobalt 60** by Mark Bode, son of US comix artist, Vaughn Bode.

Despite the closure of Tundra UK, plus Peter Pavement's innovative Slab-O-Conrete and Fast Fiction disappearing, there remains a thriving UK small press indie scene. However, the angry cutting edge of an underground born out of injustices in the Sixties and the violent backlash of punk in the late-'70s seems to be woefully lacking.

Art by Brendan McCarthy and Carol Swain, Skin [1991].

Art: Brian Bolland, Suddenly at 2 o'clock in the morning [1974].

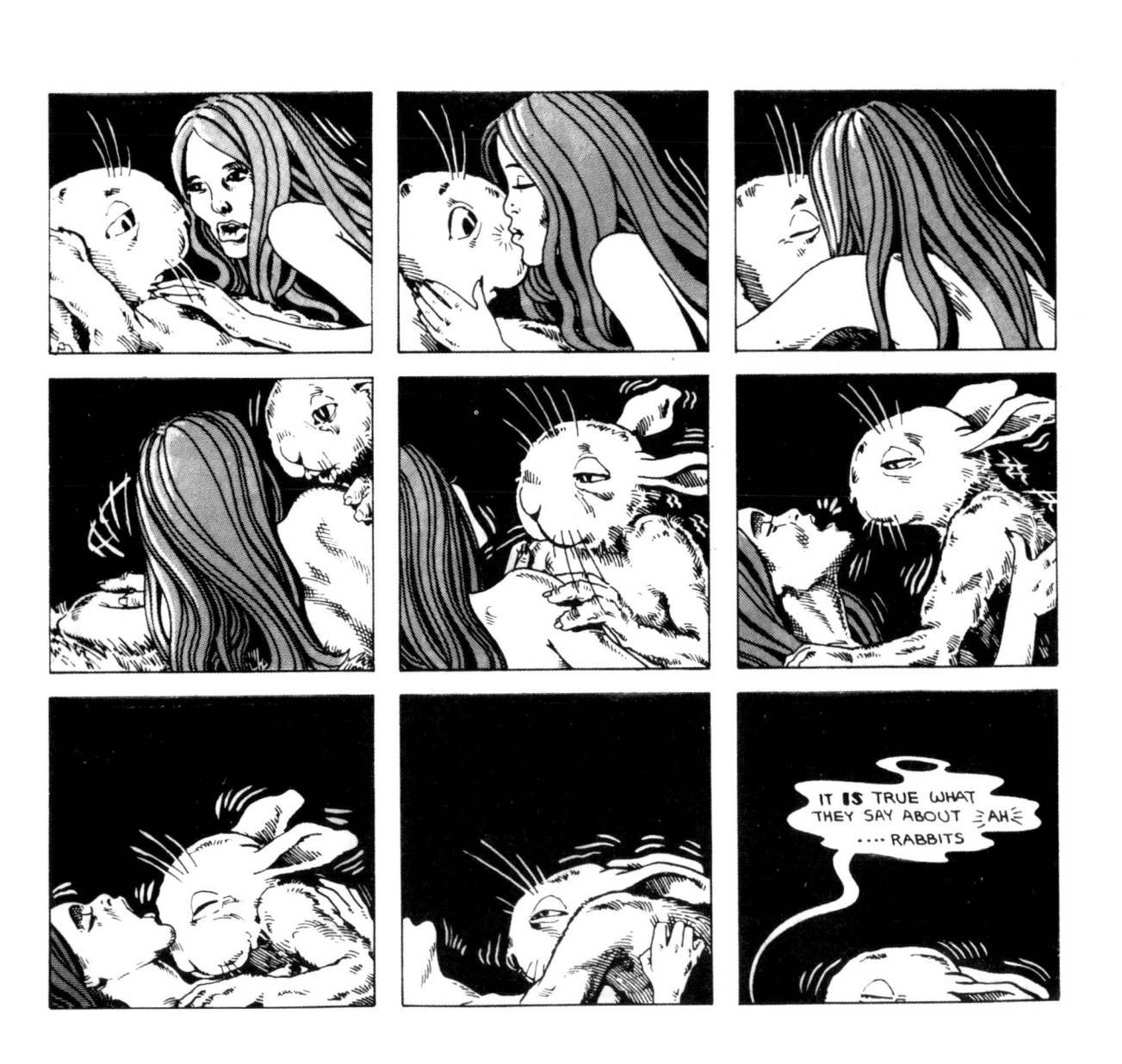

The Maus that RAWed

*In 1974 Art Spiegelman said, "As an art form, the comic strip is barely past its infancy. So am I. Maybe we'll grow up together." In 1992 his **Maus** graphic novel won him a Pulitzer Prize.*

ART Spiegelman, the man behind the ground-breaking anthology **RAW**, the Kafka of comics, is internationally renowned for his magnum opus, **Maus**.

First serialized in **RAW** from issue two [1980] it gave a compelling and deeply moving account of Vladek—Spiegelman's father—and his experiences as a survivor of the Nazi concentration camps.

The children of those who survived the Holocaust carry the task of untangling and comprehending what happened and then passing on their parent's often confusing and distressing stories to further generations. Spiegelman used his talents and situation to brilliantly achieve such a goal.

Maus had its origins in 1972, when Spiegelman wrote and drew the gut-wrenching 4-page strip *Prisoner on the Hell Planet*. It was published a year later in Head Press' underground anthology **Short Order Comix** #1, alongside work by Rick Griffin and Robert Crumb.

Spiegelman had previously been yet another of comix's rude rebels, producing such strips as *Jolly Jack Jack-Off* ("It's a treat to beat your meat in the Mississippi mud") for 1969's **Gothic Blimp Works** #7.

But in the '70s his work took on a more meaningful and personal tone. Using his position to publicly display the complexities he faced through being a child of a Holocaust survivor, Spiegelman's *Prisoner on the Hell Planet* told of the suicide of his mother in 1968 and the tremendous guilt he bore because of it. Not knowing how to deal with his feelings or how to respond to his parents and their complicated personalities, in the comic he narrates a situation where he blames his mother for killing him with her suicide and resents his father's traditions.

The text also touches on the themes of his father's Jewishness and the terrible remorse that Holocaust survivors all had to bear. Far from traditional content for underground comix, both would be major

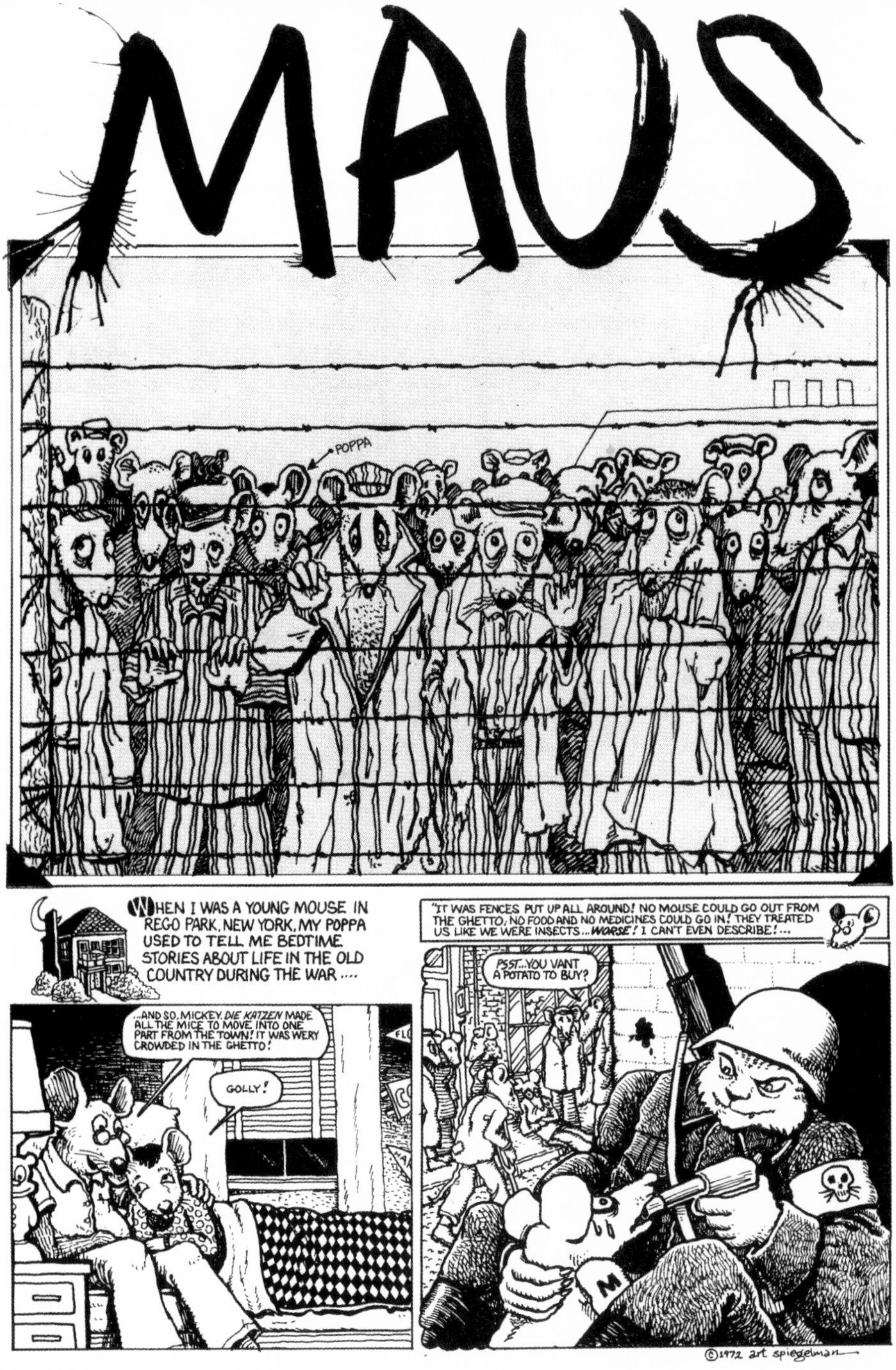

ABOVE: From behind the mask, Art Spiegelman.

LEFT: Alongside Captain Flashlight, Stinky the Pig and other outright humour strips, Maus made its inauspicious first appearance as a three page strip in Apex Novelties' Funny Aminals [1972]. The comic was edited by Terry Zwigoff, better known for his Crumb movie.

FACING PAGE: Spiegelman's self-affacing self portrait.

ABOVE: Leading Dutch artist Joost Swarte provided cover art for Spiegelman & Mouly's Raw #2 [1980], "The Graphix Magazine for Damned Intellectuals."

RIGHT: From Arcade #2 [1975], Spiegelman returned to the subject of his 1972 Prisoners of a Hell Planet strip, but less successfully using dreams rather than animals as a metaphor.

FACING PAGE: Spiegelman's Maus graphic novels.

subjects of **Maus**, which Spiegelman would fully develop in five years.

To best convey his story to generations raised on Disney, he employed the device of using cartoon stereotypes, drawing the Jews as mice and the Nazis as cats. He was also inverting Nazi propaganda which had portrayed Jews as a plague of rodents.

He did receive criticism for extending his anthropomorphic metaphor to portraying the Poles as pigs, but as the Polish attaché in New York once told him, "You know, the Nazis called us schwein, the German word for pig." Spiegelman replied, "And they called us vermin, the German word for mouse or rat."

The story of Vladek's struggle through pre-war Poland, up to the horrors of the ironically named Mauschwitz, is interspersed with conversations between father and son. These sections are equally emotionally intensive as Spiegelman Jr tries to understand his father's experiences and reconcile their differences. He finally integrated his *Prisoner on the Hell Planet* 'pilot' into the ongoing narrative of **Maus** when his father discovered the story several years later.

Vladek Spiegelman died in 1982, two years after his son had started serializing **Maus** in **RAW**. By then Spiegelman Jr had recorded numerous discussions with his father, providing the source material for the rest of the story.

The first volume of **Maus**, *My Father Bleeds History*, was collected and published by Pantheon (USA)/Penguin (UK) in 1986. It took another five years before the second and final chapter, *And Here My Troubles Began*, would be collected and published in 1991.

In 1992 **Maus** won an especially created Pulitzer Prize for fiction, the first and only comic ever to do so.

By the time Spiegelman had finished **Maus** it had taken up 295 pages and 13 years of the writer/artist's life. It stands today as one of the greatest achievements in sequential art and succeeds in transcending its humble underground comix beginnings to become a work of great literary merit, used in schools throughout the world.

Chapter 8:

Where have all the Flower Children Gone?

Long time passing, long time ago

"America wants stupid people in power. They want to remove anyone with any ideas or education, get rid of the bright people." ...GILBERT SHELTON

It's the 21ˢᵗ century. The anger has diminished, there's less hair if any, and a new generation has abandoned natural drugs for chemical cocktails. The hippie experiment has become a bywater of history except for having to step over a few old blokes you see in the street.

SO what happened to those rebellious cartoonists when they found they had nothing left to rebel against?

More than 30 years have passed since the heyday of underground comix and it's only to be expected that some of the scene's main players are no longer with us. What is surprising is that unlike such rock music contemporaries as Janis Joplin, Jimi Hendrix and Jim Morrison, so few of those who died actually crashed and burned in keeping with the 'Hope I Die Before I Get Old" credo of their generation.

First to go was **Cheech Wizard** creator Vaughn Bode. The self-acclaimed Cartoon Messiah died at his own hands in 1975 attempting an extreme autoerotic act which resulted in him hanging himself.

Flamed Out Funnies' Willy Murphy passed away the following year after a cold escalated to pneumonia. While six years later, Gilbert Shelton's **Fabulous Furry Brothers** collaborator—Dave Moriarty—fell victim to cancer. 1982 also saw the death of Rory Hayes, the **Bogeyman** cartoonist who many referred to as the Grandma Moses of the underground. True to the end, he died of a drug overdose.

> So few of those who died actually crashed and burned in keeping with the "Hope I Die Before I Get Old" credo of their generation.

In 1984 **Slow Death** and **The Legion of Charlies** artist Gregory Rodman Irons, who had gone from comix to tattooing, died in Bangkok, Thailand. Despite the exotic location, the cause was less colourful. He was killed while crossing a road. Ironically, very shortly before the accident, Irons had acquired a special "protective" magic serpent tattoo from a 100-year-old Buddhist monk. He was then hit by a bus and died. His body was later cremated but nobody other than the monk and the mortician saw his supposedly special tattoo.

Gothic Blimp Works contributor Roger Brand died of renal failure in 1986, a result of alcoholism. Another victim of a traffic accident was **Zap's** Rick Griffin who died in a motorbike accident in 1991, two years before the underground's major influence, Harvey Kurtzman, succumbed to Parkinson's disease. As Lee Marrs put it, "If all the influences on comix could be distilled into one delicious drop, its name would be Harvey Kurtzman."

Six years after Kurtzman's death, Joel Beck passed away. Often called the grandfather of underground comix by virtue of his 1965 publication of **Lenny of Laredo** (a 16-page biography of controversial comedian Lenny Bruce) he died of medical problems caused by tuberculosis and alcoholism exacerbated by a vicious mugging.

Aged 60, Canadian rebel Rand Holmes, passed away on March 15, 2002 awaiting chemotherapy treatment for Hodgkins lymphoma. Hero of the Canadian counter culture movement, Holmes regularly mocked Vancouver's mayor and violent vice squad during the early 1970s through his bespectacled stoner Harold Hedd.

Art so fine it'll blow your mind

Of the remainder, a handful appear to have gone missing in action but a number of the survivors have moved into painting and illustration, pre-eminent among them being Robert Williams.

One of the original **Zap** gang of seven, Williams sprang from the custom car culture of Southern California to the roots of the underground movement, but transcended the world of comix by forging a career as a leader among a new generation of imagist painters. Today he is best known as one of the world's most iconoclastic fine artists. Based in Hollywood, he enjoys a waiting list of hundreds of art patrons for his latest work.

Others who have carved a niche for themselves as painters and illustrators include **The Checkered Demon's** Skip Williamson (real name Mervyn, which explains the nickname—somehow the idea of a hippie trendsetter named Mervyn doesn't quite gell), as well as **The Life and Loves of Cleopatra** creator Harry Driggs, Guy (**Inner City Romance**) Colwell and **It Ain't Me Babe's** Willy—now Barbara—Mendes. Most have embraced the internet, and sell from virtual galleries as well as the more traditional bricks-and-mortar art houses.

Another who found fame as a painter is Frank "Foolbert Sturgeon" Stack. Now a Professor of Arts at the University of Missouri in Columbia, the **New Adventures of Jesus** writer/artist also still finds time for comics, most notably as a collaborator on Harvey Pekar's autobiographical **American Splendor**.

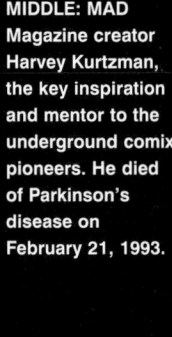

TOP: Glam rocker Vaughn Bode, who called himself "the pop-mystic transvestite and one man band." By mistake, he hanged himself on July 18, 1975. The king of hip hop art, his work inspired grafitti artists everywhere.

MIDDLE: MAD Magazine creator Harvey Kurtzman, the key inspiration and mentor to the underground comix pioneers. He died of Parkinson's disease on February 21, 1993.

LEFT: Surf fanatic and psychedelic poster wiz Rick Griffin died on August 18, 1991 on his classic Harley Softail. As a friend summed him up, "A great artist but a mediocre rider."

ABOVE AND RIGHT: Difficult to believe that he was ever involved in the development of underground comix—for which he created over 200 pages of art—Robert Williams is now one of the world's most iconoclastic fine artists with collectors of his work including Yoko Ono, Leonardo DiCaprio and Nicholas Cage. His 1993 created Juxtapoz is the second highest selling art magazine in the US with domestic sales alone topping 60,000.

223

RIGHT: A self portrait of Frank "Foolbert Sturgeon" Stack [2001], currently a Professor of Art at the University of Missouri.

FACING PAGE: Bill Griffith in his studio seeking inspiration while his world-famous creation, Zippy (right), finds his in a bottle of TNT.

When Rich Corben saw the underground dwindling he self published as Fantagor. But his profile has been greatly enhanced by work for Marvel (on **Hulk**) and DC (on **Hellblazer**), as has **Pudge, Girl Blimp** writer/artist Lee Marrs who began as an assistant on *Little Orphan Annie* but recently worked for DC's Vertigo "Mature Readers" imprint. Co-founder of the Alternative Features Service, distributing news, features and comics to underground newspapers, she is now established as an animator and computer graphics designer.

Pirates to the end

Closer to their underground roots are **Air Pirates** founder Dan O'Neill and *Zippy's* Bill Griffiths. While O'Neill continues his 1963 launched *Odd Bodkins* strip for a handful of San Francisco newspapers, Griffiths' *Zippy* goes from strength to strength. The pinheaded character

introduced in **Real Pulp Stories #16** [1970] has appeared in London's **The Guardian** newspaper and **National Lampoon**. Collections abound, produced by Last Gasp-Eco Funnies (**Pindemonium,** 1986), E. P. Dutton (**Kingpin,** 1987; **Pinhead's Progress,** 1989) and Penguin Books (**From A to Zippy,** 1991) while Fantagraphics Books has been producing **Pinhead Annuals** since 2000.

Jay Lynch has managed to keep one foot in the alternative humour camp. The **Nard 'n' Pat** creator's recent work has been for **MAD Magazine** as well as **The Simpsons** comics. He also contributes to the wholesome Archie Comics titles but, redressing the balance, for Art Spiegelman he designed many of Topps incredibly successful ugly children trading cards, the *Garbage Pail Kids.*

Captain Pissgums and his Pervert Pirates artist S Clay Wilson has moved into book illustration. Without compromising his style he has

produced a children's book called **Wilson's Grimm** (2000, Cottage Classics). "I always wanted to be a children's book illustrator," he says. "But I took some LSD and took a left turn graphically."

Kinney: From anarchy to spiritualism

Co-author of the book **Hidden Wisdom,** Jay (**Young Lust**) Kinney discovered Islamic Sufism, became editor of **Co-Evolution Quarterly** (1983-84) then editor-in-chief and publisher of the esoteric spiritual magazine **Gnosis** from its first issue in 1985 until it folded in 1999. In 2001 along with Paul Mavrides, his co-creator of many things

including **Anarchy Comics** (of which they never speak), he drew for *Infinite Matrix,* a shortlived online science-fiction magazine.

Mavrides was art director on *Grass*, a 1999 fast and funny docu-movie starring Woody Harrelson and Richard Nixon. Directed by Ron Mann, better known for his 1989 *Comicbook Confidential*, it tells how smoking grass began as a recreational activity of Hispanic and African minorities, but after being outlawed the number of pot smokers has risen from 60,000 to over 30 million. Mavrides has since completed *The Night Sky in the Dark Hotel,* a computer-generated 12-episode web comic for *Salon,* another online magazine.

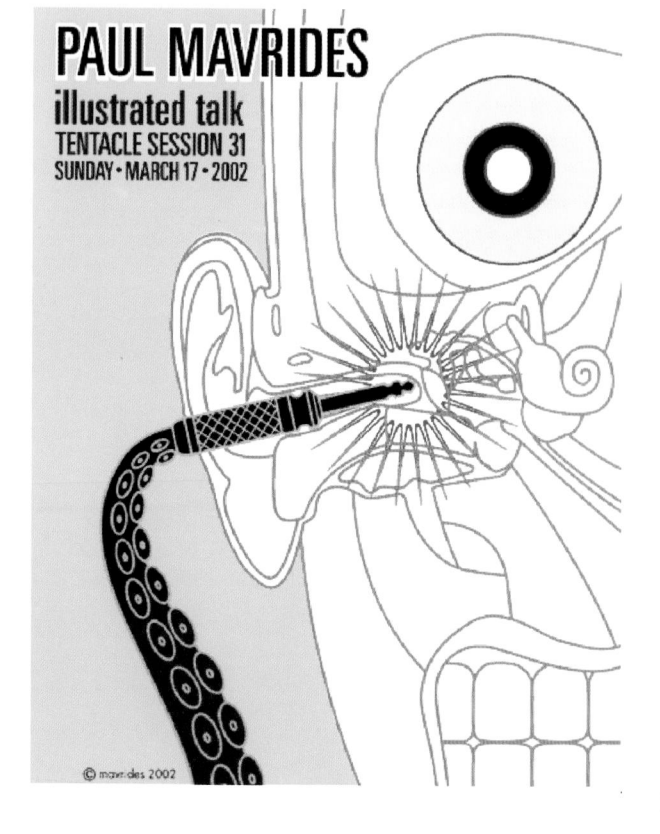

THIS PAGE: Looking somewhat out of place at a recent San Diego Comics Convention, S. Clay Wilson (left) displays his wares to a bewildered audience, keener on comics about spandex than sex. The king of gothic horror strips Rich Corben (above) looks as young as ever. He obviously keeps a portrait in his attic.

FACING PAGE: Paul Mavrides, better red than dead, alongside a poster for his 2002 Tentacle Session 31 illustrated talk.

The True Story of Famed Texas Gunslinger John Wesley Hardin

Lost Cause

Jack Jackson

ABOVE: Spain Rodriguez quickly removes his glasses for the camera.

RIGHT: Samuel Yates' cover to Jack Jackson's 1998 graphic novel John Welsey Hardin, a gunslinger made famous to hippies everywhere by the 1968 Bob Dylan album.

FACING PAGE: George Metzger introduces his 1978 lost continents comic (top). Victor Moscoso poses in front of his world of psychedelia with even the wall getting in on the act (bottom).

Like Kinney and Mavrides, Ted Richards is a comix cartoonist who has embraced new technology. The creator of **The Forty Year Old Hippie,** he is now a web designer and marketing consultant.

Waldo creator Kim Deitch is a frequent contributor to today's alternative comics and a regular in **Nickelodeon** magazine as is **Air Pirates** artist Bobby London, whose cartoons have appeared in a wide variety of magazines including **National Lampoon, Rolling Stone, Village Voice** and, more traditionally **The New York Times** and **Playboy**.

George (**Moondog**) Metzger emigrated to Canada in the mid-1970s to work in animation and is now a silkscreen printer while Justin Green—who created almost 100 underground comix—produces a regular strip, *Musical Legends Comix,* for Tower Records' **Pulse** magazine, and *Sign Game* for **Sign of the Times**. He also creates oil paintings and writes songs, playing the guitar a lot. "One of these days I'm going to Nashville," he declares.

When not still drawing comix, thanks to his extensive formal art training which included Yale and New York's Cooper Union, Spanish-born Victor Moscoso has reverted to his pre-**Zap** career, teaching art. He also sells reproductions of his classic rock posters through his online Neon Rose company. As he says, "The legacy lives on, man."

Ex-tax Jax and his Tex text

A taxman before his underground work, Jack Jackson is now a renowned expert on Texan history. He still produces comix, although they are of an historical nature. "If anything pays worse than comics, it's doing books for the university press circuit," he said. He came to the subject via his Commanche Moon trilogy, **White Commanche, Red Raider** and **Blood on the Moon,** all published by Last Gasp-Eco Funnies [1977-1978]. Based once more in the Lone Star State, his most recent was the 168-page **Lost Cause: The True Story of Famed Texas Gunslinger John Wesley Hardin**. Kitchen Sink Press published it in 1998, the year they went bankrupt.

THIS PAGE: Art Spiegelman and two of his eclectic creations.

FACING PAGE: From Spain's autobiographical collection, My True Story [1994].

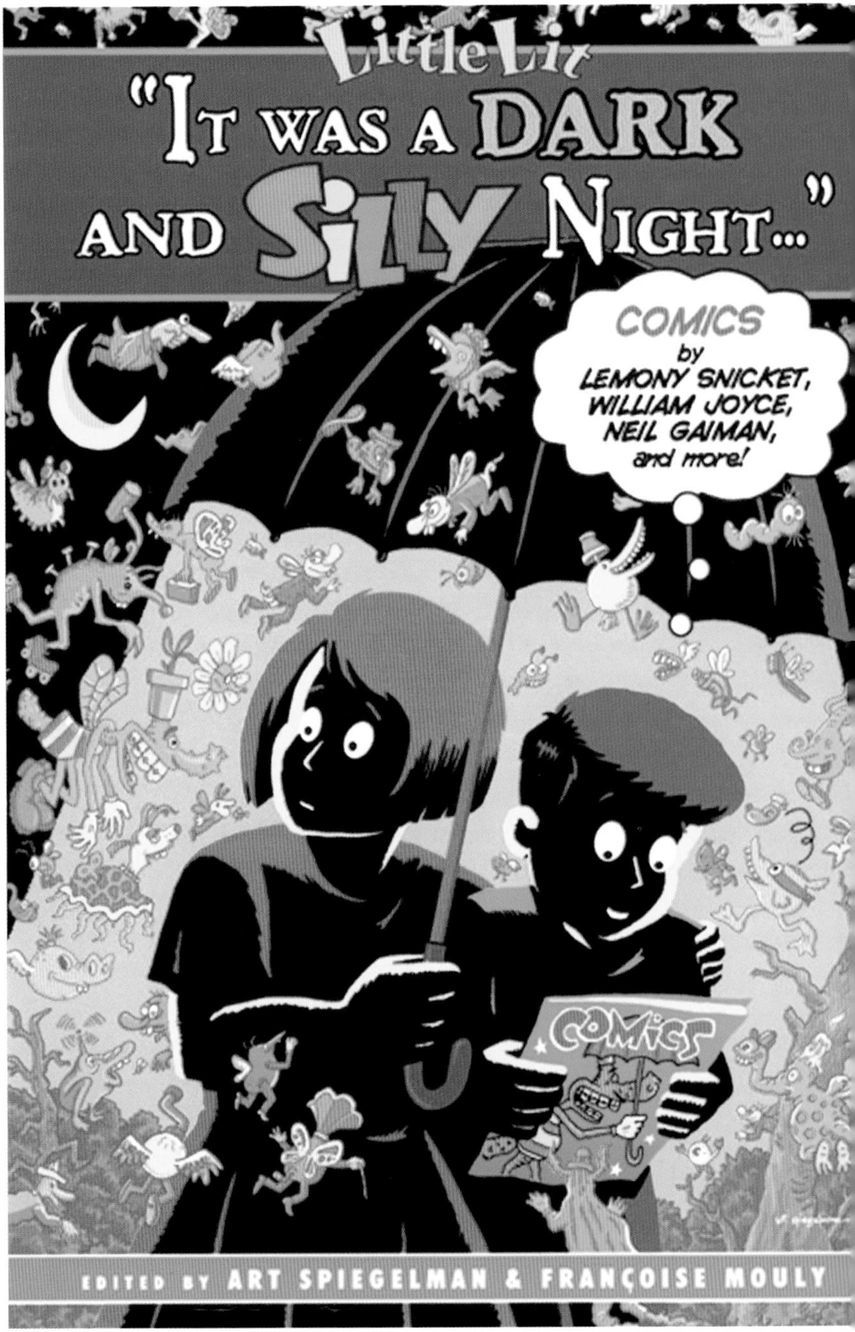

Trashman's Spain continues to draw comics, contributing to the sporadically published **Zap**. In 1991 Word-Play/Cottage Classics published the Conan Doyle book **Sherlock Holmes Strangest Cases** with cover art and ten interior pages by Spain. He recently produced a 144-page graphic novel adaptation of William Lindsay Gresham's 1946 cult novel **Nightmare Alley** [2003] for Fantagraphics Books, who collected his classic **Trashman Lives** in 1989 and his more personal work in **My True Story** [1994]. His new strips often appear in Fantagraphics anthology titles.

Arcade, the Comics Revue's Art Spiegelman is a regular contributor to the **New Yorker.** With his co-founder of **RAW Magazine,** Francoise Mouly, he also produces **Little Lit,** a series of 64-page hardcover RAW Little Books published by HarperCollins. The Pulitzer Prize-winning cartoonist continues to draw comix, his current project being a graphic novel about the September 11 attacks on New York's World Trade Center.

It Ain't Me Babe's Trina Robbins ("the goddess of comix") is now widely known as an historian through her books, which include **A Century of Women Cartoonists, The Great Women Superheroes, From Girls to Grrlz** and her most recent, 2001's **The Great Women Cartoonists**. She has also produced the **Legend of Wonder Woman** [1986] mini-series for DC Comics, and for Image has written a **Go Girl** comic [2000].

Dope springs eternal

Gilbert Shelton on leaving the States: "The Christian fundamentalist right are ... scary. The tide of creeping conservatism was something I preferred to avoid. The whole way that America wants stupid people in power, and the way they want to remove anyone with any ideas or any education, get rid of the bright people. "

R.V.M.C.
27th Reunion
SHADE'S

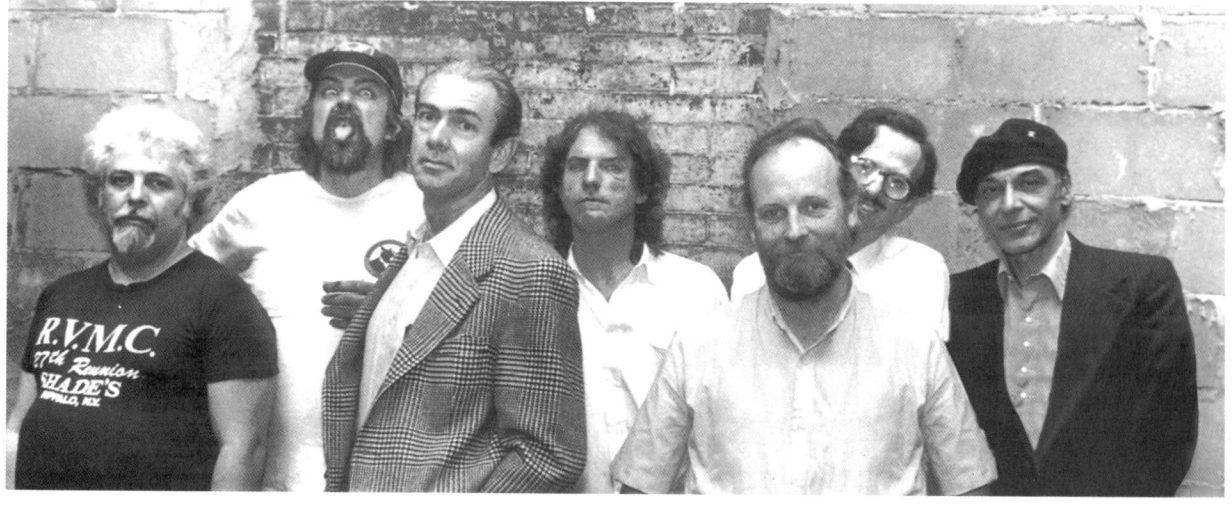

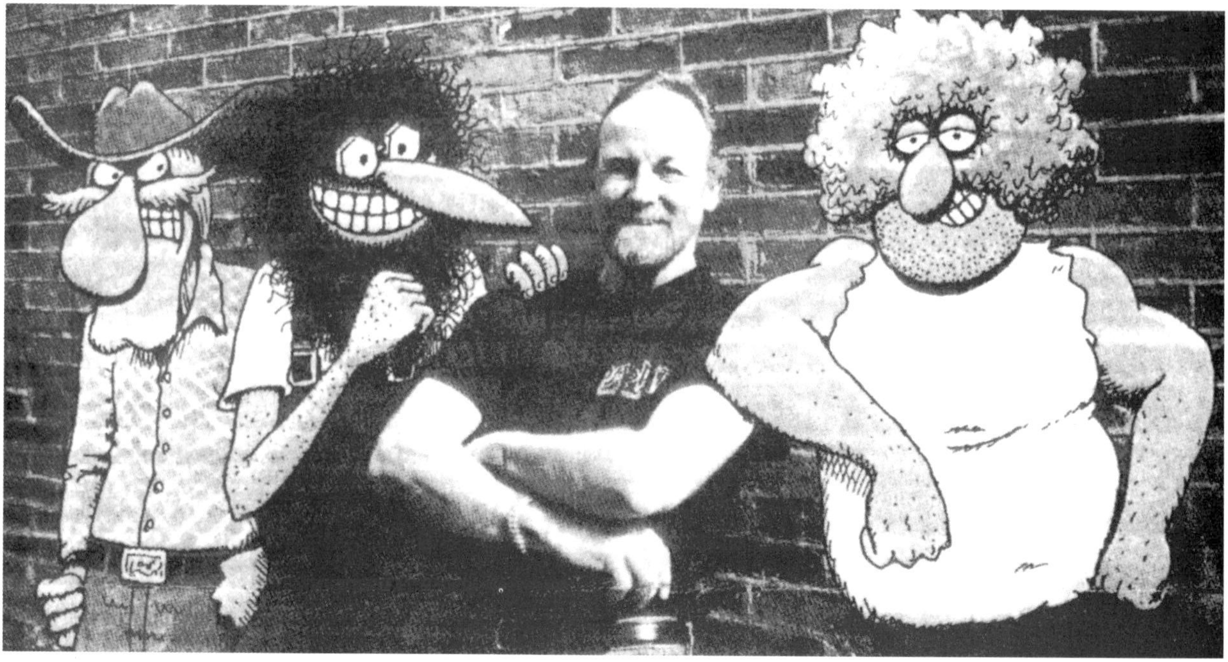

After finding himself at odds with his homeland, Shelton left the States in 1985 and landed in Paris. His most recent material has been the **Not Quite Dead** series with French artist Pic, a comic about the world's most famous band that never recorded. Benefitting from his move to Europe, the French government paid Shelton for the use of his Fat Freddy's Cat character in an AIDS awareness campaign while his Fabulous Furry Freak Brothers have been used in a promotional World Cup soccer poster campaign. As for preferred comics reading, his choice is even freakier than his creations, " I would say that my favorite cartoonist is a British guy called Leo Baxendale. He invented the Bash Street Kids and Lord Snooty for the UK comic **The Beano**."

His work remains in print in the States through Rip Off Press, in the UK through Knockabout and in France through Editions Tete-Rock Underground, as well as in Germany, Denmark, Spain, Brazil and more. A massive 432-page **Complete Freak Brothers** Volume 1 was published in 2002 by Knockabout. Sadly, the Freak Brothers movie project from Film Roman is definitely dead. When recently asked if his famous quote, "Dope gets you through times of no money better than money gets you through times of no dope" was still true, he replied, "You'll find out, when all your money becomes worthless."

Crumb tit-bits

In 1991, R. Crumb relocated to Cache, in the south of France with his wife Aline Kaminski-Crumb and their daughter Sophie, after trading six of his sketchbooks for a house. Lauded as one of the

RIGHT: Baxendale's Bash Street Kids (top) and Skip Williamson's "I Remember LSD" montage.

FACING PAGE: Up against the wall, hippies! A double dose of Shelton. Surrounded by the Freak Brothers (below) and with his six Zap pals (top) in 1989: Spain, Wilson, Williams, Griffin, Crumb—peaking from behind Gilbert—and Moscoso.

20th century's greatest cartoonists, he still produces occasional comix work. His most recent appeared across three issues of **Mystic Funnies**, two of **Self-Loathing Comics** and **Art & Beauty** #1-2 as well as a second volume of **Waiting for Food** and the **Mr Natural Postcard Book**.

Crumb's originals command increasingly high prices in galleries, and his work has recently been seen on the cover of **Art Forum**. A considerable number of books about Crumb have been published, such as **The Life and Times of R. Crumb** and his most obscure work has been collected in **Odds & Ends**, while Fantagraphics Books is nearing completion of their large format 112-page **Complete Crumb** series.

The publishing people

Since the demise of Kitchen Sink Press, artist and publisher Denis Kitchen has focused primarily on his agency business, representing clients including Crumb and Will Eisner as well as the estates of Harvey Kurtzman and Al Capp. He has also revived his underground pseudonym for his online mail order company, *Steve Krupp's Gallery and Curio Shoppe.* His Denis Kitchen Publishing is a new venture, manufacturing a selection of merchandise. As Kitchen admits, "I simply can't pull my foot entirely out of the publishing tar baby."

Of the other comix publishers, Last Gasp continues with founder Ron Turner at the helm as does Rip Off Press under co-founder Fred Todd. Apex Novelties, still headed by Don Donahue, is a mail order enterprise for underground ephemera. Gary Arlington still runs San Francisco Comic Book Company, having gone back to its retail origins.

The Brit brigade

The bulk of the Brit underground has disappeared, totally soaked up by major publishers—now more liberal than they were in the 1960s. Although some of its heroes are no longer around.

Mick Farren, on the late John Edward Barker: "My friend, my creative accomplice through much of the 1970s, and my co-defendant

in the **Nasty Tales** trial, Edward may have drunk himself to death in 1997, but he was also one of the gentlest and most innocent beings who ever walked this Earth, which is possibly why the same Earth proved too much for him. He also had a unique gift, or maybe a curse, which enabled him to see the human race as cartoon animals. When Edward was on form his drawings were up there with the best, the product of a lurid and hilarious sensibility. They were adored by we who got them, misunderstood by the benighted who scratched themselves and looked worried, and, although he has gone and I miss him, his work is still around, scattered but surviving."

The underacknowledged Mike Matthews produced some of the UK's most disturbing work in the 1970s and 1980s. He discovered Rich Corben's underground comix and was inspired. Within months he had cartoons published in a local punk fanzine, **Penetration**.

His friend and collaborator Steve Gibson takes up the story: "We worked together on **Napalm Kiss** #1 and #2 (October '77 and August '78). It was named after a poem, *Napalm Sticks To Kids,* written by a couple of disillusioned Vietnam vets and published in **Slow Death** #4. **Napalm Kiss** was mostly produced in the basement of David *(Meng & Ecker)* Britton's England's Glory, a comic shop and porn emporium (you can't get much more underground than that!) and printed by Hunt Emerson at the Arts Lab Press in Birmingham.

"As well as in fanzines, Mike had comic strips published in **Pssst!**, **Graphixus**, **Street Comix** and various Knockabout publications. He also produced a solo book, **Horrific Romance** [1984], comprising mainly of work rejected or ignored by publishers.

RIGHT: Two examples of the cartoon work of Edward Barker, a genius of the medium whose potential was never realized.

FACING PAGE: Crumb thumbs while Denis Kitchen mellows.

"By the time Knockabout was putting **Outrageous Tales From The Old Testament** together [1989], Mike was developing schizophrenia. This affected his ability to draw, which is why I was asked to illustrate the *Journey to Bethlehem* segment. After Mike finished Alan Moore's *Lust* script for **Seven Deadly Sins** his illness got out of control. By late '89, he'd stopped drawing completely and was suffering from blackouts."

Matthews disappeared just before Christmas '93. He was walking his dog by a canal not far from his home. After blacking out, he fell in and drowned. His body was not recovered for almost a month.

It ain't what you say...

Another unsung hero is Antonio Ghura. In 1972 he met Jonathan Holland-Gems who had produced the magazine **Student** with Richard Branson and who offered him work alongside Steve Parkhouse, John Bolton and reprints of Robert Crumb in his new title **It's All Lies**.

In his only recorded interview, Ghura told editor David Kerekes in **Headpress #18** (www.headpress.com), "Gems said that he would pay us after issue 6. I understood this to mean that after #6 he would pay us for all our work to date, but what he meant was that he would pay us for #7 onwards. Issues 1 to 6 we would do for free. But, of course, there was no issue 7." Seven seemed his unlucky number...

In 1977, issue 7 of **Libertine** (The New Journal of Authentic Victorian and Period Erotica) was tried and found Not Guilty of obscenity. *Home on Leave,* an Antonio Ghura comic strip in the issue, was singled out by the prosecution. As Ghura told Kerekes, "That was the first strip I did for **Libertine,** and they got busted! They lost about £10,000."

As well as ads for head shops, he drew for **Home Grown** and the music indie **Zig Zag**. He began publishing his own comix with **Bogey** [1975] featuring a lengthy drug strip *The Peyote Connection* and an incest-themed strip *Fatherly Love*. Ghura's next title, **Truly Amazing Love Stories** [1977] was even stronger.

It was a send-up of 1950s romance comics, but with lesbianism, homosexuality, VD and bestiality. Despite its 3,000 copies selling out quickly, by the time he produced a second issue [1983], the market had collapsed, resulting in it taking him 15 years to sell a mere 200 of the 3,000 printed.

Following his **Raw Purple** [1977], **Hot Nads** [1979], **The Laid-Back Adventures of Suzie and Jonnie** [1981] and **Bogey** #2 [1984], Ghura tried a third issue of **Truly Amazing Love Stories**, but nobody would publish it. Disenchanted, he bought a small van in 1998, intending to travel around Rome sleeping in it, while finding somewhere to settle in his native Italy. Before leaving he got a parking ticket and, unable to pay

MAXWELL THE MAGIC CAT
by Alan Moore

the ever-growing fine, lost the vehicle. But he eventually made it to Rome, and became a street artist, producing portraits for tourists.

Welch, Emerson & Talbot

Ogoth & Ugly Boot's Chris Welch has emigrated to Australia where he works in graphic design and fine art.

Hunt Emerson continues to produce comix, his most recent work includes **Citymouth** [2000] and a collection of his *Firkin* strips [2002] for the London-based bastion of underground publishing Knockabout Comics. For the same publisher he has produced a range of graphic novels including an adaptation of **Rime of the Ancient Mariner, Thunderdogs** and **They Call Me Puss Puss**. His work has appeared in such diverse titles as **Fortean Times** and **The Wall Street Journal**.

He is currently drawing *Little Plum,* a weekly strip in **The Beano**, a mildly subversive humour comic which enjoys a circulation in excess of 200,000 copies. His *Firkin the Cat* continues to run in **Fiesta**.

Bryan Talbot worked through Dark Horse Comics on such highly regarded series as **Heart of Empire**—a sequel to his *The Adventures of Luther Arkwright*—and **The Tale of One Bad Rat**, his multi award-winning story of an abused child who seeks refuge in the works of Beatrix Potter. His current major project is **Alice in Sunderland**.

LEFT: Before becoming comics' media darling, Watchmen's Alan Moore found early fame writing and drawing for local and rock music papers with Maxwell the Magic Cat (left), Ruscoe Moscoe and The Stars My Degradation.

RIGHT: Last seen heading for LA after co-writing Mad Max 4, Brendan (Skin) McCarthy started his comics career drawing Sometime Stories [top, 1977], co-produced with Brett (Deadline) Ewins and Peter (X-Static) Milligan. The visual below shows his development into Neo-McCarthyism [1989] before being sucked into the world of TV CGI with Reboot. "What pop music is to classical music, comics are to painting," says he.

Pop Goes the Artist

While the 'low art' of underground comix was taking off in the '60s, a new generation of pop artists was rediscovering the non-hip comicbooks and appropriating them for 'high art.'

INFANT terrible of the new wave of pop artists was Andy Warhol, a master of media manipulation. Some of Warhol's earliest paintings in the '60s used popular graphic motifs, icons made into fine art. Comics were a bountiful source of small illustrations he selected from, to convert into paintings.

In 1960 Warhol made his first comics art based on newspaper strips he'd read as a child including Chester Gould's **Dick Tracy**, Ernie Bushmiller's **Nancy** and EC Segar's **Popeye**, along with superhero icons Superman and Batman. For Warhol it was about taking powerful and popular imagery and twisting it to create a new perspective on 'found art.'

Warhol's work was meant to make the viewer stop and look at images that had become invisible through their familiarity. While he 'borrowed' such from other sources, some of his images were total steals of other people's work, yet the public loved it.

It was this attitude that underground and pop art alike had in common, as many comix artists took American icons and placed them in unusual and unsettling situations. Unlike Warhol, in a high art world,

lowly comix artists usually got sued for their infringement.

Warhol returned to his icons in 1981 for his *Myths* series, repainting his 1960 image of Superman, a world-wide symbol of all that is honourable and true. In 2002 the Superman print sold for an impressive $1,769,500.

By contrast, another pop artist—Roy Lichtenstein—was also experimenting with the often cliched world of comicbook imagery in the early Sixties, however neither of the artists was aware of each other at the time. Unlike Warhol, Lichtenstein strained the harsh language of the comic strip to its utmost limits of perfection and artificiality.

Lichtenstein's work portrayed the trivialization of culture rife in contemporary America. Using vibrant colours and techniques borrowed from what at the time was basic letterpress printing, he incorporated mass-produced emotions and objects into highly sophisticated references to art history. He selected comic-strip scenes, recomposed them, projected them onto his canvas and stencilled in the dots of colour. "I want my painting to look

FACING PAGE: The Art of Mickey Mouse by Andy Warhol [1980]. Mickey was Warhol's role model for the fame he craved.

BELOW: Warhol's Superman [1981]. He sprinkled a layer of diamond dust onto the prints, giving them a sparkling texture.

ABOVE: Roy Lichtenstein's M-Maybe [1965, top], borrowing from romance comics artist Tony Abruzzo.

FACING PAGE: Art Spiegelman's savagely satirical attack on Lichtenstein's work. [The Comics Journal Special Edition Volume One, Winter 2002].

as if it had been programmed," Lichtenstein explained.

His 16-piece series of *Girl* and *Woman* paintings [1963-65] copied, enlarged, adapted and reframed comicbook images of pretty girls from popular '60s romance comics such as **Secret Hearts** or **Girls' Romances**. While each of his derivations commanded fantastic prices, their out-of-context nature and value created a resentment among many commercial artists who had to produce at least ten similar images every single day to earn a liveable wage. But Lichtenstein never produced exact replicas of original comic panels. He crudely—some would even say clumsily—simplified the art, made trivial character name changes and accentuated the benday dot colour tints (named after inventor Benjamin Day), making his images "more like the comics than the comics were themselves."

Another of his major themes was war, with no less than 19 battle images taken from World War II comics at a time when America was involving itself in a new conflict. Arguably, he trivialized their death in combat content through highlighting their Batman-like sound effects for titles, *Whamm!, Blam, Bratatat!, Crak!* et al.

When Lichtenstein died in 1997, he was one of the most popular American artists. *Kiss 2* had sold in auction for over $6m in 1990, but a record was set when his *Happy* Tears sold for $7.1m in 2002—far more than the original artist (industry mainstay Mike Sekowsky) or any other comics creator would make from their entire life's work.

Despite spending many hours seeking out cheap old comics across Manhattan for source material, he once commented derisively, "All my art is in some way about other art, even if the other art is cartoons."

This has always been resented by Art Spiegelman, the most visible comics artist of his generation, that Lichtenstein considered his income source trash which he consecrated through his recreations.

"I liked Lichtenstein and a lot of his stuff," said a more forgiving Spain. "What he did was draw attention to comics. I think art of the 20th century has tried to break down the idea of high-brow or low-brow."

OH, ROY, YOUR DEAD HIGH ART IS BUILT ON DEAD LOW ART!... THE REAL POLITICAL, SEXUAL AND FORMAL ENERGY IN LIVING POPULAR CULTURE PASSES YOU BY. MAYBE THAT'S -SOB- WHY YOU'RE CHAMPIONED BY MUSEUMS!

Chapter 9:

Children of the Revolution

The kids are alright

"The underground milieu seemed even more bankrupt."
... ART SPIEGELMAN

The Summer of Love was long over, the hippy movement was dead and comix were on the wane. But a new generation of emerging artists was about to re-invent the undergrounds as alternatives and push the boundaries further than their parents ever dared.

BY the late '80s the underground comic scene was dying out. Many cartoonists found it difficult to support themselves on such a meagre income and turned to other means of support. Publishers also found it hard going with many fading away. Despite this there were a few die-hard determinists who kept the spirit of the underground alive. US publishers and editors such as Art Spiegelman and Gary Groth fervently believed that the underground movement could genuinely usher in a new era of comicbooks for adults and in turn engender the fine art and literary acceptance that the medium deserved. Not only that but there was a new generation of alternative comic creators growing up. Inspired by the old guard this new wave of creators was about to take the undergrounds overground and wombling free.

I spy for the FBI

In 1976 two comic entrepreneurs, Gary Groth and Mike Catron formed Fantagraphics Books Inc. (ironically abbreviated to FBI, considering their many future brushes with decency laws) with the sole purpose of publishing **The Comics Journal**, a critical art magazine focusing on the comics industry. **The Comics Journal** and Groth soon gained a reputation for being hypercritical of the industry. Small and wiry, Groth has been accused of being elitist, egotistical and has been lampooned as "Mr. Anger" by cartoonists Dan Clowes and Peter Bagge. Groth revelles in his *agent provocateur* role and continues to do his best to offend everybody and anybody in the comics industry. He has loudly scorned lowbrow superhero comics and has frequently written manifestoes calling for higher artistic standards. Considering his savage verbal attacks it's amazing that Groth has never had his lights punched out.

> Considering his savage verbal attacks it's amazing that Gary Groth has never had his lights punched out.

So, sue me

In its 27 years of tumultuous existence, Fantagraphics has been sued (and cleared) three times for libel and defamation of character—most famously in the '80s by comicbook writer Michael Fleischer because of comments made by SF novelist Harlan Ellison during a **Comics Journal** interview. The case dragged on for seven years and polarized much of the comics industry. Groth and Ellison even had their own falling-out during

No. 1

$2.95
$3.50
Canada

LOVE AND ROCKETS

ABOVE: Fantagraphics Books' acerbic founder and co-owner, Gary Groth. "We may be perceived as the 'House of Bile' because we're more honest and forthright in expressing our unorthodox opinions..."

LEFT: Cover to Love And Rockets #1 by Jaime Hernandez [1982].

For DECADES I DREW COMICS **CONSTANTLY.** I WAS A MAN ON A MISSION. I **HAD** TO DRAW COMICS!

...JUST WAIT 'TIL THE WORLD GETS A LOAD OF **THIS**!

I'LL SHOW 'EM **ALL**!

I HATE EVERYONE **OH** SO MUCH...

I USED TO **EXPERIMENT** WITH MANY DIFFERENT STY. I WOULD **CHALLENGE** MYSELF TO BE THE **BEST I COULD**

I SPENT A **WHOLE WEEK** ON THIS PAGE, AND IT **STILL** DOESN'T LOOK RIGHT...

THIS "**CHARLES BURNS**" TECHNIQUE ISN'T WORKING OUT FOR ME...

MAYBE I SHOULD A MULTIPLE SHADES O **ZIP-A-TON**

I ALSO USED TO TURN DOWN GOOD-PAYING WORK OUT OF **PRINCIPLE.** I WAS **ABOUT** SOMETHING, **MA-AN**!

...I **REFUSE** TO DO AN AD FOR YOUR MOVIE! I DON'T **CARE** HOW MUCH IT PAYS!

I'M AGAINST EVERYTHING IT **STANDS** FOR!

I HAVE A **REPUTATION** TO UPHOLD!

TODAY, HOWEVER, I'M NOT ABOUT **ANYTHING.** SO G ME A CALL! IF THE PRICE IS RIGHT THEN I'M **YOUR M**

...YOU WANT ME TO INK AN ISSUE OF "MY LITTLE PONY"?!

WHAT DOES IT **PAY**?

HMMM... THAT'S NO MUCH, BU **OKAY**!

© 2001 P. BAGG

the lawsuit against Fleischer. Fantagraphics won the case, legally confirming Ellison's statement that Fleischer was "bug-fuck crazy"

Kim Thompson became the new co-owner of Fantagraphics when Catron left to head up his own Apple Comics line. Thompson had joined Fantagraphics soon after its inception and had worked in various areas of the company as well as stints as editor and in production on **The Comics Journal**. He brought a slight tempering to Groth's rampant ranting, but was by no means less passionate about elevating comics beyond the

ABOVE: The Hernandez brothers, Jaime (left) and Gilbert, mug for the camera. The brothers' mother was a life-long comic fan who encouraged them to draw and their older brother, Mario, introduced them to underground comix by sneaking copies of the classic Zap into the house.

FACING PAGE: Hate creator Peter Bagge vents his spleen in his strip, Comics: A Young Man's Game? from The Comics Journal.

confines of the "Hey look, Kids! Comics!" mentality most adults had about the medium.

Under the new partnership of Groth and Thompson, Fantagraphics published its first comic in 1982, **Love & Rockets**. The magazine-sized anthology was written and drawn by Los Angeles-based brothers Gilbert (AKA Beto), Jaime and Mario Hernandez. The eldest,

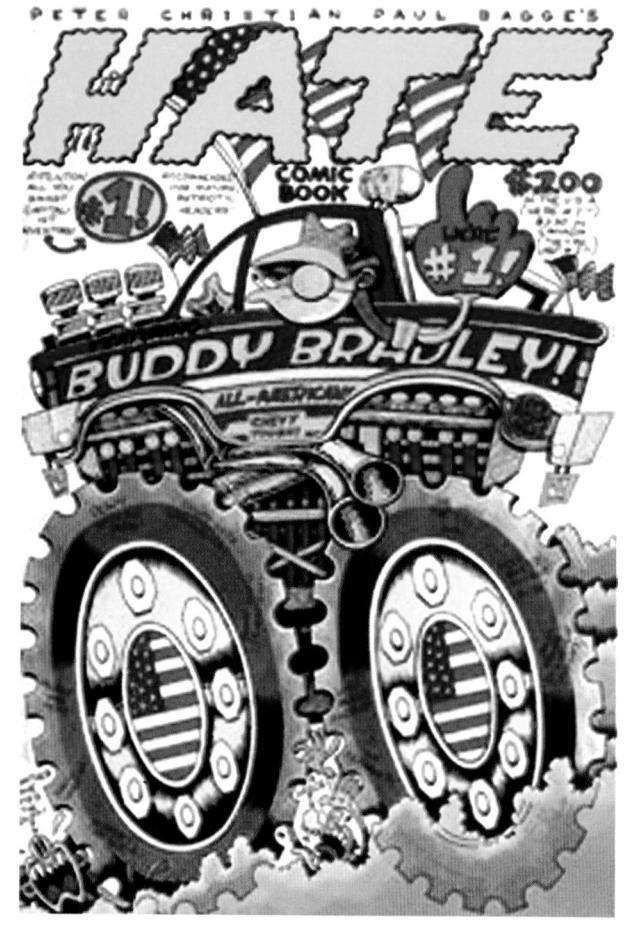

Mario, was initially the driving force behind the title but left shortly after the magazine's launch.

Los bros

The Latino brothers weaved character-driven semi-fantastical tales firmly rooted in their personal experiences of late '70s punk rock and life as Mexican/Americans. Jaime (pronounced Hymie) filled half of the comic with the moving tale of two close friends, Maggie and Hopey, and followed their life in the barrio from teens to adulthood.

Gilbert's tales of 'magic realism' explored the inhabitants of the small Mexican town of Palomar and in particular the huge-breasted Luba and her large family. Interestingly **Love and Rockets** didn't take off nearly as well in the US as it did in the UK where it became a cult hit, particularly within the gay community for its positive portrayal of lesbianism in Jaime's stories.

LEFT: Dan Clowes' strips from Eightball are a direct homage to the Sixties' undergrounds, using outrageous situations to both shock and amuse.

FACING PAGE: Hate by Peter Bagge (bottom) focused on the writer/artist's own love of America's disposable trash culture and pop music ephemera.

One of the newest cartoonists on the 'alternative' scene is Dave Cooper. His Dan and Larry graphic novel (top) deals with two friends' relationship as it develops very disturbing overtones. While the setting and characters are surreal, the story has an everyday feel to it.

Inspired by **Love And Rockets**, other artists soon flocked to Fantagraphics, and in the next few years the company published dozens of young talents who became linchpins of the burgeoning alternative comix movement.

Weirdos

By the late '80s Fantagraphics was riding high on the explosion of independent comics as readers sought out more diverse material. The company moved to Seattle, where the nascent grunge music movement was coalescing and a growing base of cartoonists was developing, including Peter Bagge. Bagge's first professional work appeared in **Weirdo** magazine [1981] published by underground survivor Last Gasp.

The anthology was originally edited by the ubiquitous Robert Crumb until issue 10 when Bagge took over the helm. **Weirdo** had all the hallmarks of the original undergrounds with work from such luminary artists as Bill Griffith and Kim Deitch, but it also saw new talents explode on to the scene like Drew Friedman, JD King and Mary Fleener. But not everyone was happy with the new wave of artists. "Crumb told me there was an awful lot of paranoia from the other **Zap** artists," recalled Bagge. "They would say, 'They're no good' or 'They don't have any

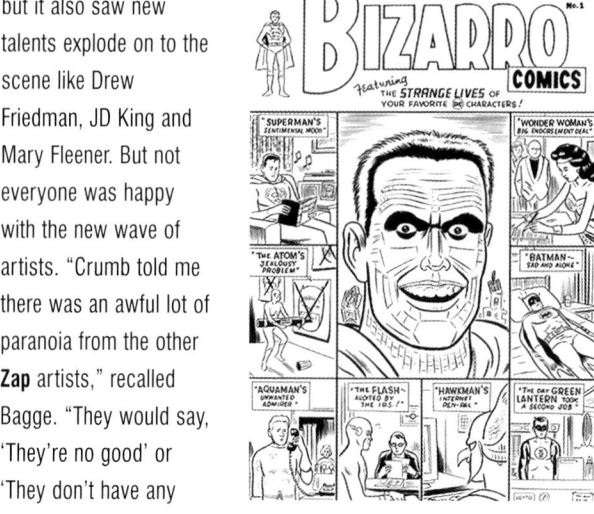

technique'—exactly what the old-timers said about them. I don't think they realized that to us the biggest thing was to be in the same comicbook as S Clay Wilson."

Issue 14 saw the debut of Bagge's *The Bradleys*, a strip he would develop over several years. By issue 18 Bagge went off to produce his own title, **Neat Stuff** [1985] for Fantagraphics, leaving the editorship of **Weirdo** in the capable hands of Crumb's wife, Aline Kominsky-Crumb.

Pure hate

Neat Stuff was a collection of hilarious stories about losers and freaks including Girly Girl, Studs Kirby and Chuckie Boy, but it was here that the gruesome Bradley family shone. Set in New Jersey, The Bradleys were the antitheses of every wholesome American family and who firmly put the 'dys' back into function. **Neat Stuff** threw Peter Bagge into the limelight and in 1990

Fantagraphics Books published his cruel and acerbically titled **Hate**. The title focused on the Bradley's oldest son, Buddy, and his attempts at living the 'slacker' lifestyle in Seattle. The tragically funny series ran for eight years evolving from black and white to a full colour comic as sales grew through word of mouth alone.

Things were going

ABOVE: The final issue of RAW [1991] featuring a cover by R. Crumb.

LEFT: The nightmarish visions of Charles Burns' Fifties-inspired artwork. Like a lot of the underground comix artists, Burns was heavily influenced by the early EC horror comics.

FACING PAGE: The unpublished cover of the Bizarro Comics anthology by Dan Clowes (left). DC Comics rejected it, possibly because it shows their greatest superheroes as mundane, angst-ridden boobs; "Batman - Sad and alone," "The Flash - Audited by the IRS!" and "The day Green Lantern took a second job."

Cover to Blab #7 by Dan Clowes (right). The anthology contained work from many top alternative artists like Drew Friedman and Richard Sala.

well for Bagge and Fantagraphics, but then the boom turned to a bust. Despite the valued input and diverse range of material Fantagraphics had published over the years, the company had been continually plagued with financial problems. This was due to the fact that both Groth and Thompson gleefully admitted they woefully lacked any business sense whatsoever—they merely wanted to encourage more people to follow the path of literate, iconoclastic figures like Crumb and Art Spiegelman.

"Every month we were losing ground, and there was nothing we could do," Groth recalled. Looking for a quick cash-flow fix Fantagraphics turned to sex comics and in 1990 created a new

subsidiary, Eros Comix, in order to cash in on the then-current trend towards pornographic comics. "Porn came to us in a vision," joked Thompson.

Many saw this as a highly hypocritical move by Groth and Thompson. **The Comics Journal** mandate was all about raising comics to an acceptance as literature and fine art, not as an excuse to peddle smut. When asked why Fantagraphics didn't simply move into publishing the great cash-cow of superhero comics Groth simply replied, "I like sex. I don't like superheroes."

Despite others' misgivings, Eros saved Fantagraphics from bankruptcy within a year and even managed to lure **Love & Rockets**

RIGHT: Joe Sacco (in the middle with glasses) visits the Balkans conflict in Safe Area Gorazde.

FACING PAGE: Montreal-based Julie Doucet's collection of strips, bizarrely titled Lift Your Leg, My Fish is Dead (left).

Crumb's cover to Weirdo #17 (right). Weirdo helped launch many artists careers including Sacco's.

co-creator Gilbert Hernandez over to create the tit-fest **Birdland** for it. Eros now thrives as an independent revenue raiser for the more esoteric projects its parent company publishes.

Cool Cat Clowes

One of the more unusual Fantagraphics projects was **Lloyd Llewelyn** [1986] by Dan Clowes. Llewelyn was a beatnik PI who spoke 'hep' and the series was resplendent in retro '50s cool. A lot of Clowes'

future themes can be seen here, from the love of left-of-centre collectibles to bizarre characters and seemingly non-sequitor storytelling. Despite—or perhaps because of—this the comic didn't take off and was cancelled after six issues and a oneshot. However, Clowes' next series for Fantagraphics, **Eightball** [1989] was a completely different story.

Eightball had a surreal dreamlike quality, reminiscent of the work of director David Lynch, populated by deeply-flawed, grotesque protagonists. It was a collection of short stories and longer serialized

RIGHT: Chester Brown's Yummy Fur wore its outlandish underground influences on its sleeve. Here, Ed the Happy Clown has some trouble with his genitalia.

FACING PAGE: Cover to Cerebus #100 [1987] by creator Dave Sim, showing the earth pig character's development over the years.

pieces, most notably *Like a Velvet Glove Cast in Iron*, *David Boring* and *Ghost World*. All were collected into graphic novels with the latter being turned into a successful cult film. Clowes described **Eightball** as "an orgy of spite, vengeance, hopelessness, despair and sexual perversion," but this ignores the fact that it is also savage and darkly funny. The comicbook series has proved to be a huge success and looks to spawn another film shortly based on the strip, *Art School Confidential*. This is a series of observations made by Clowes while honing his craft. Typically the strip is filled with the flotsam and jetsam of life's freaks that fascinate him so much.

Tumour humour

Another Fantagraphics success was Chris Ware's acclaimed **Acme Novelty Library** [1993]. Ware cut his teeth, like so many others, on **Blab!** [1986] and in Art Spiegelman's **RAW** before launching his own title. His artwork was crisp, clean and made up of dozens of intricate panels which were a masterstroke of design. All this belies grimly humourous stories of loneliness and alienation. The first collection of strips, **Jimmy Corrigan**, **the Smartest Kid on Earth** told the tragically

funny story of the young Jimmy's superheroic aspirations crushed by the mundanity of middle age. It went on to win **The Guardian** newspaper's award for Best First Book in 2001, the first graphic novel to do so.

Comics journalism

While Ware focused on the tedium and drudgery of an empty fictional existence, Joe Sacco's work looks at the terrifying and tragic consequences of real life war and conflict. Maltese-born Sacco studied journalism at the University of Oregon before becoming a full-time cartoonist, contributing to a wide range of anthologies including **Drawn & Quarterly**, **Prime Cuts** [1987], **Real Stuff** [1990] and **Weirdo** magazine.

In late 1991 the former Fantagraphics employee spent two months in Israel and the occupied territories. When he returned to the USA he combined the techniques of eyewitness reportage and comics to create **Palestine** [1993], an eight-issue mini-series for Fantagraphics. The series was collected and gained widespread praise, setting new standards for the use of the comicbook as a documentary medium and was the first

non-fiction graphic novel to rank alongside Art Spiegelman's Pulitzer Prize-winning **Maus**. In 1996 Sacco won the prestigious American Book Award for **Palestine**.

In 2000, Sacco finished **Safe Area Gorazde: The War In Eastern Bosnia 1992-1995**, an exploration of a small Muslim enclave in Serbia called Gorazde. Based upon Sacco's travels to the war-torn region it gained major coverage from **Time** magazine, **The New York Times**, **The Los Angeles Times Book Review** and eventually led to Sacco being commissioned to do a strip for **Time** magazine. Sacco has since released a highly regarded collection of his shorter works, including observations on the Gulf War, in **Notes from a Defeatist**.

Show me the money!

But critical acclaim doesn't pay the bills and once again Fantagraphics found themselves in financial difficulty when they lost $70,000 when their distributor went bankrupt and, over-excited by the success of Ware, Clowes, and Sacco, Groth and Thompson made a near fatal (and all too frequent) publishing error, printing too many books and leaving themselves severely short of cash.

In 2003 they were forced to put out a desperate plea on the Internet for readers to purchase $80,000 worth of books in order for Fantagraphics to pay off their immediate debt. It's a sign of the loyalty and high regard that Fantagraphics has in the industry when

LEFT: The pensive and unsure Acme Novelty Library creator Chris Ware. "I still have overwhelming self-doubt about my ability to handle any sort of situation with any kind of literary maturity," worries the artist.

FACING PAGE: Chris Ware's semi-autobiographical Jimmy Corrigan The Smartest Kid on Earth.

they managed to raise the money in just eight days. Thompson said, "Sometimes I literally think we're like the coyote who's run off the cliff and is not aware that he's run off the cliff yet. That's why we're still here."

Independent survivor

"It points out the inherent financial instability of publishing alternative comics," Groth ruminated. Profit margins are very tight and the genre's fan base is compact. It has always been hard to reach customers since many comics stores shun alternative comix in favour of the bread-and-butter superhero stuff. Mainstream bookstores were slightly more open to graphic novels, but still didn't really get how to sell and promote them. Which explains why "every other remotely independent comics publisher has gone out of business over the last 16 years," Groth pointed out. "Pacific Comics, Eclipse, First Comics, Kitchen Sink—any company that had staff and overheads has gone out of business, which makes it even more miraculous that we have 30 employees."

However Groth is aware of his company's strengths as well as weaknesses, "I think that generally we'll support a book that may lose money, which is of considerable value to an artist.

There is strength in numbers and we have a little more clout with distributors than an unknown artist self-publishing for the first time and may be able to secure more promotion for his work. Retailers may be more inclined to try new books because of our track record. Our expertise in production values, design, and promotion can be of enormous help. Then there's the intangible but very real value of being published by someone who appreciates good work and who's created a context where such work is valued by an educated readership."

Despite anti-authoritarian and self-sabotaging tendencies and very little cash Fantagraphics have somehow managed to survive nearly three decades through sheer passion and luck.

Canuck Comix

North of the border in Canada there was an equally strong alternative comics movement happening, the 'big daddy' of which is, without doubt, Dave Sim. In December 1977 he self-published his black and white **Conan the Barbarian** parody, **Cerebus** under the imprint Aardvark-Vanaheim. Not only did Sim write, pencil, ink and letter the series, but he also declared that it would run for a staggering 300 issues. "If you read 300 issues of **Superman** or **Spider-Man**," said Sim, "they don't make sense as a story or a life. When I started **Cerebus**, uppermost in my

LEFT: Life after RAW. Spiegelman and Mouly switched from producing comics for adults to children's fairy tales with their Little Lit range of books. However they continued to use RAW contributors like Lorenzo Mattotti and Dan Clowes.

FACING PAGE: Dan Clowes' Ghost World, originally serialized in Eightball, was turned into a successful art house film. The central protagonist, Enid Coleslaw, is an anagram of the artist's full name.

RIGHT: Artbabe creator Jessica Abel's fictional autobiography as a cartoonist. The man sitting on the desk in the second panel is Stan Lee, who was responsible for the creation of many of Marvel Comics' superheroes, such as Spider-Man and The Hulk.

FACING PAGE: Peepshow artist/writer Joe Matt's self-portrait (left).

Palookaville by Canadian cartoonist, Seth (right).

mind was the thought that I wanted to produce 300 issues of a comicbook series the way I thought it should be done—as one continuous story documenting the ups and downs of a character's life."

Not so funny animal

Cerebus began as a 'funny animal' series about an aardvark set in a mythical fantasy world, but after 25 issues Sim realized there was far more to talk about and expanded his scope to cover the entire variety of human existence. He has weaved in references to current social and political events, from electoral politics to abortion, and many familiar icons like Oscar Wilde, Groucho Marx and The Rolling Stones as well as parodying many of the mainstream superhero icons like Batman, Wolverine and Captain America. Cerebus is not a likeable character. He is greedy, ill-tempered, selfish and often self-defeating

and it's obvious he doesn't really comprehend a lot of what is happening around him. "I think everybody knows someone like Cerebus," said Sim, "someone who you wish wasn't your friend, who makes you so mad you swear you'll never speak to him again, and then he does something unexpectedly nice and you can't help liking him." Sim soon realized how daunting the project would be and brought in fellow collaborator Gerhard to pencil and ink the backgrounds and colour the covers. **Cerebus** is the longest running self-published comic of all time. It has survived a very public and bitter divorce between Sim and Deni Loubert (**Cerebus**'s then publisher) and numerous attacks on Sim's seemingly apparent misogyny. Both praised for his stand on creator rights and vilified for his uncompromising views in the same breath, Sim is undoubtedly one of the most important influences in modern comics, bridging the old school to the new wave. The epic 6,000-page story will eventually stretch over 26 years ending in March 2004 with the death of Cerebus. After that Sim intends on taking "a long nap."

Drawn & Quarterly

The rise of the black and white comics in the late Eighties and the inspiration of Dave Sim saw a string of Canadian cartoonists emerge onto the scene. Many started out simply by self-publishing mini-comics—the same way Crumb, Shelton et al started—but were soon grouped together and published by Montreal's Drawn & Quarterly. D&Q was formed by Chris Oliveros in 1990 and was Canada's answer to Fantagraphics. "I realized that a comic could be about anything—any viewpoint, any kind of graphic approach. In other words, it could be a kind of literature. After Spiegelman's **Maus**," Oliveros said, "cartoonists became more ambitious. Instead of 24-page comicbooks with one story, they began serializing longer stories that could be collected into book form." It took Oliveros almost two years to put together the first issue of the **D&Q anthology**. "My goal was to create a regular magazine that would sort of be like The **New Yorker** or **Harper's** of comics."

Soon after, he began to publish important titles such as **Yummy Fur** [1986] by Chester Brown (originally released by another Canadian publisher, Vortex), **Palookaville** [1991] by Seth and **Dirty Plotte** [1990] by Julie Doucet "... a female Robert Crumb." Doucet was also based in Montreal and had just been turned down by Fantagraphics when Oliveros agreed to publish her own series. The title, **Dirty Plotte**,

RIGHT: Art Spiegelman's re-telling of a classic Hasidic parable, Prince Rooster. The strip appeared in his fairy tale anthology, Little Lit [2000].

FACING PAGE: Toxie and Moxie, two characters from Dylan Horrocks' Hicksville [1998].

is slang for female genitalia. Another Montreal-based cartoonist, Joe Matt, appeared in **D&Q** #1, and shortly after spun-off his painfully honest and ire-raising autobiographical stories into the series **Peepshow** [1992]. Matt was almost certainly inspired by Crumb's comicbook confessionals where he laid bare his soul for all to see.

Evolution

Drawn & Quarterly magazine evolved into an annual coffee-table anthology featuring new writers and artists, old favourites, translations and reprints. Shortly after the company then published its very first graphic novel **The Playboy** by Chester Brown in 1992. Brown's autobiographical strip originally appeared in **Yummy Fur** and told of his guilt and angst at gaining a copy of Playboy in his pubescent youth. Drawn & Quarterly continues to be an important publisher of alternative comics producing great works such as **Atlas** [2001] by New Zealand cartoonist Dylan Horrocks and **Berlin** [1996] by Jason Lutes. Much of Fantagraphics and Drawn & Quarterly's inspiration was drawn from the ground-breaking work done by Art Spiegelman on **RAW** magazine. Spiegelman was a long time contributor to underground comix throughout the Seventies and was co-editor—alongside Bill Griffith—of **Arcade**. The leading-edge anthology was designed, as Spiegelman phrased it, "As a life-raft for lots of people involved in underground comix when that whole movement seemed to be sinking." Between 1975 and 1976 they published seven issues featuring founding fathers of the underground such as Robert Crumb, Spain Rodriguez, S Clay Wilson and Gilbert Shelton. Despite the quality of work and modest success Spiegelman felt "It was a tremendous headache and a lot of work and when it ended I swore I'd never be involved with a magazine again."

RAW Talent

In 1980 Spiegelman moved from San Francisco to New York and met his future wife, Françoise Mouly. Spiegelman worked on several publications including **Playboy**, **The New York Times** and **Village Voice** editing or acting as a consultant for their various comics projects.

ABOVE: James Kolchaka's Monkey vs Robot has spun-off a sequel book, a music CD and a puppet show.

RIGHT: Jaime Hernandez's cover for the 2003 SPX convention booklet. The magazine acts as a showcase for new alternative cartoonists as well as raising funds for the Comic Book Legal Defense Fund. The CBLDF helps defend comic creators' rights to freedom of speech and against censorship laws.

FACING PAGE: Ivan Brunetti's darkly comedic Schizo #2 [1996] updates the savage satire of the undergrounds.

Mouly finally persuaded Spiegelman to get back into magazine publishing and together they co-edited the first issue of **RAW**. Despite Spiegelman's reservations, "The underground milieu seemed even more bankrupt," and planning it as a oneshot, the first issue soon sold out of its 4,500 print run.

Art for Art's sake?

RAW's format was unique from the start. Over-sized it had a fine art slant with early issues being deliberately torn or individual inserts on coloured paper (including Spiegelman's *Maus* strip—see the Raw Emotions feature on page 214). "**RAW** was a demonstration of just how luxurious comics could be. It was replete with surprises. It was Pioneering."

RAW's publishing schedule was erratic to say the least with only eight issues published between 1980-1986, but what it lacked in quantity it made up for in quality. It launched the careers of dozens of cartoonists and artists from Charles Burns and Gary Panter to Drew Friedman and Chris Ware. But Spiegelman and Mouly weren't simply satisfied with home-grown US creators, they actively sought out European artists and writers such as Jacques Tardi, Joost Swarte and Lorenzo Mattotti, intending to give them wider exposure to an American audience. The co-editors also reprinted lesser-know classic strips from Basil Wolverton and George Herriman's *Krazy Kat*. "It helped launch a generation of different comics for adults," said Spiegelman.

After the success of the first collected edition of **Maus**, Penguin Books took over publishing **RAW** in 1989. The format was changed from a large over-sized magazine to a 200-page paperback format. The extended width allowed for a greater variety of material and for longer stories. "We had a backlog of stuff. And a lot of it was long," recalls Spiegelman. "So we decided to go with a smaller format but more pages. Where the original format had concentrated on art, and presented that in a dramatic fashion, we decided to make **RAW** more of a literary magazine."

Despite the critical success of the Penguin editions, Mouly and Spiegelman had always stated that each issue would be the last one as the workload involved meant that **RAW** could only be published on an annual basis. After three issues of the Penguin edition **RAW** finally closed its doors in 1991.

Even today it remains one of the most important and influential comics anthologies and was instrumental in comics gaining credibility amongst the literati and intelligentsia.

Rise of the independents

Since the late-Eighties to mid-Nineties increasingly more independent alternative publishers have appeared telling non-superheroic tales as audiences tastes have grown more sophisticated and comics have become more acceptable. Companies of note in recent years have included Slave Labour Graphics (SLG), Caliber, Larry Young's AiT/Planetlar, Oni Press and Brett Warnock and Chris Staros' Top Shelf Productions.

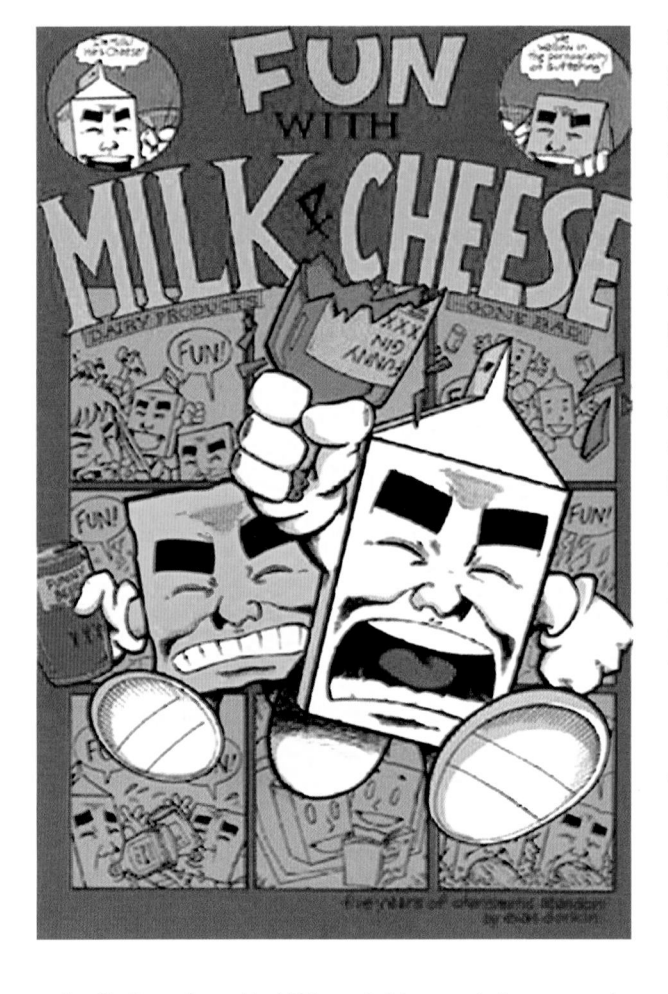

and white explosion of self-published comics meant that SLG's **Samurai Penguin** #1, by Vado and Mark Buck, sold a staggering 58,000 copies. However, the numbers soon dropped back to more realistic levels (5-8,000 copies). Other successes included Evan Dorkin's **Pirate Corp$**! and **Milk & Cheese**.

Unconventional conventions

Warnock and Staros launched Top Shelf Productions at the first Small Press Expo (SPX) in Maryland, USA. The event was designed as a convention to help publishers consolidate their work and gain a stronger voice and has grown from strength to strength and has its own prestigious and coveted awards, The Ignatz's, in honour of Herriman's *Krazy Kat*.

Two years earlier, in 1995, SPX's West Coast cousin, the Alternative Press Expo was launched in San Francisco. APE was a colourful mingling of Bay Area punks and activists, underground comix creators and established stars of the independent scene. The indy comics market is expanding and in 2003 APE's gate had grown to 3,400 attendees.

Underground comics legend Robert Williams has praised the new talent, while believing his generation had more of an outlaw presence but that today's alternative cartoonists have established themselves both artistically and economically.

But still many of the existing independent publishers perpetually hover on the brink of financial disaster, including Canadian Black Eye who stopped publishing and moved into design. In 2002 both Top Shelf and Drawn & Quarterly nearly folded when their distributor went out of business. They survived by appealing to their fans to buy their books, just as Fantagraphics would have to do a year later.

While there have been casualties along the way, the days of wondering whether alternative comics have an audience are past. The question now is just how big can the audience grow.

Top Shelf was formed in 1997, created to promote the careers of up-and-coming cartoonists. Notable releases include: Craig Thompson's **Good-Bye Chunky Rice**, Scott Morse's **The Barefoot Serpent**, James Kochalka's **Monkey vs Robot**, Ed Brubaker's **Lowlife** and Peter Kuper's **Speechless**.

SLG Publishing was founded by Dan Vado in 1986 and the black

LEFT: Beach Safari by Markus Mawil Witzel [2002] is part of the new wave of alternative comics, the natural successor to the undergrounds. Published by Top Shelf Productions, it tells the story of a ship-wrecked rabbit who spends the Summer hanging out with three girls.

FACING PAGE: Evan Dorkin's brutally funny Milk and Cheese: Dairy Products Gone Bad are published by Slave Labor Graphics. The vitriolic duo have been merchandized on to T-shirts, lighters, lunch boxes fridge magnets and beer mats. Today's cartoonists have a lot more business acumen than their predecessors.

Comix Go Arthouse

Over the last 10 years comicbooks have gained increasing mass market credibility and have begun to be assimilated into mainstream culture, and in particular film.

JUST as Hollywood blockbusters have looked towards superhero comics for inspiration, so too have independent film-makers sought out comics, albeit more esoteric underground ones, as source material. However, one major difference between tinseltown and the mavericks shines through in the end product: the passion the indies have for the source material. Unlike most Hollywood adaptations, these films have managed to remain faithful to their origins while raising awareness in the subject matter among arthouse cinema-goers.

In 1988 Ron Mann co-wrote and directed the documentary *Comic Book Confidential,* which was the first serious piece of film-making to study the distinctly American phenomenon of the comicbook industry. Mann succeeded in interviewing almost every key underground cartoonist including Robert Crumb, Bill Griffith, Paul Mavrides, Dan O'Neill, Victor Moscoso, Gilbert Shelton and Spain Rodriguez.

Mann also looked at the artists who were spawned from Art Spielgeman and Françoise Mouly's **RAW**. Creators such as Lynda Barry, Charles Burns and Sue Coe were interviewed alongside old school stalwarts including Will Eisner, Al Feldstein, Jack Kirby, Harvey Kurtzman and Stan Lee. The result was a well crafted documentary successfully encapsulating the entire breadth of the comics industry from newspaper strips and superheroes to the Sixties underground movement and the next wave of artists.

Zwigoff's *Crumb*

In 1994 Terry Zwigoff showed his talent for giving real life outsiders their cinematic due in his award winning documentary, *Crumb*. A San Francisco resident, Zwigoff had previously made a documentary short *Louie Bluie* [1985] about an obscure blues/jazz player. Zwigoff was a long time friend of Robert Crumb and together they co-wrote two screenplays in the late '80s, but neither made it to production. Instead Zwigoff turned the cameras on his friend and made a moving (if not entirely tragic) documentary on the bizarre Crumb family.

The film was a Sundance Film Festival sensation and art house hit, revealing a family utterly divorced from mainstream "normalcy" and presenting a warts-and-all portrait of a uniquely twisted artist. Crumb's emotionally disturbed brother Maxon was a poignant reminder of the suffering that dysfunctional families

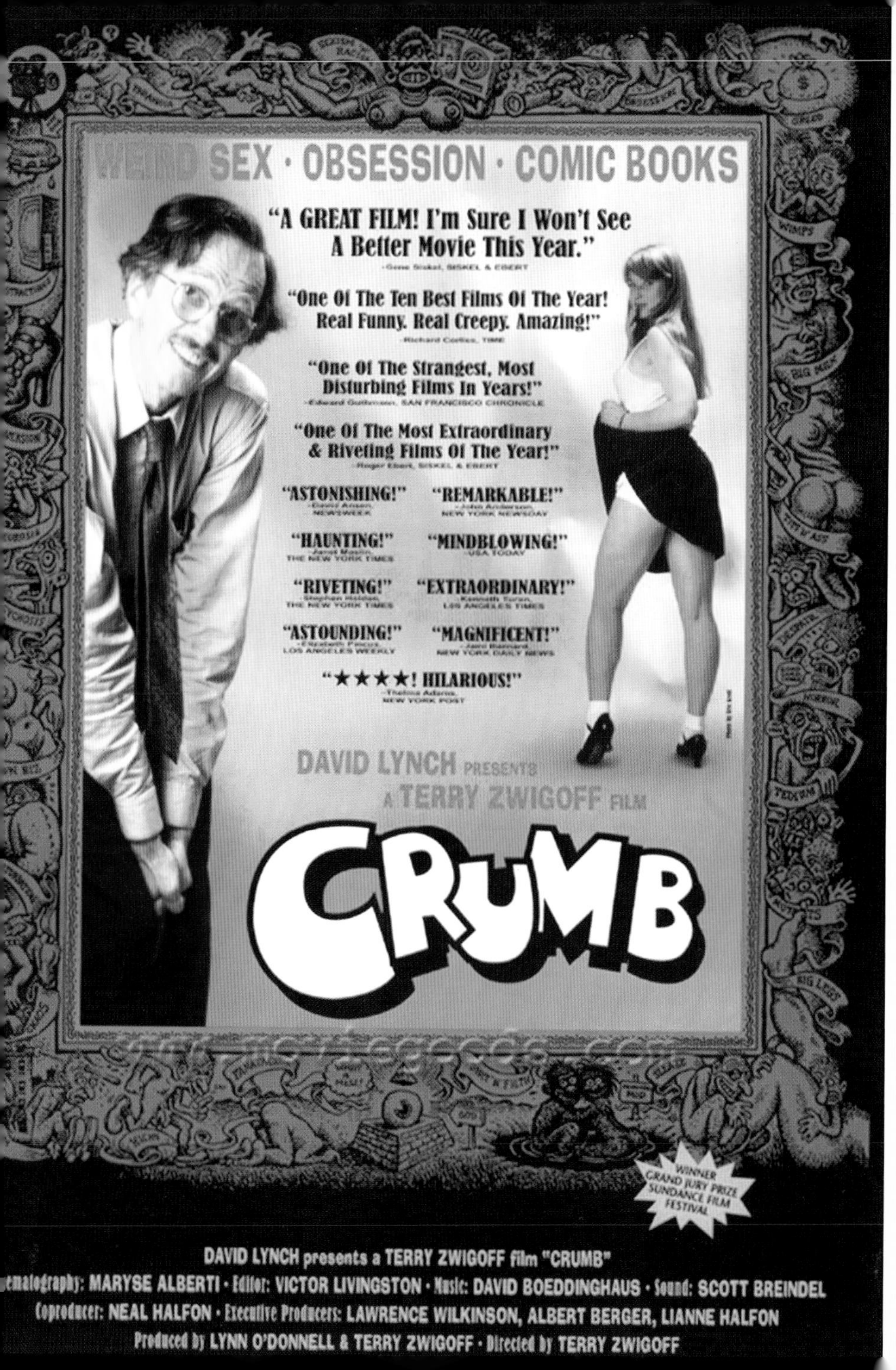

WEIRD SEX · OBSESSION · COMIC BOOKS

"A GREAT FILM! I'm Sure I Won't See A Better Movie This Year."
— Gene Siskel, SISKEL & EBERT

"One Of The Ten Best Films Of The Year! Real Funny. Real Creepy. Amazing!"
— Richard Corliss, TIME

"One Of The Strangest, Most Disturbing Films In Years!"
— Edward Guthmann, SAN FRANCISCO CHRONICLE

"One Of The Most Extraordinary & Riveting Films Of The Year!"
— Roger Ebert, SISKEL & EBERT

"ASTONISHING!"
— David Ansen, NEWSWEEK

"REMARKABLE!"
— John Anderson, NEW YORK NEWSDAY

"HAUNTING!"
— Janet Maslin, THE NEW YORK TIMES

"MINDBLOWING!"
— USA TODAY

"RIVETING!"
— Stephen Holden, THE NEW YORK TIMES

"EXTRAORDINARY!"
— Kenneth Turan, LOS ANGELES TIMES

"ASTOUNDING!"
— Elizabeth Pincus, LOS ANGELES WEEKLY

"MAGNIFICENT!"
— Jami Bernard, NEW YORK DAILY NEWS

"★★★★! HILARIOUS!"
— Thelma Adams, NEW YORK POST

DAVID LYNCH PRESENTS A TERRY ZWIGOFF FILM

CRUMB

WINNER GRAND JURY PRIZE SUNDANCE FILM FESTIVAL

DAVID LYNCH presents a TERRY ZWIGOFF film "CRUMB"
Cinematography: MARYSE ALBERTI · Editor: VICTOR LIVINGSTON · Music: DAVID BOEDDINGHAUS · Sound: SCOTT BREINDEL
Coproducer: NEAL HALFON · Executive Producers: LAWRENCE WILKINSON, ALBERT BERGER, LIANNE HALFON
Produced by LYNN O'DONNELL & TERRY ZWIGOFF · Directed by TERRY ZWIGOFF

ABOVE: Displaying the root of his friendship with Crumb, director Zwigoff amidst his collection of music memorabilia.

LEFT: "Weird Sex - Obsessions - Comic Books"… it could only be one man. The domestic release poster for Crumb, a Terry Zwigoff movie, aptly presented by the equally self-obsessed film-maker turned cartoonist David Lynch.
For nine years [1983-92], Lynch had produced a strip The Angriest Dog in the World for various alternative news-papers including the L. A. Reader.

FACING PAGE: The film poster to Ron Mann's widely acclaimed 1988 docu-movie, Comic Book Confidential.

can inflict. *Crumb* won several critics awards as well as being one of the best-reviewed films of the 1990s. Sadly, Zwigoff's unflinching film caused a rift between him and Crumb for several years but eventually they were reconciled.

Ghost World

Zwigoff's next foray into comic movies was Ghost World (2001). Rejecting the compromise of Hollywood and with a long-standing aversion to corporate commercialism, Zwigoff struggled for five years to get an adaptation of cartoonist Daniel Clowes' graphic novel **Ghost World** made. Co-scripted with Clowes and starring the deadpan Thora Birch (Enid) and Scarlett Johansson (Rebecca) as two alienated teens stuck in a generic suburban city, *Ghost World* was wiser, funnier, and more moving than the usual teen film.

Suffering from a more than average case of adolescent angst, Enid's journey toward an alternative life is aided by Steve Buscemi's gently eccentric collector, Seymour. Zwigoff directed with his assured low-key style that suited both the subject and its source, showing that he could handle a fictional narrative as well as documentaries.

Ghost World became a critical art house success in the summer of 2001 and Zwigoff has since collaborated with Clowes on another adaptation of his work, *Art School Confidential* (2004), with John Malkovich starring and producing.

American Splendor

In 2003 it was the turn of social commentator and comix writer Harvey Pekar to make it to the big screen. Taking the comic of the same name as its source, *American Splendor* is a bio-pic of Pekar's life as a Cleveland filing clerk. The simplistic and heartfelt vérité vignettes, drawn by various artists for the irregularly published comic, belie their emotional intensity. As Pekar said, "Ordinary life is pretty complex stuff."

Pekar began self-publishing the title in 1976 until the early '90s when Dark Horse Comics took over publishing. Again the directors, Shari Springer Berman and Robert Pulcini, remained faithful to the source, portraying Pekar as a cartoon as well as being played by actor Paul Giamatti and by Pekar himself.

Pekar's long-time friend Robert Crumb also appears, played with uncanny realism by James Urbaniak. The film, like *Crumb*, went on to win the Grand Jury Prize at the Sundance Film Festival.

While Hollywood scours superhero comics for new ideas, the small indie directors not only remain loyal to the alternative new wave, but win well deserved awards for doing their job so well.

Accentuate
the
negative.

GHOST
WORLD
A SCREENPLAY
BY DANIEL CLOWES & TERRY ZWIGOFF

GHOST WORLD

THIS PAGE: A story of extreme teen angst, Ghost World. The movie poster [left, 2001] and the Clowes cover art for the book (above) adapting the film that adapts the Clowes comic!

FACING PAGE: Paul Giamatti, who shares the lead role with a cartoon version and the real life Harvey Pekar in the award-winning screen version of the comic book, American Splendor [2003].

The Cartoon History of the Universe

Larry Gonick likes the big picture. Thanks to Jacquie Onassis he's still telling his epic tale, which started 25 years back with the Big Bang and still has another five or six centuries to go!

BEING personal little pamphlets, underground comix have a habit of covering the interests or frustrations of their creators; sex, drugs and rock 'n' roll. But not all. Some have dealt with politics, sexism and racial discrimination while others are in a category all of their own.

One such is **The Cartoon History of the Universe,** considered one of the top 100 comics of the 20th century by the elitist **Comics Journal**. Launched from the home of Gilbert Shelton's **Fabulous Furry Freak Brothers** in the twilight years of the underground comix scene, the Rip Off Press series takes a witty but authoritative look at history, from day one on.

Exhaustively researched, **Cartoon History** first appeared in 1978. It is meticulously produced by Larry Gonick, who refers to Shelton as his comics' midwife but is the last person you'd expect to be a cartoonist—he holds a masters degree in mathematics from Harvard University. Also nurturing a passion for the past and for drawing, Gonick has lovingly detailed the events that have shaped our world, from prehistory to 564AD and the Fall of

Rome across a 13-issue series finishing in 1994.

But that was not to be the end of **Cartoon History,** which found a champion in Jacqueline Onassis, President John F Kennedy's widow. An editor at Doubleday, she was responsible for the series being repackaged for the mainstream book trade. **From the Big Bang to Alexander the Great** and **From the Springtime of China to the Fall of Rome** collected the original 13 issues.

With those two compilations under his belt, being widely praised for his even-handed rather than Anglo-centric handling of world cultures and having already produced the 400-page **Cartoon History of the United States** in 1991, Gonick ploughs on in book form. **Cartoon History of the World III,** subtitled **From the Rise of Arabia to the Renaissance** is a 320-pager that was published in 2002.

Through Onassis, Gonick's opus has transcended its underground roots, drawing praise from all quarters with astronomer Carl Sagan calling it, "A delight. Charming, irreverent, with a true global perspective. A better way to learn human history than school textbooks."

ABOVE: The cover to The Cartoon History of the Universe III, the first volume in Gonick's graphic novel series to consist entirely of material not reprinted from the original comic.

LEFT: From issue #1, Larry Gonick's comix avatar—a narrator guiding the reader down the ages—introduces The Cartoon History of the Universe.

FACING PAGE: The cover to the 1978 first issue of the Rip Off Press series.

Comix checklist

During the past four decades, almost 1,000 underground comix have been produced, with many running to multiple editions. Following is the major output, listing all key artists involved.

AARDVARK
(1971, Dave Faggioli)
#1-2; 28 pages.
Art: Holman, Neilson, Passey

ABDUCTION OF DOT DARLING
Oneshot. Art: Cabarga

ABORTION EVE
(1973, Nanny Goat)
Oneshot; 36 pages.
Art: Chevli, Sutton

ABYSS
(1970, self published)
Oneshot. Art: Jones, Wrightson, Kaluta

ACE HOLE MIDGET DETECTIVE
(1974, Apex) Oneshot.
Art: Spiegelman

ACE OF SPADES
(1973) Oneshot.
Art: Blamire

ACNE PIMPLES
(1975) Oneshot.
Art: Adams

AFTERWORLD
(1975)
#1-4. Art: Blake

AIR PIRATES FUNNIES
(1971, Air Pirates Collective/Northern

California Power Failure/Hell Comics)
#1-2; 36 pages.
Art: London, Hallgren, O'Neill

AIR PIRATES FUNNIES TABLOID
(1972, Air Pirates Collective) Oneshot;
8 pages. Art: London, Hallgren, O'Neill, Todd, Flenniken, Richards

ALL-AMERICAN HIPPIE COMIX
(1995, Kitchen Sink)
Reprints Dope Comix 1

ALL-ATOMIC COMICS
(1976, Educomics)
Oneshot; 28 pages.
Art: Rifas, Weber, Sampson, Rippee

ALL CANADIAN BEAVER COMIX
(1974, Last Gasp Eco-Funnies)
#1; 36 pages. Art: Holmes, Falcioni, Boates, Knuut

ALL DUCK
(1972, Co. & Sons)
#1; 36 pages. Art: Hatchman, Bramley, Epstein, Kinney

ALL GIRL ROMANCE
(1975) Oneshot.
Art: Adams

ALL GIRL THRILLS
(1971, Print Mint) #1;
36 pages. Art: Wood, Robbins, Mendes

ALL STARS
(1970, San Francisco Comic Book Co.)
#1-2. Art: Griffin

ALL NEW UNDER-GROUND COMIX
(1972-74, Last Gasp Eco-Funnies)
36 pages.
#1-3 *Armageddon*
Art: Steel
#2 *Hot Crackers*
Art: Clapp, Corbett
#3 *High School Funnies & The Mountain* (52 pages)
Art: Hubbell, Todd, Silverberg, Richards,
#4 *Big League Laffs*
Art: Himes
#5 *Two-Fisted Zombies*. Art: Veitch

ALTERNATE MEDIA COMICS & STORIES
(1970) Oneshot.
Art: Shelton

AMAZING DOPE TALES
(1967, Greg Shaw)
#1. Art: Shaw

AMAZON COMICS
(1972, Rip Off Press)
Oneshot; 28 pages.
Art: Stack, Graves

AMERICAN FLYER FUNNIES (1972,
The Print Mint) #1-2;
44 pages. Art: Welz, Sutherland, Todd

AMERICAN SPLENDOR
(1976, Harvey Pekar)
#1-17; 52 pages.
Art: Dumm, Budgett, Pekar, Crumb

AMPUTEE LOVE
(1975, Last Gasp Eco-Funnies)
Oneshot; 36 pages.
Art: Boates, Kosinki, Rene & Rich Jensen

ANARCHY COMICS
(1978, Last Gasp Eco-Funnies)
#1-4; 36 pages.
Art: Kinney, Seyfried, Spain, Gebbie, Shelton, Epistolier

AN AMERICAN REVOLUTION (1/2 BURNT TOAST)

(1976) Oneshot.
Art: Rifas

AN ARMY OF PRINCIPLES
(1976, Kitchen Sink)
Oneshot; 36 pages.
Art: Rifas, Rippee, Wright, Price, Collins

ANDROMEDA
(1977, Andromeda)
#1-6; 52 pages.
Art: Motter, Allison, Meers, Tiptree, Ross

ANIMAL BITE COMIX
(1979, Everyman Studios) Oneshot;
36 pages.
Art: Hansen, Erling, Nordberg, Kennedy

ANIMAL 8 PAGER
(1974) Oneshot.
Art: Hansen

ANOMALY
(1972, Bud Plant)
#1-4; 36 pages.
Art: Corben, Kline, Strand

A+PLUS
(1977, Megaton)
#1-2; 68 pages.
Art: Stolinsky, Nino, Orzechowski, Liembieda, Siembieda

ARCADE: THE COMICS REVUE
(1975, The Print Mint) #1-7; 44 pages.
Art: Spiegelman, Lynch, Griffith, Crumb, Spain, Osborne, Armstrong

AREBA KOALA
(1977, Kep Productions)
Oneshot; 36 pages.
Art: R. Wozniak, M. Wozniak

ARE YOUR HIGHS GETTING YOU DOWN?
(1980, Last Gasp Eco-Funnies)
Oneshot; 32 pages.
Art: Wings

ARIK KAHN
(1977)
#1. Art: Reyes

ARMADILLO
(1969, Rip Off Press)
#1-2. Art. Franklyn

ARMAGEDDON
(1970, Last Gasp)
#1-3. Art: Steel

ARMPIT OF FEAR, THE
(1972, San Francisco Comic Book Co.)
Oneshot. Art: Shaw

ART 2000
(1980, Everyman Studios) Oneshot;
20 pages.
Art: Lynch, Romero, Whitney, O'Neill, Punchatz

ART & BEAUTY MAGAZINE (1996,
Kitchen Sink) #1-2;
36 pages. Art: Crumb

ARTISTIC COMICS
(1973, Golden Gate)
Oneshot; 68 pages.
Art: Crumb

ARTSY FARTSY FUNNIES (1974)
Art: Rosenkranz, Baren

ATOMIC COMIX
(1975)
Oneshot. Art: Karrow

ATOM ROBOT ADVENTURER
(1976) #1. Art: Terry

ATTIC SENTINEL; PROMETHEUS UNBOUND
(San Francisco Comic Book Co.) #1. Art: Anderson, Senauke

AUSTIN COMIX
(1976, Limestone

Press) Oneshot.
Art: Bates

AUSTIN STONE
(1975) #1-2.
Art: Garrett, Juke

AUSTENTATIOUS
(1973) Oneshot.
Art: Bradley, Banman, Turner, Priest

AUTHENTIC VISIONARY COMIX
(1976, Prairie Tales)
Oneshot; 52 pages.
Art: Petertil, Crook Jr., Cohen

AUTO-BE-RECYCLED
(1980, Last Gasp Eco-Funnies)
Oneshot; 36 pages.
Art: Irons, Boxell, Ballard, Kemmerer

AVENGING WORLD
(1973; Monster Times)
Oneshot. Art: Ditko

AWAKE (ANNOUNCING JEHOVA'S K) (1972,
San Francisco Comic Book Co.) Oneshot.
Art: Deitch, Kinney, Ripp, Arlington

BACKWATER BABIES
(1975, Last Gasp)

Oneshot. Art: Caldwell

BACTERIA
Art: Ripp

BAEGLES LOONEY HEARTS CLUB
(1977, Karma Komix Ko)
Oneshot 36 pages.
Art: Oliver

BAKERSFIELD KOUNTRY KOMICS
(1973, Last Gasp)
Oneshot; 36 pages.
Art: Welz, Sutherland

BALLOON VENDOR
(1971, Rip Off Press)
Oneshot; 28 pages.
Art: Schreir, Sheridan

BALONEY MOCCASINS COMICS (1969)
#1. Art: Anderson

BANZAI!
(1973, Kitchen Sink)
Oneshot; 36 pages.
Art: Beck, Brand, Deitch, Poplaski

BARBARIAN COMICS
(1972, California Comics) #1-4; 36 pages. Art: Hale, Loudin, Crumb

BARBARIAN KILLER FUNNIES (1974, Bud Plant) #1; 36 pages.
Art: Bird

BARBARIAN WOMEN COMICS (1975/1977, California Comics)
#1-2; 36 pages.
Art: Sidebottom, Redondo, Han, Steel, Robbins

BAREFOOTZ FUNNIES
(1975, Kitchen Sink)
#1-3; 36 pages.
Art: Cruse

BARN OF FEAR, THE
(1978, Comic Art Gallery) #1; 44 pages.

Art: Alcala, Shell, Moench, Costanza, Hunt, Renz

BEANTOWN FUNNIES
(1973) Oneshot.
Art: Lippincott

BEASTIALITY
(1976, Apandamandis Productions)
#1; 32 pages. Art: Spagnola, Treacy, Hansen, Erling, Wilber, Buniak

BEER COMICS (1976)
#1. Art: Spagnola

BENT
(1971, The Print Mint) Oneshot; 28 pages. Art: Wilson

BEST BUY COMICS
(1979, Apex Novelties)
Oneshot; 36 pages.
Art: Crumb, Kominsky

BEWILDERING INTIMACIES (1977)
Oneshot. Art: May

BEYOND TIME AND AGAIN (1972, Los Angeles Staff)
Oneshot. Art: Metzger

BICENTENNIAL GROSS-OUTS (1976, Yentzer and Gonif Comic Production)
Oneshot; 36 pages.
Art: Stout, DiCaprio, Greenwood, Serpiellow

BIG APPLE COMIX
(1975, Big Apple)
Oneshot; 36 pages.
Art: Steinberg, Hama, Kirchner, Wood

BIG ASS COMICS
(1969, Rip Off Press)
#1-2; 28 pages.
Art: Crumb

BIG LEAGUE LAFFS
(1973, Last Gasp)
Oneshot. Art: Himes

BIG TRUCKER, THE
(1978, Dancing Rock)
#1; 36 pages.
Art: Dunn, Abbott, Sigfried

BIG YELLOW DRAWING BOOK
(1974, Hugh O'Neill & Associates) Oneshot.
Art: M & H O'Neill

BIJOU FUNNIES
(1968, Bijou Publishing)
#1-8; 36 pages.
Art: Lynch, Lieberman, Williamson, Crumb, Shelton

BINKY BROWN MEETS THE HOLY VIRGIN MARY (1972, Last Gasp Eco-Funnies)
Oneshot; 44 pages.
Art: Green

BIZARRE SEX
(1972, Kitchen Sink)
#1-10; 36 pages.
Art: Kitchen, Boxell, Green, Clyne, Pugh, Pound, Geary, Stiles Loebs, Cruse, Kinney

BLACK-LITE COMIX
(1972, San Francisco Comic Book Co.)
#1. Art: Jerry

BLACK AND WHITE COMICS (1973, Apex Novelties) Oneshot; 28 pages. Art: Crumb

BLAZING VIOLENCE
(1975) #1-2.
Art: Blamire

BLOOD ON THE MOON
(1978, Last Gasp)
#1; 36 pages.
Art: Jaxon

BLOWN MIND, THE
(1966) Oneshot.
Art: Yampolsky

BOGEYMAN
(1970, Co. & Sons)
#1-3; 28 pages.
Art: Jaxon, Hayes, Lynch, Rodgriguez, Deitch, Griffin, Irons

BOOK OF DREAMS
(1977) Oneshot.
Art: Thompson

BOOK OF RAZIEL, THE
(1969, The Print Mint) Oneshot.
Art: Thompson

BOOK OF ZOMXATBXIA
(1976) Oneshot.
Art: Snow

BRAIN FANTASY
(Last Gasp Eco-Funnies)
#1 (1972,); 36 pages.
Art: Shubb, Metzger, Inwood, Parker
#2 (1975); 36 pages.
Art: Turner, Todd, Smith, Becker

BREAKDOWNS: AN ANTHOLOGY OF STRIPS
(1977, Nostalgia Press) Oneshot.
Art: Spiegelman

BRIDE'S MEMORIES, A
(1975)
Oneshot. Art: Adams

BRIDGE CITY BEER COMIX (1973, Public Publications/Bridge City Booger Co.)
#1-3. Art: Geary

BUCK BOY
(1976, San Francisco Comic Book Co.)
Oneshot. Art: Hayes

BUM WAD
(1971, Yahoo Productions)
Oneshot; 28 pages.
Art: Geiser, Stalker

BUZZARD
(1970, Co. & Sons)
#1. Art: Wink

CALIFORNIA COMICS
(1974, California Comics)
#1-3; 36 pages.
Art: Watson, Williams, Shaw, Meugniot

CANARSIE CREEPS
(1974)
Oneshot. Art: Newman

CAP'N RETRO
(1977, Texas)
#1-3. Art: Bryson

CAPTAIN, THE
(1972, The Print Mint)
Oneshot; 44 pages. Art: Vogrin

CAPTAIN GUTS
(1969, The Print Mint) #1-3; 28 pages.
Art: Welz

CAPTAIN JOINT COMICS (1966)
#1. Art: Beckman

CARTOON HISTORY OF THE UNIVERSE, THE
(1978, Rip Off Press)
#1-9; 52 pages.
Art: Gonick

CAZCO
(1976,self published)
Oneshot. Art: Yeh

CHANGES
(1972, San Francisco Comic Book Co.)
#1. Art: Jordan

CHECKERED DEMON
(1977, Last Gasp)
#1-3; 36 pages.
Art: Wilson

CHEECH WIZARD
(1986, Rip Off Press)
#1-4; 36 pages.
Art: Bode

CHERRY POPTART
(1982, Last Gasp/ Kitchen Sink)
#1-22; 36 pages.
Art: Welz, Todd, Kinney, Boxell

CHICANOS, THE
(1973, North American Congress on Latin America) Oneshot.
Art: Rius

CHOCOLATE ALPHABET (1978, Last Gasp)
Oneshot; 28 pages.
Art: Todd, Ellison

CHOICE MEATS
(1971, Peanut Juice/ Adams Apple) #1-2;
Art: Hansen, Schnadig

CLASS WAR COMIX
(1979, Kitchen Sink)
#1; 36 pages.
Art: Harper, Kinney

CLEARLAKE COMIX
(1981, Polaris Adventures)
#1; 44 pages.
Art: Cunningham, Leach

CLOUD COMICS
(1971, Kitchen Sink)
#1-2. 32 pages
Art: Bramley, Skurski

CLOWNS
(1972, Yahoo)
Oneshot; 28 pages.
Art: Geiser

COCAINE COMIX
(1976, Last Gasp Eco-Funnies)
#1-4; 36 pages. Art: Stout, Chidlaw, DiCaprio, Boates

COCHING KOMIX
(1976, San Francisco Comic Book Co.)
Oneshot.
Art: Bulandadi

COLLECTIVE UNCONSCIENCE OF ODD BODKINS
(1973, Volcano)
Oneshot. Art: O'Neil

COLLEGIATE COMIX
(1971, The Print Mint) Oneshot.
Art: Mcgehee

COLOR
(1971, Victor Moscoso)
Oneshot; 36 pages.
Art: Moscoso

COME OUT COMIX
(1974, Portland's Women Resource Center) Oneshot;
36 pages. Art: Wings

COMIX BOOK
(1974, Marvel Comics
#1-3, Kitchen Sink
#4-5) 68 pages.
Art: Kitchen, Poplaski, Meltzer, Robbins, Stiles, Spiegelman

COMIX UNLIMITED
(1975, M&M) #1-2.
Art: Kimszal, Erlin

COMMIES FROM MARS
(1973, Kitchen Sink)
#1-6; 36 pages.
Art: Boxell, Poplaski, Stiles, Crawford, Griffen, Crumb

COMPLETE FART AND OTHER BODY EMISSIONS, THE
(1977, Kitchen Sink)
Oneshot; 36 pages.
Art: Marrs, Poplaski

COMPOST COMICS
(1973, Gasparotti, Tellez, Todd & Reece)
#1; 36 pages. Art: Todd, Gasarotti, Tellez, Metzger, Reece, Boyce

CONCEPTUAL FUN
Art: Adams

CONAN (1/2 DR. STRENGE) (1973)
Art: Thompson

CONSPIRACY CAPERS
(1969)
Art: Williamson

COOCHY COOTY MEN'S COMICS
(1970, The Print Mint) #1; 28 pages.
Art: R & S Williams

CORN FED COMICS
(1972, Kim Deitch)
#1; 36 pages. Art: Deitch

CORPORATE CRIME COMICS
(1977, Kitchen Sink)
#1-2; 36 pages.
Art: Rifas, Irons, Driggs, Poplaski, Robbins, Colwell, Rudahl, Deitch

CORRUPTION COMICS
(1972, San Francisco Comic Book Co.)
Oneshot. Art: Nordey

COUNTRY HITS JAMBOREE (1977)
Art: Buckler

COSMIC CAPERS
(1972, Big Muddy Comics) Oneshot;
36 pages.
Art: Kelly, Dameron, Wright, Frolich

COSMIC CIRCUS
(1977, Cosmic Brain Trust) #1-4.
Art: M. Bode, Burnham, Roper, V. Bode, King, Todd

COVER-UP LOWDOWN
(1977, Rip Off Press)
Oneshot; 52 pages.
Art: Mavrides, Kinney

CRYSTAL NIGHT, ADVENTURES OF
(1980, Kitchen Sink)

Oneshot; 36 pages.
Art: Peters

CUNT COLORING BOOK
(1975, Pearchild)
Oneshot; 44 pages.
Art: Corinne, Shelly

CUNT COMICS
(1969, Apex Novelties)
#1. Art: Hayes

CUNT FART FUNNIES
(1973) Art: Hosier

**DAN O'NEILL'S
COMICS AND STORIES**
Vol. 1 #1-3 (1971,
Company & Sons);
52 pages. Art: O'Neill
Vol 2 #1-2 (1975,
Comics and Comix).
Art: O'Neill, London

DAS KAMPF
(1963, Walter Bachner
and Bagginer)
Oneshot; 52 pages.
Art: Bode, Todd

DEADBONE
(1976, Northern
Comfort) Oneshot; 80
pages. Art: Bode

DEADEARTH KOMIX
(1972, Zondervan)
Oneshot. Art: Niblick

DEATH RATTLE
(1972, Kitchen Sink)
#1-3; 36 pages.
Art: Corben, Boxell,
Pound, Poplaski

DEEP 3D COMIX
(1970, Kitchen Sink)
#1; 36 pages. Art:
Glassford, Lynch,
Kitchen

DEMENTED PERVERT
(1971, Yahoo)
#1-2; 36 pages.
Art : Geiser, Carson,
Stalker

DESPAIR (1969, The
Print Mint)

Oneshot; 28 pages.
Art: Crumb

**DEVIANT SLICE
FUNNIES** (1972,
The Print Mint)
#1-2; 36 pages.
Art: Irons, Veitch

DIE GRECHEN
(1973) Art: Harter

DIRTBALL FUNNIES
(1972, Krupp Comic
Works) Oneshot;
Art: Lantzy, Molider

DIRTY DUCK
(1972, Co. & Sons)
Oneshot; 36 pages.
Art: London

**DIRTY LAUNDRY
COMICS** (1974,
Cartoonists Co-Op
Press) #1-2; 36 pages
Art: Crumb, Kominski

**DIRTY LAUNDRY
COMICS, THE
COMPLETE**
(1993, Last Gasp)
Oneshot; 118 pages.
Art: Crumb, Kominski

D.O.A. COMICS
(1976, Saving Grace)
#1; 44 pages.
Art: Jim Osborne

DOLL
(1989, Rip Off Press)
#1-8; 36 pages.
Art: Colwell

DOPE COMIX
(1978, Kitchen Sink)
#1-5; 36 pages.
Art: Steffan, Stiles,
Rudahl, Deitch,
Kitchen

DOPIN' DAN
(1972, Last Gasp
Eco-Funnies)
#1-4; 36 pages.
Art: Richards, Murphy,
Hallgren, Flenniken,
London

DORMAN'S DOGGIE
(1979, Rip Off Press)
Oneshot; 52 pages.
Art: Stack

DOUGLAS COMIX
(1972, Douglas
Communications)
Art: Spiegelman

DR. ATOMIC
(1978, Last Gasp
Eco-Funnies) #1-6;
36 pages. Art: Todd

**DR. ATOMIC'S
MARIJUANA
MULTIPLIER**
(1974, Kistone Press)
Oneshot; 20 pages.
Art: Todd

DREAMS
(1974) #1. Art: Beck

DROOL
(1972, Co. & Sons)
#1; 36 pages.
Art: Surski, Hatchman,
Burwen, Reece, Hama

**DR. WIRTHAM'S
COMIX & STORIES**
(1976, Clifford Neal)
#1-10; 36 pages.
Art: Neal

DT'S (1974, Yahoo)
Oneshot; 32 pages.
Art: Geiser

DUTCH TREAT
(1977, Kitchen Sink)
Oneshot. Art: Geradts

DYING DOLPHIN, THE
(1970, The Print
Mint) Oneshot; 36
pages. Art: Evans,
Griffin, Cobb

DYNAMITE DAMSELS
(1976 self published)
Oneshot. Art: Gregory

EBON
(1970, San Francisco
Comic Book Co.)
#1. Art: Fuller

EL PERFECTO

(1973, Print Mint)
Oneshot; 36 pages.
Art: Crumb, Hayes,
Green, Deitch

ENERGY COMICS
(1980, Educomics)
#1; 36 pages.
Art: Rifas, Kitchen,
Farmer, Zarsky, Crumb

ENIGMA!
(1973, Last Gasp
Eco-Funnies)
Oneshot; 36 pages.
Art: Tellez, Gasparotti,
Todd, Boyce, Reece

ETERNAL COMICS
(1973, Last Gasp
Eco-Funnies)
#1; 36 pages.
Art: Thompson,
Crumb, Bowers,
Ginsberg

ETERNITY
(1975) Art: Gordon

**EVERYDAY IS
SUNDAY FUNNIES**
(1970) Art. Abbott

**EVERYTHING YOU
WANTED TO KNOW
ABOUT YOGA
BUT WERE AFRAID TO
ASK** (1972, San
Francisco Comic Book
Co.) Art: Kinney

**EXILE INTO
CONSCIOUSNESS**
(Rip Off Press)
Oneshot. Art: Jaxon

EXTRA! COMIX
(1969) #1. Art: Peck

E.Z. WOLF
(1977, Rip Off Press)
Oneshot; 52 pages.
Art: Richards, Gonick,
Leonard

**E.Z. WOLF'S
ASTRAL EXPRESS**
(1977, Last Gasp)
Oneshot; 36 pages.

**FACTS O' LIFE SEX
EDUCATION FUNNIES**
(1972, Rip Off Press)
Oneshot; 36 pages.
Art: Fountain,
Shelton, Brand,
Frutkoff, Crumb

FAERIE STAR
(1977, Moon Press)
#1; 44 pages. Art:
Cothran, Raney,
Giovanni, Kirby, Sim

FALL
(1972, San Francisco
Comic Book Co.)
Oneshot. Art: Horton

FANBOY
(1972) Art: Hudson

FANTAGOR
(1971, Last Gasp
Eco-Funnies)
#1-5; 36 pages.
Art: Corben, Armitage,
Arnold

FAN FREE FUNNIES
(1973) #1-3.
Art: Trumbo, Bennett

FARK COMIX
(1969)
Art: Guadalupes

FAR OUT WEST
(1976, Performing
Arts Social Society)
#1; 36 pages. Art: Eve

**FAT FREDDY'S CAT,
THE ADVENTURES OF**
(1977, Rip Off Press)
#1-7; 52 pages.
Art: Shelton, Sheridan

**FAT FREDDY'S
COMICS AND STORIES**
(1983, Rip Off Press)
#1-2; 36 pages.
Art: Shelton,
Mavrides, Robins,
Jaxon, Spain

FEAR AND LAUGHTER
(1977, Kitchen Sink)
Oneshot; 36 pages.

Art: Shaw, Stout, Wray

FEDS 'N' HEADS
(1968, The Print
Mint) Oneshot;
28 pages.
Art: Shelton, Adkins

FEELGOOD FUNNIES
(1972, Rip Off Press)
Oneshot; 28 pages.
Art: Stack, Frutkoff,
Hatcher, Shelton

FELCH COMICS
(1975, Keith Green)
#1; 36 pages. Digest
sized. Art: Williams,
Wilson, Crumb,
Osborne, Spain

FEVER DREAMS
(1972, Kitchen Sink)
Oneshot; 36 pages.
Art: Corben, Strand,
Richardson

**FICTIONAL
NARRATIVES
BY DENNIS FUJITAKE,
A SELECTION OF**
(1971, Fantagraphics)
Oneshot; 16 pages.
Art: Fujitake

50'S FUNNIES
(1980, Kitchen Sink)
#1; 44 pages.
Art: Shell, Stout,
Yeates, Bissette

FIREWORXARIS
(1977) Art: Todd

FIRE SALE
(1989, Rip Off Press)
Oneshot; 52 pages.
Art: Bode, Kinney,
Ellison, Todd, Spain

FIRST KINGDOM
(1974, Comics
and Comix)
#1-24; 36 pages.
Art: Katz, Scortia

**FLAMED
OUT FUNNIES**
(1976, Rip Off Press)

#1-2; 28 pages.
Art: Murphy

FOG CITY COMICS
(1977, Stampart)
#1-3; 36 pages.
Art: Hamilton, Holmes,
Newton, Boates

FOLK FUNNIES
(1973, New Morning
Talent Union/Co. &
Sons) #1-2; 36 pages.
Art: McKenna

FOOD COMIX
(1980, ducomics/
Leonard Rifas)
#1; 36 pages.
Art: Rifas, Driggs,
Chalkley, Boxell

**FORBIDDEN
KNOWLEDGE COMICS**
(1975, Last Gasp)
#1-2; 36 pages.
Art: DiCaprio,
Williams,
Chidlaw, Golden

**FORTY YEAR OLD
HIPPIE CATALOG, THE
WHOLE**
(1976, Rip Off Press)
#1-2; 52 pages.
Art: Richards

FOUR STAR FINAL
(1970, Rip Off Press)
Oneshot. Art: Scudder

**FREAK BROTHERS,
THE FABULOUS FURRY**
(1971, Rip Off Press)
#1-13; 52 pages.
Art: Shelton

**FREAK BROTHERS,
THOROUGHLY
RIPPED WITH THE**
(1976, Rip Off Press)
#1-2. Art: Shelton

FRED FOIL TALES
(1977, New Wave
Comics) #1; 4 pages.
Art: Sherman

FRESCAZIZIS
(1977, Last Gasp)
Oneshot; 36 pages.
Art: Gebbie, Dubin,
Warren

**FRESH BLOOD FUNNY
BOOK**
(1979, Last Gasp Eco-
Funnies)
Oneshot; 36 pages.
Art: Leonard

FREZNO FUNNIES
(1973, Doug Hansen)
#1-2. Art: Hansen

FRITZ BUGS OUT
(1972, Ballantine Books)
Oneshot; 100 pages.
Art: Crumb

FUKTUP FUNNIES
(1972, Head Imports)
Oneshot; 36 pages.
Art: Nelson, Potts

FUNNY AMINALS
(1972, Apex Novelties)
Oneshot; 36 pages. Art:
Crumb, Green,
Spiegelman

FUNNYBOOK
(1971, Almighty
Publishing)
#1; 28 pages.
Art: Shelton, Welz

**FUNNY BOOK, THE
NEW** (1977, Larry Fuller
Presents) #1-3; 36
pages. Art: Fuller, Nino,
Plumb, Davis

FUNNY PAPERS, THE
(1975, Funny Papers)
#1-3; 24 pages.
Art: Bode, Brubeck,
Crumb, Richards,
Holman

GAG REFLEX
(1994, Skip
Williamson)
#1; 36 pages.
Art: Williamson

GALAXY
(1972, San Francisco Comic Book Co.)
#1, Art: Santos

GAMUT
(1976, Sheridan College)
#1-2; 52 pages. Art: Hansen, Eisner, Bilinsky, Stephens, Ploog

GANG BANG
(1980, Nuance)
#1-3; 52 pages. Art: Wood

GARBAGE COMIX
(1973) Oneshot.
Art: Krus, Mcdonald

G.A.S. LITE
(1973) Oneshot.
Art: Crumb

GATES OF EDEN
(1982, Fantaco)
#1; 52 pages. Art: Marrs, Jones, Russell, Geary

GAY COMIX
(1980, Kitchen Sink)
#1-25; 36 pages. Art: Cruse, Holmes, Marrs, Fugate, Waller, Worley, Mangels, Franson

GAY HEARTHROBS
(1976, Ful-Horne)
#1-3; 44 pages. Art: Spade, Plumb, Borg, Orchid, Corona, Bold, Remington

GHOST MOTHER COMICS
(1968) #1. Art. Peck

GIMMIE
(1972, Head Imports)
#1; 36 pages. Art: Rifas, Ciampi, Garcia, Rippee

GIRL FIGHT COMICS
(1974, The Print Mint)

#1-2; 36 pages.
Art: Robbins

GIVE ME LIBERTY
(1976, Rip Off Press)
#1; 52 pages. Art: Shelton, Richards, Murphy, Halgren

GJDRKZLXCBWQ COMICS (1973, Glenn Bray) Oneshot; 36 pages. Art: Wolverton, Williams

GLASS CITY GIGGLES
(1974)#1-4. Art: Kelley

GOD NOSE: SNOT REEL (1971, Rip Off Press) Oneshot; 44 pages. Art: Jaxon

GOOD JIVE
(1972, Pooo Bear)
#1-2; 36 pages. Art: Green, Bevacqua, Foss

GOOGIEWAUMER COMICS (1969, The Print Mint) Oneshot; 36 pages. Art: Pugh, Jones

GOPHER FREEDOM COMIX
(1975; Trans-Prairie Gopher Freedom Propoganda Press)
#1. Art: Geary

GOTHIC BLIMP WORKS (1969)
#1-8. Art: Crumb, Spain, Williams, Shelton, Deitch

GRAND JURY (1975, Edge City) #1.

GREASER COMICS
(1971, Half Ass Press)
#1-2; 28 pages.
Art: DiCaprio, Down Jacomma, Bloomer

GREAT MARIJUANA DEBATE
(1972, Kitchen Sink)

Oneshot. Art: Poplaski

GREAT DIGGS OF 77: THE YEAR IN CARTOONS
(1977, Rip Off Press)
#1-2; 68 pages.
Art: Driggs, Bordett

GRIFFITH OBSERVATORY
(1979, Rip Off Press)
#1; 36 pages.
Art: Griffith

GRIM WIT
(1973, Last Gasp Eco-Funnies)
#1-2; 36 pages.
Art: Corben, Jaxon, Moench, Holman

GRITS (1977)
Oneshot. Art: Tomasic

GROSS OUT COMIX
(1969)
#1-2. Art: Baker

GROUND POUND COMIX (1987, Blackthorne) #1; 52 pages. Art: Pound, Evanier, Clark

GRUNT
(1972, Grunt Records)
#1-2; 12 pages.
Art: Irons, Veitch

GUANO COMIX
(1973, The Print Mint)
#4; 44 pages. Art: McCleery, Narum, Sharp

GUNFIGHTER
(1971, Ivan's Press)
#1-4. Art: Ivan

HAIRY WHO/HAIRY WHO SIDESHOW
Oneshots. Art: Nutt

HALF TON PICKUP
(1972, San Francisco Comic Book Co.)
Oneshot. Art: Schenkman

HAPPY ENDINGS COMICS
(1969, Rip Off Press)
Oneshot. Art: Jaxon

HARDBOILED ANIMAL COMICS
(1982, Brouhaha Studio)
#1; 52 pages.
Art: Fuller, Vojtko, Erling, Kochell, Armstrong

HARD TIMES
(1971, Adams Apple)
Oneshot. Art: Hansen

HAROLD HEDD
Art: Holmes
#1 (1972, Georgia Straight): 36 pages
#2 (1977, Last Gasp Eco-Funnies)

HAROLD HEDD HITLER'S COCAINE
(1984, Kitchen Sink)
#1-2; 36 pages. Art: Holmes

HAWGFAT FUNNIES
(1972) Oneshot.
Art: Sheldon

HEAD COMIX
(1970, Ballantine Books)
Oneshot; 68 pages. Art: Crumb

HEART
(1973, John Aulenta)
Oneshot; 36 pages.
Art: Aulenta

HEAR THE SOUND OF MY FEET WALKING
(1969, Glide Urban Center)
Oneshot. Art: O'Neil

HEAVY TRAGI-COMICS
(1969, The Print Mint)
#1; 44 pages. Art: Irons

HEEBY JEEBIES
(1976, Stray Cat Comix Studio)
#1. Art: Milke

HEEHEE COMICS
(1970, Co. & Sons)
Oneshot. Art: Ripp

HEMP FOR VICTORY
(1993, Starhead Comics) Oneshot; 28 pages. Art: Penn, Carbajal, Baisden

HIEROGRAPHS
(1970)
Oneshot. Art: Conrad

HIGH ADVENTURE
(1971, Kitchen Sink)
#1. Art: Kline

HIFI COMIX (1973)
Oneshot. Art: McGhee

HIGH ADVENTURE
(1973, Kitchen Sink)
#1. Art: Kline

HIGH FLYIN' FUNNIES COMIX & STORIES
(1970, The Print Mint) #1; 36 pages. Art: Crawford, Askew

HIGH SCHOOL FUNNIES
(1973, Last Gasp)
#1. Art: Hubbell, Silverberg

HIT THE ROAD: A COMIX FOR & ABOUT HITCHIKING
(1972, The Print Mint) #1; 36 pages. Art: Ryan, Rosander

HOBO STORIES
(1979, Everyman Studios)
#1; 44 pages. Art: Taylor, Romero, Adams, Hansen

HOME GROWN FUNNIES (1971, Kitchen Sink) Oneshot; 44 pages. Art: Crumb

HONKYTONK SUE
(1979, Bob Boze Bell)
#1-4; 76 pages.
Art: Bell, Lovejoy,

Harshberger, Giannatti

HOT CRACKERS
(1973, Last Gasp)
#1. Art: Clapp

HOTSHOT
(1974, James Glenn Productions)
#1. Art: Perez

HOT STUF'
(1974, Sal Quartuccio)
#1-8; 60 pages.
Art: Barr, Maher, Perez, Corben, Buckler

HUNGRY CHUCK BISCUITS (1971, Kitchen Sink)
Oneshot; Art: Clyne

HUP
(1987, Last Gasp)
#1-4; 36 pages.
Art: Crumb

HYDROGEN BOMB AND BIOCHEMICAL WARFARE FUNNIES
(1970, Rip Off Press)
#1; Art: Shelton

HYPER COMICS
(1979, Kitchen Sink)
Oneshot.

I AM (1972, Cosmic Comics) Oneshot.
Art: King

IF THE SHOE FITS
(1971) #1-2. Art: Hayes, Griffith

IKE AND MAMIE
(1979, Rick Geary)
Oneshot.
ID #1-3

ILLUMINATIONS
(1971, The Print Mint) Oneshot.
Art: Mendes

IMAGE OF THE BEAST
(1973, Last Gasp Eco-Funnies)
Oneshot. Art: Boxell

IMAGINE
#1-6. Art: Russell

INCREDIBLE ROCKY, THE (1975)
Art: Andreai

INFAMOUS FUNNIES
(1973) #1.
Art: Mooney

INNER CITY ROMANCE
(1972, Last Gasp Eco-Funnies)
#1-5. Art: Colwell

INSECT FEAR
(1969, The Print Mint) #1-3. Art: Spain

INSTANT COMIX AND DRAWINGS
(1977, Stray Cat Comix Studio)
#1-3. Art: Milke, Vojtko, Edgar

ISMET (1981, Canis Publications) #1-5.
Art: Wadsworth

IT AIN'T ME BABE COMIX (1970, Last Gasp Eco-Funnies)
Oneshot. Art: Robbins

IT'S A DOG'S LIFE
(1970, Last Gasp Eco-Funnies)

JAM JAR
(1972, San Francisco Comic Book Co.)
Oneshot. Art: Shaw

JAXON'S ILLUSTRATED TALES
(1984, FRT Publishing)
#1. Art: Jaxon

JESUS MEETS THE ARMED SERVICES
(1970, Rip Off Press)
Art: Sturgeon

JESUS, THE NEW ADVENTURES OF
(1971, Rip Off Press)
#1-3; 44 pages.
Art: Stack, Shelton

JIZ COMICS (1979, Apex Novelties) #1.
Art: Crumb, Wilson

JOEL BECK'S COMICS AND STORIES
(1977, Kitchen Sink)
Oneshot. Art: Beck

JOURNAL OF POPULAR CULTURE
(1977) Oneshot.
Art: Bissette, Veitch

JUDY TUNAFISH
(1973, Adams Apple)
Oneshot, Art: Hansen

JUICY (1974)
#1. Art: Macmillan

JUICE CITY (1977)
Oneshot. Art: Phillips

JUNIOR JACKALOPE
(1982, Nevada City)
#1-2. Art: Various

JUNK COMIX
(1970, Do City Productions)
Oneshot.

JUNKWAFFEL
(1976, Last Gasp/Print Mint) #1-5; 36 pages.
Art: Bode, Todd

KAMPUS KAPERS
(1975, Art Comics)
#1-6. Art: K. Jackson

KANNED KORN KOMIX
(1969, Total Entity Pub.) Oneshot.
Art: Schnepf

KAVER KOMIX
(1972, self published)
#1. Art: Kristofferson

KING BEE
(1969, Apex Novelties)
#1 Art: Crumb

KING BISCUIT ENTERTAINERS KOMIX
(1974)Oneshot. Art: Lee

KINGDOM OF HEAVEN IS WITH YOU

(1969, The Print Mint) #1.
Art: Thompson

KISSER COMIX
Art: Thibeault

KOAN COMICS
(1969) Oneshot.
Art: Boldrick

KOMMA-KAZI KOMICS
(1972, Starflower Inc.)
#1. Art: McGurl

KOSMIC CITY KOMIX
(1973, Kosmic City)
#1. Art: Womelduff

KUKAWY COMICS
(1969, Print Mint)
#1. Art: Thompson

KURTZMAN KOMICS
(1976, Kitchen Sink)
#1. Art: Kurtzman

L.A. COMICS
(1971, Los Angeles Comic Book)
#1-2. Art: Trujillo

LAIR OF MADNESS
(1972, DB Features)
#1. Art: Broadhurst

LAND OF HEROES
(1977) Oneshot.
Art: Marais

LAKE COUNTY COMIX
(1982, County Comix) Oneshot; 44 pages.
Art: Cunningham, Leach

LAST TOQUE, THE
(1971) Oneshot.
Art: Reece

LAUGH IN THE DARK
(1971, Last Gasp Eco-Funnies)
#1. Art: Deitch

LEAN YEARS
(1974, Cartoonist Co-Op Press)
Oneshot; 36 pages.
Art: Siegel, Simon, Deitch, Pound

LEFT FIELD FUNNIES
(1972, Apex Novelties)
#1. Art: London

LEGEND OF THE WOLFMAN (1976)
#1-2. Art: Zegri

THE LEGION OF CHARLIES (1971, Last Gasp Eco-Funnies)
Oneshot; 36 pages.
Art: Turner, Irons, Veitch, Sheridan, Wilkie

LENNY OF LAREDO!
(1965, Sunbury)
Oneshot. Art: Beck

LET'S NOT 'N SAY WE DID FUNNIES
(1972, Adams Apple)
Oneshot. Art: Hansen

LICENTIOUS INGESTIA
(1975) Oneshot.
Art: Adams

LIFE AND LOVES OF CLEOPATRA, THE
(1967 Communication Co.) Oneshot

LIGHT COMITRAGIES
(1971, Print Mint)
Oneshot; 28 pages.
Art: Irons, Vietch, Sheridan

LIGHTNINGWAR
(1976, Texas)
Oneshot. Art: Bryson

LIKE NOBODY'S BIZNESS FUNNIES
(1972, Adams Apple)
Oneshot. Art: Hansen

LITTLE BOOK OF INNER SPACE, THE
(1972, California Comics) Oneshot
Art: Ormandu

LITTLE GREEN DINOSAUR, THE ADVENTURES OF
(1972, Last Gasp)
#1-2. Art: Chambers

LITTLE GRETA GARBAGE
(1990, Rip Off Press)
#1-2. Art: Crab

LIVING IN THE U.S.A.
(1975)
Oneshot. Art: Fagen

LIZARD ZEN (1973)
Oneshot. Art Bode

LOST CAUSE COMIX
(1976) Oneshot.
Art: Willis

LOW BUDGET FUNNIES
(1977, self published)
#1. Art: Vojtko

LOVE RANGERS
(1977, self published)
#1. Art: Grant

LULLABY FOR A SPEED FREAK
(1972, San Francisco Comic Book Co.)
Oneshot. Art: Rip

MACHINES, THE
(1967) Oneshot.
Art: Bode

MAH FELLOW AMERICANS (1968, Sawyer Press) Oneshot.
Art. Cobb

MAN, THE
(1975, The Print Mint) Oneshot;
28 pages. Art: Bode

MAN FROM UTOPIA
(1972) Oneshot.
Art: Griffith

MANHUNT
(1973, Print Mint)
#1-2. Art: Griffin

MAXWELL MOUSE FOLLIES
(1978, Mad Hatter)
#1. Art: Sinardi

MEAN BITCH THRILLS
(1971, Print Mint)
Oneshot. Art: Spain

MEAT EATERS, THE
Art: Burkhart

MEEF COMIX
(1972, Print Mint)
#1-2. Art: Schrier

ME GUSTA
(1977) Oneshot.
Art: Bryson

MELODY
(1988, Kitchen Sink)
#1-8 Art: Rancourt

MELOTOONS
(1972, Peter Kuper)
#1-2. Art. Crumb

MENDOCINO COUNTY COMIX (1982, County Comix Group)
Oneshot; 44 pages.
Art: Cunningham, Leach, Tapia, Estrada, Steele

MENDOCINO FUNNIES
(1982, County Comix Group) #1; 44 pages.
Art: Cunningham, Leach, Tapia, Estrada

MERTON OF THE MOVEMENT
(1972, Last Gasp Eco-Funnies)
#1; 36 pages. Art: London, Richards, Hallgren, Flenniken

MICKEY RAT
(1972, Los Angeles Comic Book Co.)
#1-4; 36 pages.
Art: Armstrong, Crill

MIDDLE CLASS FANTASIES (1973, Cartoonists Co-op Press) #1-2. Art: Lane

MIDGET WORLD OF VENUS
(1977, Walter Bachner Mini-comics)
Art: Bachner, Coleman

MIGHTY HIGH
(1974, self pub.)

#1-4. Art: Balun

MINDWARP
(1974) Oneshot.
Art: Sheridan, Schrier

MINI LUST COMICS
(1972, San Francisco Comic Book Co.)
Oneshot. Art: Mary

MOM'S HOMEMADE COMICS
(1969, Kitchen Sink)
#1-3. Art: Kitchen, Poplaski, Mitchell

MONA
(1999, Kitchen Sink)
#1. Art: Kurtzman, Mattotti, Hart, Johnson, Guest

MONDO SNARFO
(1978, Kitchen Sink)

MONOLITH
(1972, Last Gasp Eco-Funnies)
Oneshot. Art: Weltz

MOONCHILD
(1968, Forbidden Fruit) #1-3. Art: Cuti

MOONDOG
(1969, Print Mint)
#1-4. Art: Metzger

MOTHER'S OATS
(1969, Rip Off Press)
#1-3; 28 pages.
Art: Schrier, Sheridan

MOTOR CITY COMICS
(1970, Rip Off Press)
#1-2. Art: Crumb

MR. A
(1973, Monster Times) #1. Art: Ditko

MR. NATURAL
(1970, Apex Novelties)
#1-3. Art: Crumb

MU, THE LAND THAT NEVER WAS
(1978, Kitchen Sink)
Art: Metzger

MUTANTS OF THE METROPOLIS
(1972, Los Angeles Comic Book Co.)
Oneshot. Art: Sernuik

MY FELLOW AMERICANS (1970, Price/Stern/Sloan)
Oneshot. Art: Cobb

MYRON MOOSE FUNNIES (1971, MM Comic Book Works)
#1-3. Art: Foster

MYRON MOOSE FUNNIES (1987, Fantagraphics)
#1-3. Art: Foster

MYSTIC FUNNIES
#1-3

NARD N' PAT
(1974, Cartoonists Co-op Press)
#1-2. Art: Lynch

NATURE COMIX
(1970) #1-2.
Art: Geary

NEIL THE HORSE
(1983: Aardvark-Vanaheim; Renegade: 1984) #1-10 (A-V)
#11-15 (Ren)
Art: Saba

NEUROCOMICS
(1979, Last Gasp)

NEW GRAVITY
(1969, San Francisco Comic Book Co.)
#1-2. Art: Abraham

NEW PALTZ COMIX
(Moods Pub. Empire)
Art: Gilbert, Venzina, Young, Buniak.
#1 (1973)
#2 *Amazing Adult Fantasies* (1974)
#3 *Iron-Soul Stories* (1977)

NICKLE BAG
(1976)

#1-2. Art: Edgar

NO DUCKS
(1977, Last Gasp Eco-Funnies)
#1-2. Art: Larson, Bosell

NOO FUNNIES
(1970) #1.
Art: Greene

NOWHERE IN PARTICULAR (1976)
Oneshot. Art: Mcgehee

OAT WILLIE
(Rip Off Press)
#1. Art: Jaxon

OCCULT LAFF PARADE
(1973, Print Mint)
#1. Art: Kinney

O.K. COMICS
(1972, Kitchen Sink)
#1-2. Art: Walters

OMAHA THE CAT DANCER (1984 #1-2 Steel Dragon Press; 1986: #3-21 & #0 Kitchen Sink; 1994: Fantagraphics v2 #1)
#0-21; v2 #1-6
Art: Waller

OMAHA THE CAT DANCER, COLLECTED
(Steel Dragon/Kitchen Sink/Fantagraphics)
#1-6. Art: Waller

ONE (1977)
Oneshot. Art: Garris

ORANGE
(self published)
Oneshot. Art: Bode

OUTSIDE A SLEEPY VILLAGE (1972, San Francisco Comic Book Co.) Oneshot. Rudahl

PAGFEEK PAPERS
(1973, Kitchen Sink)
#1. Art: Morrison

PAIN (1977, Bagginer)

Press) #1. Art: Geiser

PANDEMONIUM EXPRESS FUNNIES
(1974) #1-12.
Art: Greenfelder, East, Banks, Dizzer, Melvin

PANDORA'S BOX COMIX (1973, Last Gasp Eco-Funnies)
#1. Art: Lyvey

PARADISE – AN INTERPLANETARY FANTASY (1975)
Oneshot. Art: Aulenta

PARANOIA (1972, Co. & Sons) Oneshot.
Art: Dallas, Moodian, Todd, Knight

PEER PRESSURE
(1977) #1. Art: Orr

PEOPLE'S COMICS, THE (1972, Golden Gate) Oneshot.
Art: Crumb

PEOPLE ARE PHONEY
(1976) Oneshot.
Art: Siegel, Simon

PERVERTED PRIMER, THE (1972, San Francisco Comic Book Co) Oneshot. Art: M.R.

PHOEBE & THE PIGEON PEOPLE
(1979, Kitchen Sink)
#1-3. Art: Lynch, Witney

PHUCKED UP PHUNNIES
(1968) Oneshot.
Art: Spiegelman

PIECE OF CAKE (1976)
Oneshot. Art: Luisi

PIG HEAD
(1993, Williamson)
#1; 36 pages.
Art: Williamson

PLAIN TALK WITH PUERTO RICANS

(1972, San Francisco Comic Book Co.) Oneshot. Art: Garbaga

PORK (1971, Cartoonist Co-op Press) Oneshot. Art: Wilson

PORTIA PRINZ (1976) #1-4. Art: Howell

POWER PACK COMICS (1979, Kitchen Sink) #1-2. Art: Phillips

PREMIUM CRACKERS (1974) #1. Art: Adams

PRESTO (1976) Oneshot. Art: Mcgehee

PRISCILLA PUMPS (1976) Oneshot. Art: Butzner

PROJUNIOR (1971, Kitchen Sink) Oneshot. Art: Crumb

PROMETHIAN (1971, Enterprises) #1-5 Art: Crumb, Corben (#3 @#*!!!)

PSYCHO COMICS #1-2

PSYCHOTIC ADVENTURES (1972, Co. & Sons) #1-3. Art: Dallas

PUDGE, GIRL BLIMP (1973, Last Gasp Eco-Funnies) #1-3. Art: Marrs

PURE JOY (1975, Pooo Bear) #1. Art: Childlaw

PURPLE CAT (1973, Adams Apple) #1. Art: Lynch

PURPLE PICTOGRAPHY, THE COLLECTED Oneshot. Art: Bode, Wrightson

QUACK (1976, Star Reach) #1-6.

Art: Brunner, Leialoha, Sim, Gilbert, Richards

QUAGMIRE COMICS (1970, Kitchen Sink) #1. Art: Poplaski

QUOZ (1969) Oneshot. Art: Rifas

RADICAL AMERICA KOMIKS (1969, SDS) Art: Shelton

RAW SEWAGE (1970, Price Stern Slone) Oneshot. Art: Cobb

R. CRUMB'S CARLOAD O' COMICS (1976, Belier Press) #1-5. Art: Crumb

R. CRUMB'S COMICS AND STORIES (1969, Rip Off Press) #1. Art: Crumb

R. CRUMB'S HEAD COMIX (1968, Viking) Oneshot. Art: Crumb

REALM (1969) #1-7. Art: Anderson

REAL PULP COMICS (1973, The Print Mint) #1. Art: Brand

REAL WORLD COMIX (1974) Oneshot. Art: McCarthy

RED RAIDER (1977, Last Gasp Eco-Funnies) Oneshot. Art: Jaxon

REEFER MADNESS (1972, San Francisco Comic Book Co.) Oneshot. Art: Smad

RIC SLOANE COMICS (1969, San Francisco Comic Book Co.) #1. Art: Sloane

RIMSHOT (1990, Rip Off Press) #1-3. Art: Childlaw

RIP IN TIME

(1986, Fantagor) #1-5. Art: Corben

RIP OFF COMIX (1977, Rip Off Press) #1-31. Art: Shelton, Sheridan, Richards, Griffith, Seda, Spain, Jaxon, Robbins

RIP OFF PRESS, THE BEST OF (Rip Off Press) Vol 1 (various artists, 1973) Vol 2 (Freak Brothers, 1974) Vol 3 (New Adventures of Jesus, 1979) Vol. 4 (More Freak Brothers, 1980)

RIPT N' REKT (1972) #1-2. Art: D'amillo

ROBOT FIELDS (1977) Oneshot. Art: Weir

ROWLF (1971, Rip Off Press) Oneshot. Art: Corben

ROXY FUNNIES (1973, Head Imports) #1. Art: Lynch

RUBBER DUCK TALES (1971, The Print Mint) #1-2. Art: Lawso, Landeros

SACRED AND PROFANE (1976, Last Gasp) Oneshot. Art: Greene

SALLY STARR, HOLLYWOOD GIRL SLEUTH (San Francisco Comic Book Co) Oneshot. Art: Robbins

SALOON (1973, The Print Mint) Oneshot. Art: Geiser

SAMMY SAVED

AND AL MOST (1974) Oneshot. Art: Yog

SAND SCRIPTS (1977, Rick Geary)

SAN FRANCISCO COMIC BOOK #1 (1969, San Francisco Comic Book Co.) Art: Hays #2-7 (1970, The Print Mint). Art: Irons, Crumb, Murphy

SAVAGE HUMOR (1973, Print Mint) #1. Art: Sielel, Simon, Anthony

SCARLET PILGRIM (1977, Last Gasp) Oneshot. Art: Robbins

SCHIZOPHRENIA/ CHEECH WIZARD (1973, Last Gasp Eco-Funnies) Oneshot. Art: Bode

S. CLAY WILSON PORTFOLIO COMIX (1970, Print Mint) Oneshot. Art: Wilson

SCRABBIS TRENO (1976) #1. Art: Romero, Peterson

SEATTLE SIMPLETON (1975) #1-3. Art: Workman, London, Flenniken

SELF-LOATHING COMICS (1995, Fantagraphics) #1-2. Art: R & A-K Crumb

SELF DESTRUCT (1973, San Francisco Comic Book Co.) #1. Art: Spiegelman

SEX AND AFFECTION (1974, Family Publishers) Oneshot. Art: Himes

SEX AND VIOLENCE COMIX (1975)

#1. Art: Jaxon

SHORT ORDER COMIX (1973, Family Fun) #1-2. Art: Spiegleman

SHOW AND TELL COMICS (1973, The Print Mint) Oneshot. Art: Green

SIN CITY (1972) #1-2. Art: Mancusi

SKULL COMICS (1970, Rip Off Press #1/Last Gasp #2-6) #1-6. Art: Sheridan, Irons, Shelton, Spain, Corben

SKY BUMS Art: Jaxon

SKY RIVER FUNNIES Art: Richards

SLEAZY SCANDALS OF THE SILVER SCREEN (1974, Cartoonists Co-op Press) Oneshot. Art: Spiegelman

SLOW DEATH FUNNIES (1970, Last Gasp) #1-11; 36 pages. Art: Mendes, Shelton, Cobb, Jaxon, Deitch, Crumb, Stout, Holmes, Irons, Grimshaw, Evans

SMILE (1972, Kitchen Sink) #1-3. Art: Mitchell

SNAPPER (1972) #1-2. Art: Miller

SNAPPY SAMMY SMOOT (1979, Kitchen Sink) Oneshot; 36 pages. Art: Williamson, Petrie, Rudnick, Crumb

SNARF (1972, Kitchen Sink) #1-15. Art: Kitchen, Lynch, Eisner, Miller, Kurtzman, Crumb

SNATCH COMICS (1968, Apex Novelties) #1-3. Art: Crumb

SNOID (1979, Kitchen Sink)

SOFTCORE (1973, The Print Mint) Oneshot. Art: Landeros

SONOMA COUNTY COMIX (1982, County Comix) Oneshot; 44 pages. Art: Estrada, Cunningham, Leach, Steele, Wooldridge

SOUL TALES (1972, San Francisco Comic Book Co.)

SPACE DOG #1. Art: Greenwood

SPACED (1974, Comics and Comix) #1-3. Art: Pinkoski

SPACED OUT (1972, The Print Mint) Oneshot. Art: Bird

SPASM (1973, Last Gasp) #1. Art: Jones

SPAZ COMIX (1975, self published) #1-2. Art: Balun

SPHINX, TALES FROM THE (1972) #1-2 (Kitchen Sink) #3 (Print Mint). Art: Thompson

SPIFFY STORIES (1969, Print Mint) Oneshot. Art: Osborne

SPIRIT, THE (1973, Kitchen Sink) #1-2. Art: Eisner

STAR REACH (1974, Star Reach)

#1-18. Art: Chaykin, Jones, Adams, Smith, Mayson

STAR WEEVILS (1978, Rip Off Press) Art: Leonard

STONED OUT FUNNIES (1972, Adams Apple) #1. Art: Krueger

SUBVERT COMICS (1970, Rip Off Press) #1-3. Art: Spain

SUDS (1969, The Print Mint) Oneshot. Art: Florida

SUNDAE FUNNIES Art: Lockner

SUNPOT (1971) Oneshot. Art: Bode

SUPERBALONEY Art: Lockner

SUPER BITCH (1975) #1. Art: Harmon

SUPER CHICKS (1976) #1. Art: Sommerkamp

SUPER SOUL COMIX (1972, Kitchen Sink) #1. Art: Green

SWAMP FEVER 1972) Oneshot. Art: Dameron

TAILDRAGGER COMIX (1973, Adams Apple) #1. Art: Hansen

TALES FROM THE BERKELEY-CON (1974, UC Berkley) #1-2. Art: Geiser

TALES FROM THE FRIDGE (1973, Kitchen Sink) #1. Art: Jones, Stewart

TALES FROM THE LEATHER NUN (1973, Last Gasp) #1; 44 pages. Art: Sheridan, Crumb, Spain, Jaxon, Ryan, Brand

TALES FROM THE OZONE (1970, The Print Mint) #1-2. Art: Lundgren, Grimshaw

TALES FROM THE PLAGUE (1969, Wierdom) #1. Art: Corben

TALES FROM THE TUBE (1972, Surfer Pub) Art: Griffin

TALES OF JERRY THE STONED VAMPIRE #1-9

TALES OF BOZI-SATTVA (1973, Serious Funnies) Art: Petertil

TALES OF SEX AND DEATH (1971, The Print Mint) #1-2. Art: Brand

TALES OF THE ARMORKINS (1970, Co. & Sons) Oneshot. Art: Todd

TALES OF THE TOAD (1970, Print Mint) #1-3. Art: Griffith

TEENAGE HORIZONS OF SHANGRI LA (Kitchen Sink) #1 (1970). Art: Lynch #2 (1972). Art: Green

TEENAGE TRASH (1972, Adams Apple) #1. Art: Krueger

TEENAGE SAM (1974, Adams Apple) #1. Art: Stewart

TERMINAL COMICS (1971, Apex Novelties) #1. Art: McMillan

TESSERAE (1977) Oneshot. Art: Macklin

TEJANO EXILE (Last Gasp)

THEOLOGICAL COMICS
(1972, Apex Novelties) Oneshot. Art: Hatfield

THEY SHALL NOT PERISH
(1975) Oneshot. Art: Kennard

THREE-FISTED TALES
(1971) #1. Art: Greene

THIS IS NOT THE ZEBRA
#1-2. Art: Greenver

THRILLING MURDER TALES
(1971, San Francisco Comic Book Co.) #1. Art: Deitch

THUNDERDOGS
(1981, Rip Off Press) Oneshot Art: Emerson

TIE TAC: AN ALLEGORY
(1974, Warm Neck Funnies) Oneshot; 24 pages. Art: Gonick, Baron

TIME TWISTED TALES
(Rip Off Press) Art: Sheridan

TITS & CLITS
(1973, Nanny Goat Productions) #1-7; 36 pages. Art: Sutton, Chevli, Farmer, Trout, Powers, Mars, Sampson

TOE JAM COMICS
(1973) #1. Art: Cavey

TOONEY LOONS AND MARIJUANA MELODIES
(1971, Gold Agape Ark) #1. Art: Greene

TORTOISE AND THE HARE (1971, Last Gasp Eco-Funnies)
#1. Art: Hallgren

TOTAL EFFECT
(1974) #1-2. Art: Surasky

TRASHMAN
(1969) Oneshot. Art: Spain

TRICKS COMICS
(1975) Oneshot. Art: Crumb

TRINA'S WOMEN
(1976, Kitchen Sink) Oneshot. Art: Robbins

TRIVIAL ANNOYANCES
(1972) Oneshot. Art: Frosich

TRUCKIN' (1972, The Print Mint)
#1-2. Art: Metzger

TUFF SHIT COMICS
(1972, Print Mint) Oneshot. Art: Williams

TURNED ON CUTIES
(1972, Golden Gate) Oneshot; 28 pages. Art: Lynch, Griffith, Green, Crumb, Peck, Holmes

TWISTED SISTERS
(1972, Golden Gate) #1. Art: Komanski

2. (1975)
#1-2. Art: Wilson

TWO FOOLS
(1976, Saving Grace) Oneshot. Art: Richards

UNCLE CHARLIE'S SUMMER SLUG
(1977) Oneshot. Art: Oliff

UNCLE SAM TAKES LSD (1972, Rip Off Press) #1. Art: Schrier

UNCLE SHAM
(1970, Print Mint) #1-2. Art: Gieser

UNCLE SQUIGGLY'S COMICS Oneshot. Art: Turner

UNDERHANDED HISTORY OF THE U.S.A. (1973) #1. Art: Thorkelson, O'Brien

UNEEDA COMIX
(1970, Print Mint) Oneshot. Art: Crumb

UNDERGROUND CLASSICS (1985, Rip Off Press)
#1 Freak Brothers
#2 Dealer McDope
#3 Dealer McDope Vol.2
#4 The Early Works of Greg Irons
#5 Wonder Wart-Hog Vol.1
#6 God Nose
#7 Wonder Wart-Hog Vol.2
#8 The Forty Year Old Hippie Vol.1
#9 Early Works of Greg Irons Vol 2
#10 Jesus Vol.1
#11 Jesus Vol.2
#12 Shelton in 3D
#13 Jesus Vol.3
#14 Jesus Vol.4
#15 Art: Rudahl
#16 various artists

UP FROM THE DEEP
(1971, Rip Off Press) Oneshot. Art: Corben

VALLEY FEVER
(1975) Oneshot. Art: Hansen

VENTURE
(1972) #1-4. Art: Winnick, Cirocco

VIBRATORY PROVINCAL NEWS
(1973) #1-3. Art: May

VOLTAR (1977) Oneshot. Art: Alcala

WE HAVE COME TO SEE JESUS

(1972) #1. Art: Dunworth

WEIRDO (1981; Last Gasp Eco-Funnies) #1-28. Art: Crumb, Spain, Friedman, Caz, Sede, Worden, Bagge

WEIRD FANTASIES
(1972, Los Angeles Comic Book Co.) #1. Art: Chesly

WEIRDOM COMIX
Art: Corben

WEIRD TRIPS MAGAZINE (1974, Kitchen Sink) #1-2. Art: Kitchen

WET SATIN (1976, Kitchen Sink) #1-2. Art: Robbins

WHA..!? (1975; Monster Times) Oneshot. Art: Ditko

WHITE COMMANCHE (1977, Last Gasp Eco-Funnies) Oneshot. Art: Jaxon

WHITE LIGHTNING SPACEWAYS. (1971) Art: Lewis

WHITE LUNCH COMIX (1972) #1. Art: Holmes

WHITE RAIN (1969) Oneshot. Art: Stewart

WHITE WHORE FUNNIES
(1975) #1-2. Art: Spade

WHOLE WHEAT
(1977) #1. Art: Jaxon

WIERD TRIPS MAGAZINE
(1974, Kichen Sink) #1. Art: Geradts

WIMMIN'S COMIX
(1972, Last Gasp Eco-Funnies)

#1-17. Art: Godian, Shelby, Wilson, Flennikin, Gerbie, Marrs, Jundis

WONDER WART-HOG
(1967; Miller) #1-2. Art: Shelton

WONDER WART-HOG AND THE BATTLE OF THE TITANS! (1985, Rip Off Press) Oneshot)

WONDER WART-HOG AND THE NERDS OF NOVEMBER (1980, Rip Off Press) Oneshot

WONDER WART-HOG, THE BEST OF
(1973, #1-2 Rip Off Press/#3 Print Mint) #1-3. Art: Shelton

WONDER WART-HOG, THE HOG OF STEEL
(1995, Rip Off Press) #1-3. Art: Shelton

WORM MAGAZINE
(1973) #1-2. Art: Hosier, Green

XYZ COMICS (1972) Oneshot. Art: Crumb

YELLOW DOG
(1968, Print Mint) #1-25. Art: Crumb, White, Martin, Irons, Evans, Moscoso, Williams, Robbins

YIKES (1975, Stray Cat Comix Studio) #1-4. Art: Milke, Vojtko, Edgar

YOUNG LUST
(1970, Co. & Sons) #1-8. Art: Griffith, Todd, Kinney

YOUNG LUST READER
(1974, And/Or Press) Oneshot. Art: Kinney

YOUNG & LUSTLESS
(1972, San Francisco

Comic Book Co.) Oneshot. Art: Griffith

YOUR HYTONE COMIX
(1971, Apex) Oneshot. Art: Crumb

YOW (1978, Last Gasp) #1-2. Art: Griffith

YOYO (1972) Oneshot. Art: Jeri

YUM YUM BOOK
(1974) Oneshot. Art: Crumb

ZAM ZAP JAM
(1974, The Print Mint) Art: Wilson

ZAP COMIX
(1967, Apex Novelties) #0-14. Art: Crumb, Moscoso, Williams, Shelton, Spain

ZERO COMICS (1974) #1-4. Art: Sholly, Greenwood

ZIP-A-TUNES AND MORE MELODIES
(1972, San Francisco Comic Book Co.) #1. Art: Spiegelman

ZIPPY THE PINHEAD
(1977, Rip Off Press) #1-3. Art: Griffith

ZODIAK MINDWARP
(1967) Oneshot. Art: Spain

ZOOKS (1973) Oneshot. Art: Bode

UK TITLES

ACID HEAD ARNIE
(Knockabout) Art: Smith

ADVENTURES OF LAZARUS LAMB
(Knockabout) Large format. Art: Edney

ALIENS ATE MY TROUSERS

(1998, Knockabout) Large format. Art: Emerson

ANIMAL WEIRDNESS
(1974, H. Bunch) Oneshot; 36 pages. Art: Livingstone, Edward, Poynter, Petagno, Hancroft

BIG BOOK OF EVERYTHING (1983, Knockabout) Large format. Art: Emerson

BIJOU FUNNIES
(1974, H. Bunch) UK Edition

BLOOD, SEX, TERROR
(1978; Junior Print Outfit) #1-3; 36 pages. Art: McKie, Huxley

BOGEY (1975, self published) Art: Ghura

BRAINSTORM COMIX (Alchemy)
#1-5 (1975-1977)
#6 (Amazing Rock & Roll Adventures)
Art: Talbot, Bonk, Emerson, Bolland, Schofield, Taylor, Davies, Szostek, Luck, Berridge, Kennedy

BRYAN TALBOT'S EX-DIRECTORY
(Knockabout) Art: Talbot

CALCULUS CAT - DEATH TO TELEVISION (1987, Knockabout) Large format. Art: Emerson

CARTOON KAMA SUTRA (Knockabout) Large format. Art: Tolputt

CASANOVA'S LAST STAND (1993, Knockabout) Large

format. Art: Emerson

CITYMOUTH
(2000, Knockabout) Art: Emerson

COMMITTED COMIX
(1977, Arts Lab Press)

COZMIC COMICS
(1972, H. Bunch) #1-6. Art: Osborne, Kinney, Weller, Wilson, Renrut, Stelling

CREAM OF CONDENSED SOUP
(1992, Electric Soup/ John Brown) Best of Electric Soup #1-7

CYCLOPS
(1970; Innocence & Experience) Tabloid newspaper, 20 pages #1-4 (Edward, McNeill, Dean, Raymond)

DOGMAN
(1975, Arts Lab Press) Art: Fisher, Emerson

DOPE FIEND FUNNIES
(1974, H. Bunch) #1. Art: Livingstone, Edward, Rowley, Tyler

DYKE'S DELIGHT
(Knockabout) #1-2. Art: Charlesworth, Gregory, Byatt

EDWARD'S HEAVE
(1973, H. Bunch) Oneshot. Art: Edwards

EITHER OR COMICS
(1977, Junior Print Outfit) #1. 48 pages Art: McKie, Marshall

ELECTRIC SOUP
(1989,Electric Soup/ John Brown) #1-17. Art: Alexander, Watt, Douglas, Cardle, Singh, Mathieson, Quitely, McCallum, McAlpine, Somerville

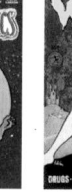

ELECTRIC SOUP 10th ANUSVERSARY ISSUE (1999, ElectricSoup)

ELRIC – RETURN TO MELNIBONE (1973, Unicorn Books) Art: Cawthorn

FANNY (Knockabout) #1-4. Art: Robbins, Charlesworth, Varty

FAT FREDDY'S CAT, FAMOUS TALES OF (Knockabout) Hardcover. Art: Shelton

FAT FREDDY'S CAT (Knockabout) #1-7. Art: Shelton

FAT FREDDY'S COMICS & STORIES (Knockabout) #1-2. Art: Shelton, Irons, Wilson

FIRKIN THE CAT (1985, Virgin Books) Art: Emerson

FIRKIN COLLECTION (Knockabout) Large format. Art: Emerson

FIRKIN GUIDE TO HUMAN SEXUALITY (1989, Knockabout) #1-7. Art: Emerson

FREAK BROTHERS, FABULOUS FURRY (1976 Hassle Free Press/Knockabout) #0-13. Art: Shelton

FREAK BROTHERS, THE COMPLETE (Knockabout) Vol.1-2; Large format. Art: Shelton

FREE COMIX (1973, Arts Lab Press) Art: Emerson

FRITZ THE CAT (1972, J. J. Flash) #1-2. Crumb reprints

FUCK OFF AND DIE (2004, Savoy) Annual; 165 pages. Art: Guidio

GRAPHIXUS (1978, Media and Graphic Eye) #1-5. Art: Bolland, Talbot, Hortelano, Lawley, Kek, Matthews, Schofield, Noon

HALF-ASSED FUNNIES (1973, H. Bunch) #1. Art: Sanderson, Edward, Boates

HARD TO SWALLOW (1988, Knockabout) Art: Dowie

HOT NADS (1979, self published) #1-2. Art: Ghura

HOW TO COMMIT SUICIDE IN SOUTH AFRICA (Knockabout) Oversize. Art: Coe

IDIOTS ABROAD, THE (Knockabout) Large format. Art: Shelton, Mavrides

IT'S ONLY ROCK AND ROLL (1975, Petagno) Oneshot. Art: Petagno

JAZZ FUNNIES (1986, Knockabout) Large format. Art: Emerson

JAZZ FUNNIES – TWO NEW STORIES (1996, Forbidden Planet) Oneshot. Art: Emerson

KAK KOMIX (1976, Arts Lab Press) #1-2 Con booklets

KNOCKABOUT (Knockabout) #1-14. Art: McKean, Deitch, Talbot, Matthews,

Irons, Emerson (#7: hardcover, Trial Special)

LADY CHATTERLEY'S LOVER (1986 Knockabout) Large format. Art: Emerson

LAID BACK ADVENTURES OF SUZI & JONNIE (1981, Creamy Thigh Enterprises). Art: Ghura

LARGE COW COMIX (1972, Arts Lab Press) #1 Large Cow #2 Outer Space Comix #3 Mr Spoonbiscuit #4 Pholk Comix #5 Zomix Comix Art: Emerson, Noon

LORD HORROR (1989, Savoy) #1-15; 40 pages. Art: Guidio, Douthwaite, Coulthart

MacBAM BROTHERS (1994, Cozmik Broth) #1. Art: Alexander, McKenna, McCallum.

MENG & ECKER (1989, Savoy) #1-9; 40 pages. Art: Guidio

MENG & ECKER, THE ADVENTURES OF (1997, Savoy) #10-11; 56 pages. Art: Guidio, Walker, Coulthart

MONOSHOCK (1992, Savoy) Oneshot. 36 pages. Art: Guidio, Coulthart

MOON COMIX (1977, Arts Lab Press) #1-3. Art: Burns, Hill, Brock, Emerson, Bicknell

MY TROUBLES WITH WOMEN (Knockabout) Art: Crumb

NAPALM KISS (1977, T. Sheridan) #1-2. 36 pages. Art: Matthews

NASTY TALES (1971, Bloom) #1-7. Art: Williamson, Welch, Edward, Sheridan, Crumb, Shelton

NASTY TALES, THE TRIALS OF (1973, H. Bunch/ Bloom) Oneshot. Art: Edward, Welch, Gibbons, Rankin

NEAR MYTHS (1978, Galaxy Media) #1-4. Art: Talbot, Haddon, Manley, Eunson, Bonk, Scott, Morrison

NEON COMIX (1978, Junior Print Outfit) #1. Art: Davidson

NORTHERN LIGHTZ (1999, Northern Lightz) #1-10 on. Art: D & J Alexander, Bisley, Boyd, Braysher, Burrows, Hall, Harris, Haward, Heffernan, Hood, Kennedy, Linden, Martin, McAlpine, McKenna, Miller, Morris, Mulder, O'Brien, Pickering, Quitely, Regan, Sibling, Sisson, Simpson, Stafford, Stewart, Talbot, Thompson, Xuasuis

NO SHIT (1969, self-published) Oneshot Art: Bonk, Talbot

NOT QUITE DEAD (Knockabout) #1-4. Art: Shelton

OGOTH & UGLY BOOT (1973, H. Bunch) Oneshot. Art: Welch

ONE-FISTED TALES (1974, Pirate Press) Oneshot. Art: Aldrich, Farnsbarns, Allerton

OPIUM (Knockabout) Large format. Art: Torres

OUTRAGEOUS TALES FROM THE OLD TESTAMENT (1987, Knockabout) Large format. Art: Matthews, Talbot, Emerson

PETER PANK (Knockabout) Large format. Art: Max

PHILBERT DESANEX' 100,000th DREAM (Knockabout) Art: Shelton

PHOLK COMIX (Art Lab Press) Oneshot. Art: Emerson

PINK FLOYD (1974, Hipgnosis) Oneshot. Art: Stubbs

PRO-JUNIOR (1970, J. J. Flash) Oneshot; 32 pages. Digest size. Art: Crumb

PUSSPUSS (1994, Knockabout) Oneshot. Art: Emerson

RAPID REFLEXES (1990, Knockabout) Oneshot. Art: Emerson

RAW PURPLE (1977, Creamy Thigh Enterprises) Art: Ghura

R.CRUMB DRAWS THE BLUES (Knockabout) Large format. Art: Crumb

R.CRUMB'S AMERICA (Knockabout) Large format. Art: Crumb

RIME OF THE ANCIENT MARINER (1989, Knockabout) Large format. Art: Emerson

ROCK 'N' ROLL MADNESS FUNNIES (1973, H. Bunch) Oneshot. Art: Welch, Gibbons, Gallagher, Irons, Livingstone

SERIOUS COMICS (1975, H. Bunch)

7 AGES OF WOMEN (Knockabout) Large format. Art: Charlesworth, Swain, Gebbie

SEVEN DEADLY SINS (Knockabout) Large format. Art: Emerson, Talbot, Gibson, Gibbons, Deitch, Matthews

SHIT THE DOG (1997, Bad Press) #1-4. Poster magazine Art (#1-3): Bisley Art (#4): Bisley, Brashill, Deighan, Esquerra, Gillespie, Haward, Sampson

SIN CITY (1973, H. Bunch) #1. Art: McKie, Raine, Simmons, Edward

SOMETIME STORIES (1977, Hourglass) Art: Ewins, McCarthy

STARTLING PLANET (1989, Knockabout) Art: Emerson

STREET COMIX (1976, Arts Lab Press) #1-6. Art: Emerson

SUDDENLY AT 2 AM IN THE MORNING (1977, self-published) #1. Art: Bolland

SUNPOT (1971, J.J. Flash) Oneshot. Digest format, UK edition. Art: Bode

TALES FROM THE FRIDGE (1974, H. Bunch UK edition) Art: Jones, Stewart

THE BOGIE MAN (1989, Fatman Press) #1-4; 28 pages (1991, John Brown). 112 page graphic novel. Art: Smith

THE BOGIE MAN: THE CHINESE SYNDROME Toxic Weekly serialization (1991) Graphic novel (1991, Apocalypse Press) Art: Kennedy

THE BOGIE MAN: CHINATOON (1993, Tundra UK) #1-4; 24 pages (1994, Tundra). 112 page graphic novel Art: Smith

THE BOGIE MAN: THE MANHATTAN PROJECT (1991, Tundra UK) Oneshot; 48 pages Art: Smith

THOROUGHLY RIPPED (Knockabout) Large format. Art: Shelton

THRRP! (Knockabout) Large format. Art: Baxendale

THUNDERDOGS (1993, Knockabout) Art: Emerson

TOXIC PIE (1996, Scotch Pie) #1-2. Art: Alexander, Flynn, Haward, Ronald, Maguire, Slater, Travers, Watson

TROMBONE (Knockabout) Art: Edika, Emerson, Goossens

TRULY AMAZING LOVE STORIES (Beyond the Edge) #1 (1977); 44 pages #2 (1983). Art: Ghura

VIEW FROM THE VOID (1973, H. Bunch) Art: Simmons, Goring, Ghura, Antonio, Frost

WIMMEN'S COMIX, BEST OF (Knockabout) Large format. Art: Robbins

WOMEN OUT OF LINE (Knockabout) Large format. Art: Swain, Lawson Charlesworth

WONDER WARTHOG (Knockabout) Large format. Art: Shelton

YARROW STALK (1967, Big O) #1-2

YOU ARE MAGGIE THATCHER (1987, Titan Books) Oneshot. Art: Emerson

ZAP (1969, publisher unknown) #0-1. Art: Crumb

ZIP COMICS (1973, H. Bunch) #1. Art: Gibbons, Raine, O'Keefe, Morris, Rankin

The author apologizes for any omissions from this listing and would welcome further information for future editions. Email: dez@comicsinternational.com

Index

Bibliography

Art of the Fillmore: The Poster Series 1966-1971
Bill Graham Presents [Thunder's Mouth, 1999]
Comic Books As History: The Narrative Art of
Jack Jackson, Art Spiegelman, and Harvey Pekar
Joseph Witek [University Press of Mississippi, 1990]
Comics, Comix & Graphic Novels:
A History of Comic Art
Roger Sabin [Phaidon, 1996]
Comics Journal Library: R Crumb
Milo George, editor [Fantagraphics, 2003]
Comix: A History of Comic Books in America
Les Daniels [Wildwood House, 1973]
Crumbology: The Works of R Crumb 1981-1994
Carl Richter, compiler [Water Row, 1995]
Crumbology Supplement
[Water Row, 1998]
Dangerous Drawings:
Interviews With Comix & Graphix Artists
Andrea Juno, editor [Juno, 1997]
From Aargh to Zap:
Harvey Kurtzman's Visual History of the Comics
Harvey Kurtzman [Kitchen Sink, 1991]
High Art: A History of the Psychedelic Poster
Ted Owen and Denise Dickson [Sanctuary, 1999]
History of Underground Comics
Mark James Estren [Straight Arrow, 1974]
Illustrated Checklist to Underground Comix
Robert K Wiener, editor [Archival, 1979]
Kitchen Sink Press: The First 25 Years
Dave Schreiner [Kitchen Sink, 1994]
Life and Times of R Crumb
Monte Beauchamp, editor [St Martin's, 1998]
Nasty Tales: Sex, Drugs, Rock'n'Roll
and Violence in the British Underground
David Huxley [Criticial Vision/Headpress, 2001]
Official Underground
and Newave Comix Price Guide
Jay Kennedy, editor [Boatner Norton, 1982]
R Crumb Checklist of Work and Criticism: With a
Biographical Supplement and a Full Set of Indexes
Don Fiene [Boatner Norton, 1981]

Rebel Visions:
The Underground Comix Revolution 1963-1975
Patrick Rosenkranz [Fantagraphics, 2002]
Richard Corben: Flights into Fantasy
Fershid Bharucha, editor [Thumb Tack, 1981]
Rick Griffin
Gordon McClelland [Dragon's World, 1976]
Underground Comix Family Album
Michael Whyte and Clay Geerdes [Word Play, 1998]
Zap to Zippy:
The Impact of Underground Comix
Bill Griffith [Cartoon Art Museum, 1990]

Keep abreast of developments
in the world of comix and comics with:
   Comics International
   345 Ditchling Rd, Brighton, Sussex BN1 6JJ, UK
   www.comicsinternational.com
   send £2/$4 for sample issue
   The Comics Journal
   7563 Lake City Wy NE, Seattle, WA 98115, USA
   www.fantagraphics.com
   send $7/£4 for sample issue

RECOMMENDED READING
Anthologies
   Apex Treasury of Underground Comics
   [Link, 1974]
   Best of Bijou Funnies [Link, 1975]
   Best of Rip Off Press volumes 1-4
   [Rip Off 1973-1980]
   Mindwarp: An Anthology [And/or, 1975]
   Outrageous Tales from the Old Testament
   [Knockabout, 1987]
   Seven Deadly Sins [Knockabout, 1989]

Bode, Vaughn
   Bodé's Erotica volumes 1-4
   [Fantagraphics, 1996-97]
   Cheech Wizard volumes 1-2
   [Fantagraphics, 1990-91]

Cobalt 60 [Donning/Starblaze,
   1988 w/Mark Bodé and Larry Todd]
Junkwaffel volumes 1-2
   [Fantagraphics, 1993-95]
Lizard Zen [Fantagraphics, 1999]
Poem Toons [Tundra, 1989]
Schizophrenia [Fantagraphics, 2001]

Corben, Richard
   Bloodstar [Morning Star, 1976]
   Bodyssey [Catalan, 1986]
   Cage [Marvel/MAX, 2002]
   Den volumes 1-5 [Fantagor, 1984-92]
   Den 2: Movovum [Catalan, 1984]
   Fall of the House of Usher [Catalan, 1985]
   Hellblazer: Hard Time [DC/Vertigo, 2000]
   House on the Borderland [DC/Vertigo, 2000]
   Jeremy Brood [Fantagor, 1982]
   Last Voyage of Sinbad [Catalan, 1988]
   Mutant World [Fantagor/Catalan, 1983]
   Odd Comic World of Rich Corben
   [Warren, 1977]
   Richard Corben Complete Works
   volumes 1-3 [Catalan, 1985-87]
   Rip in Time [Kitchen Sink, 1996]
   Richard Corben's Art Book volumes 1-2
   [Fantagor, 1991-94]
   Startling Stories: Banner [Marvel , 2001]
   Richard Corben's Funny Book
   [Nickelodeon, 1976]
   Tales of the Black Diamond [Fantagor, 1993]
   Vic and Blood [ibooks/Edgeworks Abbey, 2002]
   Werewolf [Catalan, 1984]

Crumb, R.
   Book of Mr. Natural [Fantagraphics, 1995]
   Comics [Black Sparrow, 1990]
   The Complete Crumb Comics
   volumes 1-17 [Fantagraphics, 1987-2003]
   Complete Fritz the Cat [Belier, 1978]
   Crumb Comics [Ginko, 1992]

Life and Death of Fritz the Cat
[Fantagraphics, 1993]
My Troubles with Women [Last Gasp, 1994]
Odds & Ends [Bloomsbury, 2001]
R Crumb Coffee Table Art Book
[Little Brown, 1997]
R Crumb Comics [Ginko, 1999]
R Crumb Draws the Blues [Last Gasp, 1994]
R Crumb's America [Knockabout, 1994]
R Crumb's Carload o' Comics
[Kitchen Sink, 1996]
R Crumb's Head Comix [Fireside, 1988]
R Crumb's Yum Yum Book [Scrimshaw, 1975]

Deitch, Kim
All Waldo Comics! [Fantagraphics, 1992]
Beyond the Pale! [Fantagraphics, 1989]
Boulevard of Broken Dreams [Pantheon, 2002]
Hollywoodland [Fantagraphics, 1989]
Shroud for Waldo [Fantagraphics, 1992]
Stuff of Dreams! [Fantagraphics, 2002]

Emerson, Hunt
Aliens Ate my Trousers [Knockabout, 1998]
Big Book of Everything [Knockabout, 1983]
Calculus Cat [Knockabout, 1987]
Casanova's Last Stand [Knockabout, 1993]
Citymouth [Knockabout, 2000]
Firkin Collection [Knockabout, 2002]
Jazz Funnies [Knockabout, 1986]
Lady Chatterley's Lover [Knockabout, 1986]
Rapid Reflexes [Knockabout, 1990]
Rime of the Ancient Mariner
[Knockabout, 1989]
Startling Planet [Knockabout, 1989]
They Call Me Puss Puss [Knockabout, 1994]

Gonick, Larry
Cartoon History of the Universe volumes 1-3
[Doubleday/W W Norton, 1990-2002]

Green, Justin
Binky Brown Sampler [Last Gasp, 1995]

Griffith, Bill
Are We Having Fun Yet? [Fantagraphics, 1997]

From A to Zippy [Penguin, 1991]
King Pin [E P Dutton, 1987]
Pinhead's Progress [E P Dutton, 1989]
Zippy Annual
volumes 1-4 [Fantagraphics, 2000-2003]
Zippy: Nation of Pinheads [Last Gasp, 1987]
Zippy: Pindemonium [Last Gasp, 1986]
Zippy: Pointed Behaviour [Last Gasp, 1984]
Zippy's House of Fun [Fantagraphics, 1998]
Zippy Stories [And/or, 1981]

Jackson, Jack
Commanche Moon
[Rip Off Press/Last Gasp, 1979]
God's Bosom and Other Stories
[Fantagraphics, 1995]
Indian Lover [Mojo Press, 1999]
Lost Cause [Kitchen Sink, 1998]
Los Tejanos [Fantagraphics, 1982]
Optimism of Youth [Fantagraphics, 1993]
Secrets of San Saba [Kitchen Sink, 1989]

London, Bobby
Mondo Popeye [St Martin's, 1989]

O'Neill, Dan
Collective Unconscience of Odd Bodkins
[Volcano, 1973]
Hear The Sound Of My Feet Walking
[Glide Urban, 1969]

Shelton, Gilbert
Best of Fat Freddy's Cat [Knockabout, 1983]
Complete Fabulous Furry Freak Brothers
volumes 1-2 [Knockabout, 2003]
Wonder Wart-Hog:
Battle of the Titans [Rip Off, 1985]
Nurds of November [Rip Off, 1980]

Spain (Rodriguez, Spain)
Alien Apocalypse 2006 [Frog, 2001]
Boots [Precipice, 1998]
My True Story [Fantagraphics, 1994]
Nightmare Alley [Fantagraphics, 2003]
She: Anthology of a Big Bitch [Last Gasp, 1994]

Sherlock Holmes' Strangest Cases
[Word Play, 2001]
Trashman Lives! [Fantagraphics, 1997]

Spiegelman, Art
Agony [Pantheon, 1987]
Breakdowns [Belier, 1977]
Maus volumes 1-2 [Pantheon, 1986-91]
Raw volumes 1-3 [Penguin 1989-91]
Wild Party: The Lost Classic [Pantheon, 1999]

Stack, Frank
Dorman's Doggie [Kitchen Sink, 1990]
Naked Glory [Fantagraphics, 1997]

Talbot, Bryan
Adventures of Luther Arkwright
[Dark Horse, 1997]
Bryan Talbot's Brainstorm [Alchemy, 1999]
Heart of Empire [Dark Horse, 2001]
Tale of One Bad Rat [Dark Horse, 1995]

Williams, Robert
Hysteria in Remission [Fantagraphics, 2003]
Malicious Resplendence
[Fantagraphics, 1998]
Views from a Tortured Libido
[Last Gasp, 1993]
Visual Addiction [Last Gasp, 1993]

Williamson, Skip
Halstead Street [Kitchen Sink, 1990]
The Scum Also Rises [Fantagraphics, 1997]

S. Clay Wilson
Collected Checkered Demon [Last Gasp, 1998]
Wilson's Andersen [Cottage Classics, 1994]
Wilson's Grimm [Cottage Classics, 2000]

PUBLISHERS' WEBSITES
www.deniskitchen.com
www.fantagraphics.com
www.knockabout.com
www.lastgasp.com
www.ripoffpress.com